LOVE
is a
MIRACLE

LOVE
is a
MIRACLE

BRAD STEIGER

KENSINGTON BOOKS
http://www.kensingtonbooks.com

Contents

Acknowledgments

I would like to acknowledge the assistance of the many individuals who have returned their questionnaires and have provided me with extensive research materials and exciting accounts of contemporary paranormal and mystical experiences. In particular, I would like to thank the many men and women who shared their personal love stories for this book and who generously revealed the details of how they met their destined loved ones.

Deepest regards are expressed to the memory of Fay Marvin Clark, Victor Darr, and Gael Crystal Flanagan.

In addition, I must thank Paul Dinas, editor in chief of Kensington, for his unbridled enthusiasm for this project; my editor, Karen Haas, for her cheerful willingness to work with me in smoothing out the glitches; my agent, Agnes Birnbaum, for her unfailing support of my work for over thirty years; and, of course, my inspiration, soulmate, and wife, Sherry, whose wise counsel is one of my strongest bulwarks against the stresses of life on the material plane. And I must not forget to express my warmest appreciation to the Angels of Love themselves for their inspiration and guidance during the writing of this book.

Introduction

For centuries now our poets, troubadors, composers, and romance writers have declared that the very act of falling in love may somehow transport the lovers to another dimension of reality and that the process of experiencing a true blending of two bodies and spirits is a wonderful gift sent from heaven. Cynics may caution others about the power of a moonlit night, soft music playing in the background, and the presence of an attractive man or woman in one's arms to cloud and delude the senses, and it is true that many love-struck romantics have rushed into relationships too quickly and suffered the consequences. However, those of us who have been granted the blessing of having found our soulmates, our true life partners, have been able to see clearly that the love-bond that we share with our significant other has been destined to be by forces far beyond the parameters of our limited earthly knowledge. Our love was truly fashioned by powers and principalities that are "miracles of love."

It seems that it is somehow important to God's plan for the evolution of our planet that certain humans come together as man and wife, lovers, soulmates, or parents of children. On occasion, it would seem that some intervention from beyond our human world is needed. Some people firmly believe that they have been brought together by beings that they call, "Angels of Love," entities who assume various disguises and identities in order to help couples fulfill their romantic and spiritual destinies.

The concept of a spirit being—a cupid—bringing two earthlings together is an ancient one. In the apocryphal texts, those inspired works that for one reason or another did not make the final cut to be included in the Bible, there are numerous accounts of angels shepherding certain men and women to come together as man and wife. The Book of Tobit, circa 622 B.C.E., relates a fascinating story of how the angel Raphael is assigned to the task of seeing to it that two young people are united in marriage, for they are "the children of holy ancestors." And, of course, we recall that it was the angel Gabriel who informed the virtuous young maiden Mary that she would one day bear a son named Jesus.

Can it be that our guardian angels, those heavenly beings who are to assist us in leading a good life, are also responsible for bringings us together with our beloved other half?

While the strictly orthodox religionists may have some problems associating their guardian angels with the concept of heavenly matchmakers, my research and my own personal experience have led me to conclude that there are multidimensional beings—angels, spirit guides, cosmic teachers—who not only concern themselves with the mundane activities of us mortals, but who also assume the task of bringing us together with our one special person.

In addition to the above-mentioned angels of the Judeo-Christian tradition and the spirit guide concept of numerous cultures, there are the "bodhisattvas" of Buddhism, those beings who have earned Nirvana but who elect to stay behind to help suffering humanity; the "garudas" and "asparas" of the Hindu; the "shaktis" and "peris" of the Persians; and the "daemones" of the ancient Greeks, to name only a few. And in contemporary times, we must add such titles as Light Beings, Star Beings, and

Space Brothers—all names for alleged wise and benevolent entities who come from Outer Space to take an active role in shepherding us mortals to higher consciousness and to special loving relationships.

In this book you will read many inspirational accounts of men and women who were certainly destined to be together as one. In some cases, it would seem that they were compelled to be with one another because of paranormal manifestations such as telepathy, clairvoyance, prophetic visions, out-of-body experiences, dreams, the resurfacing of past-life memories, and the intervention of guiding spirits or angels.

How many thousands of couples have been brought together by the miracle forces of love? Were you aware of angelic interaction in the creation of your own love relationship? Were you conscious of a telepathic linkup with your beloved? Had you perhaps met one another before in strangely vivid dreams?

As you read the dramatic stories in this book, you just might be reminded of a mysterious person who briefly and benevolently touched the lives of you and your loved one. You, too, may remember that you also entertained an angel unaware, and the old saying that marriages are made in heaven may seem more probable than poetic. Perhaps as you read these fascinating and inspirational stories of love found or reclaimed, you will be able to determine if you and your beloved were destined to love. My prayer for you is that your relationship is sacred and true and that the very essence of your love remains eternally beyond the ravages of time and exists forever as a miracle of love.

One

Sherry, My Gift from Heaven

In October of 1986, I could no longer endure a marriage that had steadily progressed from psychic torment to psychological torture. The beautiful home in Scottsdale, Arizona, complete with swimming pool and a lush Oriental garden on which I had invested so much time and effort, could no longer compensate for the spiritual anguish which the soured relationship had inflicted upon me. I moved out of the house and into an apartment in Phoenix, determined to reclaim my dignity and self-respect.

A few weeks later, I was beginning to yield to the entreaties of my friend, Stan Kalson, to "get back into the flow of life."

Stan, the director of the International Holistic Center in Phoenix, has always been at the cutting edge of research in nutrition and alternate health care; and on this occasion he was sponsoring a demonstration conducted by Dr. Caruso, a remarkable practitioner of polarity therapy who, though well into his eighties, was still actively engaged in the healing arts. I hadn't given Stan a firm commitment about whether or not I would attend the demonstration, but since it was being held at Herb and Ann Puryear's metaphysical center only a short distance from my apartment, I decided at the last minute to go.

I took a seat in the front row so that Stan would be certain to see that his well-intentioned urgings to pry me away from non-stop work in my apartment had been successful, but I truly did not feel at all like being social or mixing with the crowd. I knew that I would be meeting Dr. Caruso after the program for a quiet evening of conversation at Stan's home, but I really hoped that my friend had no hidden agendas up his sleeve. My basic attitude toward any member of the opposite sex at this particular time of emotional chaos was one of extreme caution and more than a little distrust.

Just before the evening's proceedings were to begin, an attractive blond lady approached me and asked if I were Brad Steiger. When I admitted that I was, she proceeded to introduce herself: "I am Mary-Caroline Meadows. Is the seat next to you taken?"

The pretty woman exuded a great deal of charm, so I was pleased to tell her that she was welcome to sit in the empty chair beside me. After all, there might as well be a pleasant person sitting next to me as someone as dour as I was feeling.

Then Mary-Caroline turned to me and uttered the words that transformed my attitude from depressed and negative to optimistic and positive. "I must tell you that I bring you greetings from our very dear mutual friend, Sherry Hansen."

My charming new acquaintance suddenly had my complete attention. I had really only met Sherry Hansen once before, and I had thought her the most beautiful, fascinating, and captivating woman that I had ever seen. What was more, even though our brief meeting had taken place over four years before, I had not been able to get her out of my mind. And one of the basic reasons for that fixation was the peculiar fact that her image had been placed in my mind after a paranormal happening when I was a boy of five—forty-five years ago.

"Is Sherry Hansen here in Phoenix?" I asked Mary-Caroline incredulously.

In 1982, Sherry had stopped by my office in the company of her producer. At that time she had been on her way to Europe on business. She had read one of my books and had wanted to meet me. She was living at that time in Los Angeles. I assumed that she still was.

"Why, yes, Sherry is here in Phoenix," Mary-Caroline said. "In fact, we take a class together. And last night in class, when I said that I would be seeing you tonight at Dr. Caruso's lecture, she said to be certain to say hello to you and to give you her love."

I was suddenly so excited to learn that Sherry Hansen was in Phoenix that my normally rational journalist's mind did not wonder how Mary-Caroline Meadows, who was meeting me for the first time, could possibly have known that she would see me at the lecture that evening. Especially since I myself hadn't known until minutes before the presentation began, that I would be there.

But my capacity for analysis had been completely suspended by my mental vision of the enchanting Sherry Hansen—and the thought that she cared enough about me to send her greetings with a friend.

Stan Kalson introduced his mentor, Dr. Caruso, and the energetic octogenarian began his demonstration.

I'm afraid that I observed with only a portion of my conscious attention. My memory was churning up some uncomfortable images of my awkward first meeting with Sherry.

I had recognized her as the fairy princess of my childhood visions the second that she stepped into my office.

But as fate would have it, when I met her in 1982, I was so miserable emotionally that I held myself aloof from her.

My marriage had disintegrated into bitter estrangement. My acute embarrassment at the failure of the relationship kept me in the relationship far too long, and I desperately attempted to keep up appearances.

At the time that I met Sherry, I was the president of Harmonious Publishing Company, producing other people's books and cassette tapes—while striving to maintain my own career as an author, lecturer, and psychical researcher.

Most evenings, after having worked on my duties for the company from ten to five, I would start work on my own writing projects after a brief dinner break. Sometime in the hours before dawn, I would often doze off at my typewriter and spend what remained of the night asleep on the floor beside my desk. Daily, I was forced to deal with the stresses arising from the financial problems of the company, the individual temperaments of the staff, the eccentricity of one of our principal backers, and the fickle demands of the marketplace.

When Sherry walked into my office that day, I treated her quite brusquely. But while I maintained a cool, unruffled exterior demeanor, inwardly I was screaming in frustration: "Dear God, why did you bring her into my life *now?* I am already nearly out of my mind trying to balance the cascading pieces of a crumbling reality. Why torment me further by parading the woman of my dreams in front of my eyes when I can't touch her or even tell her how much she means to me!"

I could scarcely look at Sherry, for fear I would suddenly leap to my feet, scoop her up in my arms, toss her over my shoulder and run off to the mountains with my prize—while advising the rest of my world where it could go.

It would have been unfair to Sherry to encourage any kind of relationship—even a platonic friendship—while I was so depressed. At this point in my life, I had begun to believe that I was living under a curse that had somehow been set in motion by my marriage—and maybe I really was.

What I did not fully realize at the time was that if the Angels of

Love *really* want to bring you together with your special person, *they will make it happen!*

That night, as soon as I left Stan's house, I hurried back to my apartment to check the Phoenix telephone book. I had to verify if Mary-Caroline Meadows had really been telling me the truth. Was it really true that Sherry Hansen was living in Phoenix?

It was true. I found the listing: Rev. Sherry Hansen.

I remembered then that in addition to a list of accomplishments as long as my arm, Sherry was also an ordained Protestant minister who had attended the Lutheran School of Theology in Chicago and had later been placed on its staff.

Now all I had to do was to call her. Just pick up the telephone and dial her number. Maybe I could even say that I needed pastoral counseling.

It would take me two weeks to summon the courage to call her. But meanwhile, as I sat alone in my apartment, night after night, I had a lot of time to think about her and the bizarre events of my life that had led me to that particular juncture on my path.

I had first seen Sherry's face after a smallish being of multidimensional or otherworldly origin visited me when I was five. The morning after I had caught sight of the alien presence at the window of our Iowa farmhouse, I found a magic circle in our grove. And while I stood in the midst of its enchanted perimeter, I could hear beautiful music and I could see the lovely, smiling face of a fairy princess who had auburn hair and unusually large blue-green eyes. At the same time, I received an inner *knowing* that one day the princess and I would be together and accomplish a special kind of work together.

Because I had had a close encounter with a being that would either be classified as supernatural or extraterrestrial, depending upon one's cosmological bias, I very early on understood that our universe is a very much more wonderful place than even our science can perhaps imagine and that there truly do exist "powers and principalities" in the seen and unseen worlds, just as the Bible informs us.

My favorite hymn as a child was "Heaven Is My Home." I seemed to especially relate to the line, "I'm but a stranger here— Heaven is my home."

And yet, while recognizing the nonphysical "heavenly" spark within, I was very keenly aware of the wonder and the challenge of being a human being—a child of Earth's dust and of God's breath.

As I reviewed such thoughts in my mind while I sat alone late at night in my apartment, I found it curious that just a few weeks before Mary-Caroline Meadows had brought me the welcome greetings from Sherry, I had experienced a very significant dream about her.

I had been visiting my childhood home in Iowa. My parents' house had suffered a fire which had not destroyed it, but had caused enough damage to encourage them to move into town after a lifetime in the country.

When I came to the spot where the place I'd called "the magic circle" had been, I was saddened to see that only one large tree remained of the once majestic grove of trees and that the highly productive orchard had been plowed under in order to enlarge the tillable area for field crops. I was especially disheartened to see that the lilac bushes which had contained my "secret place" had also been removed.

I was reminded of my experience with the alien entity that had visited our farm when I was a child of five, and I thought longingly of my vision of the beautiful fairy princess.

That night I had a profound dream of Sherry Hansen, the lovely woman who had so briefly entered my office four years before; and I saw to my complete understanding that she was, as I had suspected upon first seeing her, the human representation of the fairy princess of my childhood vision.

* * *

The days went by, and I still had not called Sherry Hansen. The more I reviewed what I knew about her, the more nervous I became and the more reluctant I was to telephone her.

Although she was an ordained Protestant minister, she had also received national attention as a model, a writer-producer of television commercials, and as a publicist for some of the top acts in show business. If she hadn't developed a fever during a crucial shoot, everyone would know her as the "Excedrin P.M. Girl." If she had not been opposed to cigarette smoking, we would all know her from billboards as the "Marlboro Woman."

She had appeared in small parts in a number of made-for-television movies, but acting was not really her thing. She even turned down an offer from Norman Lear who wanted to build his first feature film around her after he had finished his incredibly popular run with "All in the Family."

Although she had appeared on posters attired in a two-piece swimsuit, she rejected lucrative offers from both *Playboy* and *Penthouse* to reveal more.

All these things she had turned down to organize the Butterfly Center for Wholistic Education in Virginia Beach, Virginia, and to serve as a founding member of the Wholistic Healing Board through the Institutes of Health and Education, Washington, D.C.

Sherry had rejected opportunities that others would have "killed for" in order to remain true to her own vision of elevating planetary consciousness.

She was obviously a woman with a mission.

And she was only a telephone number away from me.

Over and over I had rehearsed how I would begin the conversation when I got up the nerve to call her. I decided that I would say that our mutual good friend Mary-Caroline Meadows had relayed her greetings to me at Dr. Caruso's lecture. Then I would apologize for not having called sooner, and I would explain how terribly busy I had been.

But then I got to thinking that a lady might not like to hear that it was another lady who prompted me to call her, so I was uncertain what would be the best ice-breaker.

When I finally did make the call, I found myself speaking to a woman whose very voice transmitted vibrations of love, understanding, and deep wisdom—and I forgot all about mentioning mutual friends or the latest movies or the current trends in local politics or anything, for that matter.

But it still took me another three months to ask her out on a late-night coffee date.

In the meantime, though, our telephone conversations had become increasingly deep, more confessional. We began to talk for hours, releasing veritable floodgates of communication.

One night she called me at one, and we talked until three. That was when we discovered that we were both night people.

Another night she called late to tell me of a remarkable vision that had come to her during a deep meditative experience. Although she found the imagery difficult to express in words, she had seen the two of us exploding into a living pyramid of light.

As she described her vision, I received a clear picture of the two of us surrounded by enormously powerful waves of energy.

I confessed to her that she had always been an enigma and mystery in my life. I admitted that I had flashed on her image a thousand times since we had met briefly so many years before. I even got up the nerve to tell her that I had first become acquainted with her features when I was a small boy—years before she was even born into Earth plane life.

After over three months of telephone conversations, we finally met at midnight for coffee in an all-night restaurant. The impact of seeing her again was almost too much for my senses. In my memories it was her aura, her energy, more than her physical appearance that had enchanted me. In person, however, her auburn-maned beauty and her compellingly large blue-green eyes seemed an incredible bonus.

Both of us wished that the night of endless conversation and perpetually poured cups of coffee would never end, but I had to leave the next morning for Los Angeles to lecture.

The connection had been made, however, and on some deeper level of *knowing* we perceived that it would be forever.

A few days after my return, I received a call from Mary-Caroline Meadows, who in the interim months since our meeting had been away from Phoenix conducting insightful research with dolphins.

After we had chatted for a few minutes, I informed her that I was about to enter a business and research association with a good friend of hers.

"Oh, who is that?" she asked, naturally curious.

"Sherry Hansen."

There were several moments of silence.

"Mary-Caroline?"

"Ah, yes, Brad, I don't think I know anyone named Sherry Hansen."

I was stunned. "Of course you do. The night that we met, you told me that you were bringing me greetings from our mutual dear friend Sherry Hansen."

"Ah, I don't think so."

I was growing a bit impatient. I saw no need for someone failing to remember an incident that had occurred only a few months ago. Especially when it involved people who knew each other well.

"You told me that the two of you were taking a class together. She asked you to say hello to me, to give me her love."

Keeping her voice pleasant, Mary-Caroline said patiently,

"Brad, I really do not know anyone named Sherry Hansen, so I could not have promised her that I would bring you greetings from her. Secondly, I have *taught* classes in the Phoenix area, but I have never *taken* a class from anyone in Phoenix."

I had never mentioned to Sherry the stimulus that had prompted me to call her, but after I had said good-bye to Mary-Caroline, I decided that it was time to raise the issue and to solve the mystery of why Mary-Caroline had denied knowing her.

"I just had a call from your friend Mary-Caroline Meadows," I told Sherry when she answered the telephone at her office.

"My friend, *who?*" she asked.

"Mary-Caroline Meadows. You took a class with her in Phoenix just a few months ago."

Sherry was firm in her response. "I haven't taken a class *with* anyone or *from* anyone since I've been in Phoenix."

"Sher," I said, once more getting a little impatient with the whole business and deciding to come out with it, "it was because you asked Mary-Caroline to greet me at Dr. Caruso's lecture that I even knew you were in Phoenix. It was because of her relaying your message and your wishes of love that I called you."

"That is most interesting, Brad, because I will swear to you on all things that I consider holy that I do *not* know *anyone* by the name of Mary-Caroline Meadows!"

By the time that Sherry and I had finished our conversation that afternoon, I had no question left in my mind: Sherry and Mary-Caroline definitely did not know each other.

And then, for the first time, it became clear to me. Mary-Caroline had been used by some unseen entity who had temporarily entered her in order to bring Sherry and me together. In some remarkable way, the Angels of Love had interacted in the flow of our physical lives. After all these years, they had brought my fairy princess into my arms.

That night in my meditation, I heard the voice of the Light

Being that I refer to as my guide speak clearly to my spiritual essence: *"Sherry is the one for whom you have waited for so long. She is truly your destiny."*

We were married near the airport vortex in Sedona, Arizona, by Reverend Jon Terrance Diegel on August 17, 1987, at midnight during the Harmonic Convergence. Jon's wife, Dr. Patricia Rochelle Diegel was in attendance. The Diegels are two of my oldest and dearest friends, who have always been supportive of all aspects of my research. Patricia and Jon accepted Sherry as their sister, as I have been their brother.

Patricia Rochelle, who has performed more than 45,000 psychic readings, advised us that we were not simply two entities coming together as one—we were the equal parts of a whole being.

She also warned us that now that we had come together, there would be the forces of discord and chaos that would strenuously seek to pull us apart, to break us up, to once again split the single entity in two.

Because I had been scarred emotionally deeper than I believed, I at first experienced some difficulty in being able to accept just how fully and completely Sherry loved me. I had never really believed that I could be loved unconditionally for who and what I truly am.

Soon she helped me to realize that our having been brought together by the Angels of Love had formed the Living Pyramid that she had once described to me. Sherry's quiet wisdom that issues from the vibratory energy of the Oneness enabled her to become the living philosopher's stone that was able to heal my ravaged soul.

About a year after our marriage, we were lecturing in New York City for one of Paul Andrews's Whole Life EXPOs. It was late at night, we were hungry—and nothing seemed to be open except for a few greasy spoon all-night diners. At last we spotted a Chinese restaurant that appeared to be on the third floor of a building not far from our hotel.

There were only two other customers in the place. One was a man who bore an uncanny resemblance to the actor-comedian, Steve Martin. The other was his companion—Mary-Caroline Meadows.

I had not seen Mary-Caroline for nearly two years. And now—just to set my mind at peace forever—I would soon be able to detect if, in fact, Sherry and Mary-Caroline had ever met each other.

After cheerful introductions, I explained to Mary-Caroline what had occurred in my reality the night that she had sat beside me during Dr. Caruso's demonstration at the Puryears' center. She was astonished, and I suppose it gave all of us a marvelous—yet somewhat eerie feeling—to know without question how subtly the Beings of Light and the Angels of Love can interact with us in our lives.

Mary-Caroline said that she had absolutely no memory of having been "used" in such a manner to achieve such a high purpose, that of bringing two lightworkers together as one. But there was no question that her physical vehicle had been utilized to provoke me into contacting Sherry so that our mission—far too long delayed—could at last move into high gear. She now refers to herself as our Cupid Unaware.

With each passing day, it becomes clearer to me that Sherry and I have truly become a living pyramid of mind, body, and spirit. We are living crystals of Light and Love, and I know now that there is no power on Earth that can separate us.

Oh, yes, there have been difficult times and dark nights of the soul, but we know that the Angels of Love have blessed us. We have come together to complete a wondrous mission of love and light. We are now linked together in total soul union.

Two

A Snow Angel's Sweet Intervention

In January of 1972, Gloria Siburg was a freelance writer from Chicago doing a piece for a regional magazine on picturesque vacation spots in remote Midwestern rural areas. She suddenly found herself "in the very midst of the Snow Queen's Kingdom in northern Wisconsin and in the very midst of a raging blizzard."

"Why I thought that I had to set out to do research for the article in the dead of winter was beginning to make no sense at all. I was miles from any town or city, and the snow was coming down so heavy that my windshield wipers were barely able to keep up with it. And then the wind howling through the pine trees on each side of the narrow gravel road began to sound like a starving wolf."

The "oldies" station that Gloria had turned on for cheer and comfort broadcast traveler's advisory warnings after every tune.

"I freely admit that I was becoming very nervous and worried. I knew that my car could get stuck in a snowbank and that I might freeze to death before anyone with road clearing equipment ever found me. Good Lord, I thought, I could be there until the spring thaw!"

As she made her way cautiously around a sharp curve in the road, she thought that she could make out flashing red lights ahead of her. As she drew nearer, she could see a sheriff's patrol car blocking her entrance to a narrow wooden bridge.

An officer got out of the patrol car and, pulling the hood of his parka over his head, walked quickly to Gloria's vehicle.

"Ma'am, you can't keep driving on this road," he told her. "It's completely snow-packed, and it has a lot of dangerous icy spots besides. There is a major blizzard heading this way. You need to get off the roads at once."

He stepped back, glanced at her license plate, saw that her vehicle was registered in Illinois.

"Are you staying anywhere near here?" he asked. His voice was warm and filled with concern.

Gloria fought back tears of desperation and managed to maintain her control when she told him that she was lost and had no idea where she could go for refuge against the storm.

"There's no way that you're going to get very far in this heavy snow," he appraised the situation honestly. "You don't even have snow tires or chains."

Gloria noticed that the deputy appeared to be Native American in physical appearance. That would not be unusual for that particular region of Wisconsin. His eyes were brown and warm, and his manner was courteous and concerned. A shiny metal nameplate on his thick winter coat identified him as "Deputy Maleakh," and she decided, judging by the name, that her considerate law enforcement officer was definitely a member of one of the local tribes.

"What can I do, Deputy?" she wanted to know. "I was having trouble driving before I met you. How far is it to the nearest town that would have a motel?"

He shook his head grimly. "At least fifteen miles. And you know that all the rooms are going to be taken by now."

Gloria felt her stomach sink. She had never been in such a desperate situation.

"Tell you what, though," Deputy Maleakh said. "The farmers in these parts are really friendly folk. They would certainly respond to a woman in a crisis situation and be happy to take you in to sit out the storm."

Before Gloria could express her doubts or concerns, the deputy had ordered her to follow him. Under the circumstances, she decided that she really had no choice.

"Deputy Maleakh led me to a farmhouse that was not more than a mile from the bridge where he had stopped me. Thank goodness it was no farther, because my car stalled in a snow bank right in front of the home. The deputy waved good-bye, indicating that I was on my own; and he drove back down the farmer's lane and out on the narrow gravel road. He obviously had to return quickly to the bridge to warn other motorists about the dangerous road conditions ahead."

A beautiful blonde girl of about eleven answered her desperate knock at the door and, without hesitation, helped Gloria inside.

"Her father, she said as she poured me a cup of steaming hot coffee, was outside seeing to the livestock's safety. There was a big storm coming, she told me with great solemnity. We could be snowbound for days."

Gloria admitted that her account would go on to read like a romance novel.

"Suffice it to say that an Angel of Love had directed me to the love of my life, Mike Emerick. When he came into the kitchen of the farmhouse all red-faced and covered with snow, my heart felt cupid's arrow hit a bull's-eye! To my everlasting shame, I felt my pulse quicken when I learned that his wife Martha had passed away two years ago, leaving him on the farm with only his daughter Melanie."

The next four days and nights were almost as if they had been taken from the pages of a turn-of-the-century account of being snowbound in the country. They played cards, popped corn, listened to records, and watched old movies late at night on television.

"And even though I could see, feel, and *know* that Mike felt a mutual attraction to me, we were exceedingly discreet for Melanie's sake."

The telephone lines had been down for the first couple of days of Gloria's stay with the Emericks, but as soon as she got a dial tone, she told Mike that she wanted to thank Deputy Maleakh for his courtesy and for saving her life—not to mention connecting her with the man of her dreams.

"That's when Mike told me that he knew of no one named Maleakh in the sheriff's department. Mike had lived there all of his life and knew everyone on the staff.

"Theorizing that someone unknown to Mike and someone very new to the region might have joined the department, I called the sheriff and inquired about Deputy Maleakh. With a deep chuckle, he confirmed what Mike had said, then asked if this were some kind of joke.

"So at that time, I was left completely baffled as to the true identity of the Good Samaritan who had saved my life and who had brought me together with Mike."

Although Gloria had to return to Chicago, she and Mike were soon running up huge long-distance telephone bills and writing lengthy love letters to one another. When she visited Mike and Melanie in early spring, she found the area to be breathtakingly beautiful.

She had always been a big-city girl, but the natural Earth Mother beauty of rural northern Wisconsin was becoming an ever-stronger lure. And the quiet of a country farmhouse would be an ideal place to write.

It wasn't until she and Mike had decided to be married that

Gloria told her priest about the remarkable circumstances with the nonexistent Deputy Maleakh that had brought her together with the love of her life.

"Father Donlon looked at me quizzically and then broke out into a broad smile.

"'Gloria,' he said, 'your marriage is going to be truly blessed. *Maleakh* is the Hebrew word that explains what angels are, the messengers of God. And it just so happened that that particular angelic messenger was also a cupid!'"

Three

Reunion with His Heavenly Classmate

When Robert Ferrin was seven years old, he had a near-death experience when he almost died after being struck by an automobile. As sometimes occurs, young Bob was returned to life with accelerated paranormal abilities.

"During my out-of-body journey to higher dimensions, I encountered a beautiful angel of light who told me that he was my guardian angel who would always be with me. I was told that it was not yet my time to remain in the heavenly realms, so I was returned to my battered little body in the hospital."

But it wasn't long before little Bobby noticed that he could "hear" the unspoken thoughts of others.

"This can be very disconcerting to a seven-year-old. I was really frightened at first, but I soon learned to be very discreet about my new ability.

"Then, when I was eleven or so, I discovered that I was also picking up the emotional vibrations of others. This really proved to be very difficult for me, because it took me quite a while to be truly aware of what was taking place."

* * *

One night, alone in his room, Bob was wondering what was happening to him, and his angel guide manifested before him in a glowing envelope of light.

"He told me that I was to serve as a Golden Light of Peace and Love. He said that while others around me might be spinning around in emotional and mental turmoil, I was to transmit a loving energy of tranquility and balance.

"My angel warned me that this would not be an easy thing to accomplish on the Earth plane. He said that I would have to practice diligently to achieve mental and emotional harmony.

"He certainly was correct, for I failed often in my attempts to be a kind of emotional balancer. Especially during those teenage years."

When he was thirteen or fourteen, Bob remembers being taken by his angel in dreams to a beautiful golden temple on some dimension of reality.

"I was taught many awesome and beautiful things in this temple by a hooded teacher, who never quite revealed his face. Everything was explained to me in terms of energy and vibrational patterns. I was told that there were many different levels of reality. As a human, I could only see one level at a time. As a multidimensional being, I could perceive many different levels at the same time.

"Good and evil, as we humans understood the concepts, did not truly exist. There were various levels of positive and negative energies, and whether we performed acts of 'good' or 'evil' depended upon our resonance to particular vibrational levels. Nothing would be negative (evil) forever. All energies would eventually be positive and pure and One."

One night when he was sixteen, as he tried his best to absorb these higher-level teachings in some other dimension of reality, he was suddenly able to see more of the celestial environment than ever before; and he could clearly see other human students seated around him. Almost all of the members of the class were teenagers, like himself.

"When I awakened the next morning, one powerful thought reverberated within my consciousness mind: I was not alone. There were others like me!"

Bob remembered one girl in particular—a lovely young woman of about his age who had reddish-brown hair and bright blue-green eyes. He vowed then that some day he would find her.

At the same time that he was feeling very acutely alone among his friends and classmates in Cincinnati, Ohio, he found that he was becoming increasingly popular. He overheard teachers and his peers alike talking about his "charisma," the "optimistic energy he exuded," the "positive nature" he always displayed.

"You just feel like you want to be around him as much as you can, don't you?" he heard one of the varsity cheerleaders saying to a group of her friends as he walked by them on the way to class one day. "There's something about Bob that just makes you feel good."

Bob became active in as many sports and extracurricular activities as his time would permit. He was better at some pursuits than others, of course, but that never seemed to bother him. He told his friends not to be afraid to try different projects and activities, because there was really no such thing as failure.

"There is only the state of being and the opportunity for growth and love," he said.

"Love? Even in football, when you're supposed to smash the bum on the opposing team?" a buddy asked to the amusement of the other guys in the locker room.

"Even then," Bob answered with an indulgent smile.

Bob dated only to fulfill social obligations at those events on the high school calendar when it seemed appropriate to do so, but he had no special feelings for any of the girls he escorted to those special occasions. He knew that somewhere one of his fellow classmates in the Angelic Dream School was waiting for him to arrive.

"For a while there, I thought she would never show up," Robert said in his account of his interaction with the Angels of Love. "And then one day when I was twenty-nine, something caused me to turn around to face the person behind me at a bus stop—and there she was. Reddish-brown hair, bright blue-green eyes, the same intense look that I remembered from those night classes when I was a teenager."

Although Robert was normally a reserved, self-contained kind of fellow, he knew that this was the time to put all that behind him and to seize the moment.

"I know you from somewhere," he said. "Somewhere really important. Almost heavenly, you could say."

She snapped out of her reverie, startled by the stranger speaking to her. He could read her expressions easily. She was almost ready to deal harshly with some fresh, male chauvinist on the street, but after she actually took a focused look at him, she frowned, then offered him a friendly smile.

"Why . . . why, yes," she laughed. "I believe that I do know you from . . . *somewhere.* You are also very familiar to me. Was it high school?"

"You from Cincinnati?"

"No. New York City. I'm here on business for my company. I went to high school in a small town outside of Buffalo."

"Scratch high school then," Robert said. "I'm from Cincinnati. My name is Robert Ferrin. Shouldn't we get off the street corner and go somewhere nice, have a cup of coffee, maybe a little lunch, and talk about it?"

She said that her name was Sandra Yarnell, and she agreed that they should do exactly that.

When he helped her off with her coat at the small, quiet restaurant he had selected for its lack of clientele at that particular hour of the day, he noticed that she wore a small, golden angel on a chain around her neck.

"Do you believe in angels?" he asked her.

"Yes, most definitely."

"Have you ever seen one?"

Sandra looked in his eyes for a long, silent moment as they were being seated at a small table in the back. "Yes," she answered. "As a matter of fact, I have."

She folded her napkin neatly in her lap. When she looked up again, she had tears in her eyes. "And so have you, haven't you, Robert?"

A memory of having seen Robert at their angelic classroom in another dimension had suddenly returned to Sandra, and she reached for his hand.

"I've been waiting for you . . . hoping for you . . . looking for you since I was sixteen," he told her.

"And I for you," she said softly, blinking back new tears.

"I had always known that she was out there waiting for me somewhere," Robert Ferrin concluded his report. "I had always known that I was not alone, that there were other angelically tutored kids out there who had now matured and were doing what they could to spread love and light to all the world.

"Sandra and I totally readjusted our present life patterns to accommodate each other. We now live and work in the region near Carmel, California, and we conduct workshops and seminars in creating a loving reality in a world of chaos."

Four

An Angelic
Love Story

Jonathan Scordo of Gainesville, Florida, was a sickly child who suffered from severe allergic reactions to almost everything.

"My sole form of solace came from an angel who always appeared to me as a cowled figure, much like that of a monk. His voice was gentle, soothing, and his words were filled with wisdom and love. He said that his name was Jedidiah."

Jonathan told me that he had first met his angel when he was only five years old.

"I started to fall down the stairway, and someone reached out and pulled me back to a sitting position on the landing. I looked up to see this bearded man bending over and smiling at me.

"My older sister, Sarah, who was supposed to be baby-sitting me, saw me totter at the top of the steps, start to topple, then appear to fly backward to the landing. 'You must have a guardian angel!' she exclaimed in her twelve-year-old wisdom."

When Jonathan was nine, he tripped into the fireplace and burned his left forearm terribly.

"The skin appeared charred and blistered. While Father called the doctor, Mom carried me to my room and put wet cloths on the burned area. I remember the pain was excruciating.

"When Mom stepped out of the room to get some fresh cloths, Jedidiah appeared and placed the forefinger of his right hand on my burned forearm. He simply traced a straight line with his finger—and the charred area of flesh was immediately transformed back into healthy skin."

The family doctor was a personal friend of Jonathan's father, but he was still very upset over being called out on a rainy night for nothing.

"My parents protested that I had been badly burned and that they had both seen me fall into the fireplace and had both seen the area of blackened flesh. After the angry physician had departed, my sister Sarah—who was by then an exceedingly wise sixteen-year-old—told my parents quite simply and directly that 'his angel just worked another miracle, that's all.' "

When he himself turned sixteen, Jonathan was startled one night to see a strange manifestation of a greenish, glowing ball of light that appeared in his bedroom shortly after he had finished meditating.

"The glowing object just seemed to shoot around my room at great speed, yet never hitting a wall, any of the furniture, or the ceiling.

"And then suddenly it seemed as though my spiritual essence was out of my body and racing along beside the glowing ball!

"This remains one of the most exhilarating experiences that I have ever had—zipping around the room like an accelerated ping-pong ball that never had to touch anything in order to bounce.

"And then my spiritual essence and the glowing ball seemed to soar up through the ceiling and upward into the dark night sky. We seemed to dance among the stars. The feeling was absolutely ecstatic!"

After that liberating experience, Jonathan found that all of his debilitating allergies had left him. It was as if he had left his cocoon of illness and pain and emerged as a butterfly, free of blights and blemishes.

"I still had the occasional sinus headache, but all in all, I felt wonderful. I knew that it was Jedidiah, my guardian angel, who had assumed the form of the mysterious glowing ball to set my physical body free of all those restrictive illnesses and allergies."

When Jonathan met Elizabeth Carley in 1985, she was a twenty-year-old waitress who was hoping to get the right audition with the right recording executive and emerge as a singing superstar.

Jonathan was a twenty-eight-year-old high school sociology teacher and guidance counselor, who was popular and well liked by his students.

"Jedidiah would often enter my consciousness and speak through me to the students. Of course, neither they nor my superiors on the staff knew that I was channeling an angel during some of my guidance sessions. Jedidiah had a knack for saying what people *needed* to hear, rather than what they *wanted* to hear, so while some of the students might be stung by his initial comments, the truth of his counsel always rang true. And best of all, it always seemed to help them."

Elizabeth came to Jonathan's table to take his order, and she was startled when he suddenly reached up and gently took the order pad from her hands and placed her left hand in his right.

"You have a great deal of talent, young lady. Why did you leave college?" he asked her.

In her version of their meeting, Elizabeth laughed and told me that she was at first offended. She assumed he was just some wise guy trying to get fresh with her.

"But there was something about his voice and his bright blue eyes that made me stop and listen to him. And his touch—it was soothing and electrical at the same time!"

Elizabeth asked who he was. Had they met before?

"We've only met before on the inner planes," Jonathan smiled in response to her question. "I think our guardian angels know each other."

Elizabeth thought that she had encountered a religious freak or a guy with the most original line she had ever heard.

"You have a great talent for music," Jonathan was telling her, "but you have misdirected it with a false dream. You should go back to college and be a music teacher. You would be such a good teacher."

Elizabeth said that her first impulse was to tell the nosy customer that he had some nerve trying to tell her what to do, and to mind his own business.

"But there was something about his manner that wasn't mean-spirited or fresh or smart-alecky. He just seemed to be saying these things as matter-of-factly as if he were reading the stock reports in the newspaper."

She told him that she had to take his order. The boss didn't allow the waitresses to stand around and talk to the customers.

Jonathan nodded and ordered the special.

When Elizabeth got off work in an hour, Jonathan was still there.

She collected the money for his bill, then whispered that she would like to talk to him when she got off work in a couple of minutes.

"I knew that the guy could have been some nut or serial killer or something. I had never seen him in there before, after all. But there was something about his calm, yet pointed, manner of speaking that seemed so kind and loving. I mean loving in a universal way. And I had to find out how he could know so much about me!"

Jonathan offered his car as a place to sit and talk, but the cautious Elizabeth pointed out her battered old four-door Chevrolet in the parking lot and suggested that they just ride around for a while. She figured that if they were in her car and she was at the wheel, she would have a bit more control over the situation than if she were a passenger in his car. That was if he proved to be some kind of nut or something, that is.

The two of them talked until nearly dawn. They soon abandoned the woebegone Chevy and found an all-night diner in which they could share comments, ideas, and concepts with only the occasional interruption of a tired waitress refilling their coffee cups.

"Elizabeth didn't know it at the time, of course, but I let Jedidiah do most of the talking," Jonathan said. "It was he who convinced her to go back to college."

Elizabeth was astonished by the entire evening. "I felt as if I were dreaming. Not only is this complete stranger telling me what an illusion a career as a nightclub singer would be for me to pursue, but he is praising my ability to become a serious singer and teacher of voice. What is more, he is offering to help finance my return to college!"

When Elizabeth protested such an offer, Jonathan shrugged and laughed away her objections.

He told her that he was a single man living inexpensively in a studio apartment. He had no expensive hobbies, no extravagant vices, no lavish tastes.

"No girlfriend?" Elizabeth wanted to know.

Jonathan smiled at her over the rim of his coffee cup. "I have many girl *friends*. But no one serious if that's what you mean."

It was still all too much for Elizabeth to consider in such a brief time.

"Look at it this way," Jonathan argued. "I am investing in your future. I have been very blessed in my life. The angelic law of the universe says that when one has been blessed, it is the divine obligation of that person to bless another. One day it will be your obligation to pass the blessing on."

Elizabeth agreed that he had a lovely philosophy, but he was talking about more than a blessing. He was talking about money.

"Oh, very well then," Jonathan sighed, "if you are so concerned about the money, some day you can pay me back as you are able. We'll call it a loan for now."

"A loan sounds better," Elizabeth nodded.

"Better than a blessing?" Jonathan wondered at her process of evaluation. "Extraordinary."

"How is it you know so much about blessings and angels?" she asked him.

And then, for the next two hours, Jonathan told her all about Jedidiah, his angelic mentor.

By the time that the two of them left the all-night diner at 5:15 A.M., they had agreed to a plan regarding Jonathan's pledge to enable Elizabeth to complete her final year and a half at college.

"I drove Jonathan back to the restaurant parking lot so he could get into his car and dash home to his apartment to shower and shave before he was to be at school by 8:00. I knew then, of course, that I had met the most extraordinary man in the western hemisphere—if not the entire world. I also knew that I had fallen in love in one night."

Jonathan felt completely exhilarated that entire day at school—even though he had not been able to capture one wink of sleep.

"That magical evening had brought me something far more invigorating than sleep. The moment that I had walked into that restaurant at what I thought was completely at random, Jedidiah whispered in my ear that my destiny would soon be at my side. The moment I looked into Elizabeth's eyes, I felt as if I was once again that sixteen-year-old boy soaring through the stars with my angelic mentor. After that, I just permitted Jedidiah to do all my talking for me."

Elizabeth said that Jonathan was at all times the perfect gentleman during the next two years.

"I am positive that I kissed him first. And that was after we had met for coffee and dinner half a dozen times.

"He still hung back quite a distance until I was once again well into the flow of college classes, then we began to see each other regularly. I still kept a part-time job at the restaurant, and Jonathan, of course, had his teaching and counseling assignments."

However, neither of them was very surprised when Jedidiah recommended to Jonathan that he present Elizabeth with an engagement ring on her graduation day.

Since 1988, Elizabeth and Jonathan have been teaching in the same Georgia high school, being of service and counsel to their students and their community.

Five

Drawn Together in Spirit

Anastasia and Jon Marc Hammer, the co-directors of Heartlight Ministries of Santa Fe, New Mexico, a non-profit, educational entity dedicated to personal and planetary healing, came together in a way which clearly demonstrates the helping hand of guides that often seem to know our destiny more clearly than we do. But they affirm that their story tells us more: That soulmates come together for very specific purposes—purposes which often find their origins in other times and places.

"Imagine if you will," they wrote in their account of their unusual series of experiences, "what happened to Jon Marc one incredible morning in 1987. He had been rushing about his home in the State of Washington, doing all the usual things he did to get himself out the door and to his office.

"Suddenly, he heard a voice that seemed to come from everywhere. The voice spoke with calm certainty, great authority, and a depth of love.

"Along with the voice, Jon Marc felt embraced by waves of an incredibly peaceful, nurturing energy—unlike anything he had ever known.

"The voice said calmly: *'Please sit and meditate.'* "

Without further thought concerning his busy schedule, Jon Marc put his briefcase down, proceeded to the couch, closed his eyes, and went within. As his mind became quiet, a light seemed to appear in the distance, growing brighter as it moved toward him. The waves of energy that he had felt earlier were now lifting him higher and higher into the light itself.

"Then a form of someone began to appear," Jon Marc said. "It was the form of someone a part of me knew beyond all doubt. He came so close that I could feel him merge with me. He shared many things, including his name. It is a name with which millions are familiar.

" *'I am Jeshua, whom the world knows as Jesus,'* he told me."

A part of Jon Marc knew then that his life had taken an abrupt turn, a turn that somewhere in the sleeping corners of his mind, he knew had long ago been agreed upon.

That was how Jon Marc came to find himself serving as both channel and author, sharing the message of Jeshua with people across the country.

"But I had no way of knowing that Jeshua was also working behind the scenes with someone else who was coming to a major place of awakening—someone I would come to recognize more deeply than anyone I had ever encountered."

Anastasia had been living a normal life in Chico, California. Like Jon Marc, she was in a "comfortable" relationship, one based on all the "right" reasons. But something was beginning to brew within her. There was a longing welling up within her heart.

"I remember one day in particular," she said. "My husband had gone off to work, and I had sat down on the couch. As I looked around me, everything seemed so *good!* Nice house, creature comforts, a wonderful dog, friends. But something was beginning to call me from somewhere in my soul. I lit some candles and began to meditate, gazing into a mirror in front of me."

What began to unfold was something that Anastasia could never have predicted.

"All of a sudden, I began to sob uncontrollably—deep convulsions of tears that came from my very core.

"The pain became so intense that I confess to thoughts of just wanting to die, to leave the planet."

Anastasia's thinking mind could make no sense out of what had happened to her.

"I called a friend, a nationally known psychic, who told me that I was beginning a major process of transformation, that the tears were nothing to worry about.

"Later, feeling exhausted, I went to bed and fell quickly to sleep."

But that particular night's sleep would prove to be very different from all others.

About 2:00 A.M., Anastasia felt nudged awake. When she sat up, her whole body began to tremble, to vibrate with an amazingly gentle and loving energy.

She heard a thought within her mind: *Sit and meditate.*

"When I arranged myself before the mirror, I was shocked to see that it was not my own face staring back at me. It was the face of someone for whom I had felt great fondness throughout my life. I had tucked this unexplainable fondness safely in the closet of my mind, for it had always seemed as though the world would not understand my sense of *knowing* this nonphysical friend. In the mirror was the face of Jeshua."

Anastasia said that she remembers clearly being transported to a timeless, loving space, immersed in light and love that swept away a fog that had been covering her awareness.

"I sensed that my purpose for coming to the planet was being remembered and that Jeshua was silently confirming something of importance to me. The anguish was gone, and I felt deeply at peace."

But things were only beginning. Over the next several months, both Jon Marc and Anastasia began to have dreams that were very different in quality—dreams that left each of them feeling that something was stirring just out of sight of their surface consciousness.

"I began having dreams of a woman with long blond hair and eyes filled with light coming toward me," Jon Marc said. "Each time I beheld this woman, I clearly felt my heart stirring in ways that I had never before experienced.

"Interestingly, I eventually recalled this dream as the same one that had repeated itself to me at the age of twelve. Since I had been unable to understand their meaning then, the dreams had gradually been forgotten."

In her series of unusual dreams, Anastasia was envisioning a man—a man who was definitely *not* the man with whom she was currently in a relationship.

"The energy that I felt in my heart during the dreams was unlike anything I could imagine," she recalled. "I was afraid to share them with anyone. How would I be able to describe something so hauntingly familiar that generated such a profound sense of oneness—yet it was not connected to anyone I knew. Especially not the man I was sleeping next to!"

In the coming weeks—during meditation or being nudged awake from sleep—Anastasia would suddenly see the image of this man hovering near her for just a moment. And each time the experience would always elicit the same deep feelings of ancient familiarity.

Meanwhile, Jon Marc would find himself in the midst of his normal daily activities and he would suddenly feel as though his heart was about to explode out of his chest. At the same time, he would feel immersed in warmth and in light. He, too, kept such matters to himself.

One day a friend of Jon Marc's expressed an intuitive notion that he should visit Chico, California, and share his work with Jeshua there.

The words struck him like a bolt of lightning, and he felt resistant to the idea. "Where the heck is Chico? I don't know anyone there!"

But his friend was quite insistent and said that she would make some telephone calls to get an evening group set up for his visit. Grudgingly, Jon Marc agreed to go.

At the same time, Anastasia was enjoying a vacation in the Teton Mountains.

"As was my habit," she said, "I got up one morning and found a quiet spot to meditate. As I simply enjoyed being with Mother Earth, I relaxed very quickly into a quiet space.

"Suddenly an image of Jeshua appeared in my mind, and I was immediately aware of the thought: *Go home now!* So certain and clear was the message that I awakened my partner and told him matter-of-factly that we were cutting our vacation short. Oddly, he complied without a word of objection."

When she arrived home, Anastasia had a message on her answering machine from her yoga teacher, who advised her that some fellow was coming from the state of Washington, and that he channeled Jesus. Would she like to go?

"Every cell in my body tingled," Anastasia remembered. "Of course I wanted to go. I was sure that this was why Jeshua had appeared to me in the Tetons.

"I had always pooh-poohed channeling, yet as the time for the meeting drew near, my heart was racing. At first I thought that I should call everyone in my meditation group to attend the session—but a little voice kept saying, 'No, this is for you.' "

Anastasia recalled that on her way out of the door of her home, her partner remarked, "Be sure the guy is not a charlatan!"

Without a second's hesitation, she had replied that she would know the moment she walked into the place whether or not the man was genuine.

Later, she would wonder where these words, spoken with such certainty, had come from.

When she did enter the room where the event was being held, she saw a number of people milling about chatting. Then her eyes riveted on a man in the midst of the crowd.

"My whole being stopped," she said. "I felt a *whoosh* of energy. The man turned and looked at me, and just as quickly turned away again. There was such an immediate knowing.

"I muttered something to my friend who had come with me, but I was unaware at the time that I had said anything at all.

"I do remember saying, 'There is the most beautiful being I have ever known.' And then I mumbled that I had probably better sit down before I fell down."

As the evening progressed, Anastasia felt the familiar waves of loving energy that she had experienced on those occasions when Jeshua had appeared to her.

"I did not see Jon Marc's physical form at all. It was more like light—and within the light there appeared kaleidoscopic images of various persons from different time frames. Each one felt completely familiar. I sensed that I was in a new place of awareness. The floodgates had opened—nothing would ever be quite the same."

Jon Marc stated that his responses toward Anastasia were a bit slower.

"When I felt that whoosh of energy and turned to see her, my breath stopped. I wanted to leave the room! I was in a relationship that was quite comfortable, and I did not want to feel anything that would rock the boat."

* * *

The next day, Anastasia came for a private session with Jon Marc.

"It was like a homecoming, touching the deepest part of my heart," she recalled. "And it was very clear that Jeshua knew me completely."

Near the end of the session, she asked Jeshua when she would know what part, if any, she had to play in the work that was unfolding with him.

Jeshua asked her to "tune in" and perceive the answer.

"In ninety days," Anastasia said.

Jeshua told her that her response was accurate.

Jon Marc returned to his home in Washington, but something had begun to move within him. Try as he might, he could not prevent feelings of oneness with Anastasia from arising within his very essence. Somehow his coming together with her seemed so inevitable.

As things turned out, it was exactly ninety days later when Jon Marc returned to Chico. And now the floodgates would open completely for Anastasia and him.

After Jon Marc's initial visit to Chico, Anastasia had a powerful dream of Jon Marc and her walking in a local park.

"He put his arm around my waist in a friendly sort of way. We looked at each other—and all the veils blocking recognition of our union dissolved away.

"When I awoke from the dream, I cried deeply and convinced myself that I had surely created a fantasy in my mind."

One day after he had returned to Chico for another evening event and a few days of private readings, Jon Marc was passing some free time watching Anastasia play with her German shepherd, Schatzie.

"I suddenly heard a voice that instructed me to *'pay attention,'* " Jon Marc said. "Then it felt as though fingers were prying open my forehead. I began to see images of lifetime after lifetime in which Anastasia and I had been together. The images stretched back through time and finally disappeared into a radiant golden light."

He excused himself politely and went off to bed where he begged Jeshua to help him understand what had just occurred.

"All Jeshua would say was that it was important for me to allow myself to feel everything deeply—and that there would be a time when we would be able to discuss it."

The very next day, Anastasia's precognitive dream played itself out exactly as she had experienced it.

On their walk in the park, Jon Marc put his arm around her waist, and they began to share openly all those things which they had been individually experiencing.

They were so sure of their destiny together, neither of them was surprised when Jon Marc asked, "Will you be moving to Washington, or will I move to Chico?" Anastasia simply replied, "I will move to Washington."

In retrospect, Anastasia commented that it was all quite matter-of-fact.

"It was just a given. It wasn't a walk in the park filled with romanticism. We simply *knew* in the deepest place in our shared heart that we were to be together—and that the time had finally come."

When Jon Marc flew home to Washington, it was his turn for tears.

"I sobbed all the way home, tears flowing without shame. It felt as if a dam had burst, as though the purpose of my life was just beginning."

Jon Marc felt that he needed some really specific answers, so he went to the mountain to meditate, to try to get to the bottom of all that had happened to him.

"Every time that I asked Jeshua for help, all that he would say was that it was important for me to continue to feel everything deeply—and that at the proper time, we would be able to talk about it."

Jon Marc hiked by moonlight to a favorite hot spring—only to discover someone else there.

As he turned to leave, he heard Jeshua say, "Stay and listen."

At that same moment, the man in the hot spring noticed Jon Marc and asked him to join him in the pool.

"He began sharing that something had compelled him to drive four hours to this place. On the way, he began to think about the life of Jesus, and he had felt a longing to be closer to him.

"Then he casually said that he had been gay all of his life, but that a few months ago, a woman had walked into his shop and they had experienced an instant recognition. And now they were married! He asked if I had ever heard about soul mates.

"It was clear why I was supposed to be in that hot spring at just that time."

Back in his tent, Jon Marc sat in meditation, determined to get to the bottom of all the incredible things that had been happening to him. As he went deeper into all that had unfolded, he was finally forced to see that he, too, had met his soul mate—a term that previously he had always brushed aside.

Once he had achieved that realization, he immediately felt Jeshua's presence. *"Now, we can begin to talk about these things!"*

Jeshua told Jon Marc that he was now at a major crossroads in his present life experience.

"He explained that I was undergoing an initiation of sorts, and the conflict that I was feeling was between my head and my heart and between the pressures of how the world thinks and what the soul knows. He concluded by saying that it should be abundantly clear to me after those several years with him that he would advocate the wisdom of the soul which speaks to us through the heart."

One week later, a large group of people had gathered in Seattle to hear Jeshua's message. At the end of the evening, after everyone had left, a woman named Karen came back inside and asked to speak privately with Jon Marc.

"Do you remember when I had a private session with Jeshua about seven months ago?" she asked him.

"Yes," Jon Marc replied. "Vaguely."

"Well," she continued, "Jeshua asked if I would do him a favor—to which I quickly agreed. He asked that I deliver a message to you. When I asked him *when* I should do this, he said, 'Fear not. You will know beyond doubt.'

"Just as I was getting into my car tonight to go home, I felt this very strong nudge, and I heard a voice saying that the time was now. I tried to ignore it, but it grew insistent.

"The message is, *'Trust your heart.'*"

The resistance in Jon Marc melted away when he recognized the masterful weaving of guidance that Jeshua had given him.

He cried and hugged Karen and told her that she had no idea of the blessing that she had just bestowed upon him.

Somewhat puzzled, Karen turned and walked back to her car.

Back in Chico, Anastasia remembered that she wasn't "quite finished, either." She had called two very good psychics for confirmation.

"Both of them said that they saw our soulstrands going back into infinity.

"I was told by one that she could clearly see Jesus and he was sharing with her that his blessings were upon our union and that our souls had long ago signed the 'contract' to be always together."

* * *

Within a month, the two of them had walked through their personal ordeal by fire and were together.

They knew little about one another's personality, but they considered such matters rather insignificant. Finally the world made sense to them.

They had discovered a safety with each other, a safety that has allowed each to heal deeply all "unfinished business."

Through their Heartlight Ministries, Jon Marc and Anastasia present workshops, classes, seminars, and extended retreats around the country. The essential goal of their work is to assist others to open their hearts, empower their lives, and to recognize themselves as the radiant lights they are. Their work with those requesting help with relationships is called "Sacred Intimacy."

Kendra Press, the publishing branch of Heartlight Ministries, distributes the teachings of Jeshua in communion with Jon Marc. Current titles include *The Jeshua Letters* and *The Way of the Servant.*

"We feel that we are being asked to help facilitate a new model of relationship, one based on a new paradigm of an androgynous union committed to mutual empowerment and planetary healing," Anastasia and Jon Marc told me.

"It is time to let go of the old model of relationships, which are often created from the ego's attempt to find comfort and security from the world—rather than listening to the still, small voice within. While at first it may be frightening to pay heed to that voice, it will make all the difference, as evidenced by our personal stories.

"Many people ask us how they may find that special someone, and our answer is always the same:

"When we came together, we were not seeking each other. We feel that our experiences started to unfold naturally, because on some unseen level we were ready and willing to be together.

"Know that you are whole now—and put your focus on healing your sense of separation from God.

"When you grasp the awareness that you are complete *now,* the universe is able to mirror that awareness back to you in the form of a relationship. When it is time, you simply won't be able to prevent such a union from occurring.

"Or as our friend and teacher Jeshua once put it: 'Seek ye first the kingdom, and all these things will be added unto you.'"

Six

Listen to Your Soul

Dave Ragan, who now lives in a medium-sized city in Missouri, wrote to my office to tell of the angel that first manifested in his presence when he was a child of five.

"I will never forget the image of the beautiful entity when I was playing in the woods near our home in Idaho. I couldn't really tell if the angel was male or female, but the voice that I heard inside my head seemed to be a bit more feminine. It was soft and gentle, kind of like hearing sweet music being played on a harp.

"The angel said that it would always be with me, guiding me, looking after me. I remember being really afraid, but she told me to have no fear. She said that she loved me."

The angel contacted Dave several times throughout his childhood.

"The second time, I didn't see her, but I definitely heard her voice warning me not to enter a cave. I remember that I thought, 'why not?' because I had seen some older boys crawl into the cave a few weeks before. Then I got a mental image of a rattlesnake, and I pulled out right away. A few days later, a hunter told my father that he had shot the 'granddaddy of all rattlesnakes' near that same cave."

* * *

A couple of times after that, Dave thought that he might have caught a glimpse of his guardian angel, but as the years went by, he had to be contented with only the sound of her sweet, musical voice speaking to him inside his head.

"A rather strange aspect to my story is that my family was not particularly religious. We went to church on most of the religious holidays, but not too much more. I remember one exasperated minister accusing my father of being a 'Christmas Christian.' So why I had this constant interaction with an angel was always rather puzzling to me. I mean, it wasn't as if I had done anything to deserve it."

Dave had gone steady with a girl during his senior year in high school.

"She was getting really serious, and she was quite upset when we went to different colleges. We wrote for a time and carried on a long-distance romance for most of the first semester, but my feelings for her cooled, and during the holiday break, I told her that I thought we should start seeing other people.

"I had expected a few tears, but she really tore into me. She said a lot of personal things that really hurt my feelings. I left her place feeling terribly confused, wondering if I had done the right thing. But then I heard my angel's voice clear as could be inside my head: *'Don't be disturbed. Don't despair. She is not the one with whom you'll spend your life.'* "

Dave began to get serious toward the end of his junior year in college when he actually bought an engagement ring for a stunning, dark-haired girl from Montana.

"She was vivacious, really lovely, and filled with seemingly inexhaustible energy. And when I went home with her during one vacation break to meet her parents, I saw that her daddy owned a very large spread of ranchland. She didn't seem to be in any hurry to settle down, but I had decided that I didn't want to take any chances of her getting away from me.

"I was about to pop the question. I had even memorized a couple verses of some really romantic poetry to help me create the most dramatic effect when I brought out the diamond ring after a lavish dinner at an expensive restaurant.

"Although it does seem amusing in retrospect, my angel whispered to me right after I had ordered dessert and just before I brought out the engagement ring. *'This would be a terrible mistake that you would always regret. She is not the one who will make a suitable life partner for you.'*

"With those words ringing inside my head, the night of nights became simply a marvelous dinner at a fine restaurant.

"About a week later, she broke our date to go to the movies, pleading a bad head cold and a touch of the flu. But later that evening my roommate and I saw her dancing with one of the big men on campus, a rich jerk who belonged to one of the other fraternities.

"That's when my buddy leveled with me and told me that he had heard through the rumor mill that she had been two-timing me for months. He had not wanted to hurt my feelings until he had some definite proof that she was messing around behind my back.

"I really surprised my roommate when I said I wanted to stop by the chapel before I went back to our apartment. He left me alone, thinking that I must really be broken up. Well, of course, I was hurt and upset. But what I really wanted to do was to thank my guardian angel for saving me from making a very bad mistake.

"The jeweler was decent enough to take the ring back—but he did hold back a little over a hundred dollars 'for his trouble.' But I considered that I was still money ahead. Divorces are a lot more expensive than engagement rings."

Dave continued to date—perhaps much more cautiously— always looking forward to the day when the sweet, melodic voice of his angel would give him the green light for a permanent relationship.

It didn't happen for him until he was nearly thirty and becoming quite successful as a real estate salesman.

"Tina Mattes, a very attractive young widow of twenty-eight with two small children—a boy and a girl—stopped by my office to discuss the various issues involved in listing her house with my agency. She lived in an exclusive part of the city, she explained, and because her husband had been killed in an automobile accident the year before, she did not feel that she could afford to keep up the mortgage payments on such a large house. Unfortunately, her husband, Brian Mattes, had been woefully underinsured; and now she bravely accepted her responsibility to make the necessary adjustments in lifestyle in order to protect the future welfare of her children.

"I was quite astonished when my angel spoke up loud and clear inside my head: *'This is the one. She is the one for you. She is the one selected as your helpmate on your lifepath.'* "

That night, after work, Dave sat quietly in the darkness of his apartment and asked his angel aloud if she had truly meant what she had said about the young widow.

The answering voice seemed to issue from all around him: *"She is truly the one for you. She is the one for whom we have waited."*

"I don't mean to sound insensitive," Dave apologized to his unseen guide, "but the lady has two children. I feel somewhat awkward saying this, but I think it would be difficult for me to start a marriage with two kids already there. I mean, I think I would need some time to get adjusted to married life before I could deal with kids."

"It is part of your destiny to be a father. You need such life experiences for the good and the gaining of your Soul."

Dave protested that he was not saying that he did not wish to

have children. He felt only that he would need some time to prepare mentally and emotionally for fatherhood.

*"You do not have the proper seed to father children of your own.
The only children who will grace your home will be those given to
you by another."*

Dave puzzled over his angel's words, but she would speak to
him no more that night.

The next morning he had an appointment with Tina Mattes at
her home for the purpose of writing up a complete listing of the
qualities and advantages that her residence might offer a prospec-
tive buyer.

"I arrived at ten in the morning—and by three I hadn't even
thought of my one o'clock luncheon date or of leaving the house.
I had never hit it off so quickly and so thoroughly with a woman
in my entire life. Before I completely realized what was happening, I heard myself asking Tina out for dinner that night—and
what was even more incredible, I heard her accepting."

When Dave finally left her home at four that afternoon to
drive back to his office, his angel seemed almost to be chirping
happiness: *"It is as it has been written. She is the one for whom we
have waited. She is the one for whom we have saved you!"*

Dave stated in his written account of his angelically inspired
courtship with Tina that everything seemed to work out as if some
heavenly screenwriter was daily turning out the pages of a cosmic
script that the two mortals were following to the letter.

"We loved the same music, the same movies, the same foods,
the same everything, it seemed. To use the old cliché, we truly did
seem to be two peas in the same pod. I had never felt so natural,
so at ease with a woman.

"And her kids—Tammy and Rodney—they were marvelous.
The very notion of seeing a lady with two rug rats would normally
have terrified me. But they were respectful and well-behaved—
and they genuinely seemed to like me."

Dave admitted, though, that his angel's comments about his "seed" not being proper troubled him greatly.

"I'm kind of embarrassed to admit it, but I had never really read the Bible all that much. You know, a few passages here and there. And I had never been what anyone would call a literary kind of guy.

"I called a friend of mine who had once studied for the priesthood, but who had left over his honest problem with the celibacy requirement. After the usual exchange of the social amenities, I asked him to consider, theoretically, what an angel might mean if she or he referred to a person's 'seed.'

"Once I convinced my buddy that I had not been drinking and that I was really serious, and really wanted to know, he told me the answer was easy. Throughout the Bible, a man's 'seed' referred to his semen, his ability to propagate the species, to reproduce."

Dave thanked his friend, then hung up the telephone more troubled than before.

"My angel had always seemed to know everything about me. But now she was saying that there was something wrong with my semen."

Dave decided not to distress himself any further over the matter. He left a sample of his semen at a local clinic and awaited the report from his doctor.

"My angel was right as always. The lab tests came back that I was sterile, and I remembered the really severe case of mumps that I had had as a teenager. It was just as my angel had advised me: If I wanted to be a father, I would have to adopt children. So, I reasoned, what better children to adopt than the terrific kids of the woman who I was truly beginning to love with all my heart and soul!"

Dave Ragan married Tina Mattes in December of 1987. Six-year-old Tammy was a junior bridesmaid and four-year-old Rodney walked a smooth course down the aisle as the ring-bearer.

"Just before we were married, I told Tina that my guardian angel had picked her out for me years ago and had been shepherding me into her corral ever since we met.

"Tina only smiled and said, 'Then ours should truly be a marriage made in Heaven.' "

Dave said that he still receives intuitive hunches. He is convinced that they come from his guardian angel, but the last time he heard her sweet angelic voice inside his head was when Tina was coming down the aisle on the arm of her father to stand beside him at the altar.

"Well done," I heard her say. *"Well done!"*

Seven

❖

Tender Loving Care from Heaven

William Mandel and Eve Jacobs had known each other for several years and had become good friends long before they had begun to think of each other as potential lovers.

"When that awareness did come," Eve said, "it came suddenly, to both of us at once; and it seemed so natural that we could not help chiding ourselves for the three years of high school, four years of college, and two years working together in the same real estate office—nine years in all—that we had wasted by not going out with each other!"

Eve remembered that William used to pronounce solemnly around the stem of his briar pipe that a Force-Greater-Than-They had seen fit for some reason to keep them apart—yet together—for nine years.

"I sometimes blushed at the memories of the many past occasions when I had taken my love-life problems to William, who, at the time, had seemed like an older brother in whom I could confide," Eve said.

When William proposed marriage, Eve did not hesitate to say

yes. They would both be twenty-six in July. They had known each other for eleven years and had been dating for nearly two. They had not fallen in love; they had grown in love.

Then, two months before the wedding in August of 1973, William was killed in an automobile accident.

"I was left absolutely shattered by William's death," Eve said. "It was nearly eighteen months before I even thought of dating again.

"Two years later, after I had begun to go out somewhat steadily with Owen Laverty, he asked me to marry him. We had only been dating for about three months, and I asked for some time to consider his proposal. I felt that given time I would be able to love Owen, but I did not wish to marry him just then."

Eve explained her feelings to Owen, but the man continued to court her persistently for nearly two years. Finally, she agreed to marry her patient suitor.

Then, less than a week before the wedding . . .

"I lay tossing and turning in bed, unable to sleep," Eve said. "My mind was full of thoughts of William, my dead fiancé, rather than of Owen, my living husband-to-be.

"My entire being seemed to be permeated by a strange uneasiness. How I wished that William might be there to discuss the matter with me, to give me sage counsel as he had so often in the past. In spite of myself, I began to weep."

In between her sobbings, Eve was certain that she could hear William's voice calling her name.

"I sat bolt upright in bed, struck with the sudden realization that I was not imagining the sound of his voice. *I was actually hearing William calling to me!*"

She looked in the direction from which the voice seemed to be coming, and she was startled to see William standing solid as life next to her dresser.

"So many incredible images swirled through my brain that for a moment or two, I thought that I might succumb to the shock of seeing William standing there.

"Then I became strangely pacified at the sound of his voice. *"Your marriage to Owen is a serious mistake. You must not marry Owen Laverty. He is not the man for you. He is not the man that he appears to be."*

Eve was so moved by the apparition of her dead fiancé that she feigned illness and told Owen that they must postpone their marriage in order to give her the necessary time to recuperate.

"Two weeks later, Owen was arrested on a charge of illegally possessing marijuana and of selling heroin and cocaine. During his hearing, evidence was produced that would convict him of being a drug dealer.

"As if that were not bad enough to have justified William's warning from beyond the grave," Eve added, "subsequent investigation revealed that Owen was already married and had a wife in prison. That poor woman, whose existence had been previously unknown to me, had become a drug addict under the ministrations of Owen Laverty."

Two years later, Eve said, Tom Shields asked her to marry him.

"This time I felt almost certain that an apparition of William, my guardian angel on the other side, would once again appear to advise me whether or not my choice was a wise one. I was praying that the spirit of my dear friend and lover would not manifest to inform me that Tom was some kind of secret monster.

"Three nights before our August 1978 wedding, William appeared in my room. He looked just as solid as he had when he materialized two years before. I was not shocked this time, and I waited eagerly for some sign of communication from him.

"This time William only smiled, waved a hand in farewell, and disappeared. I knew that dear William had given my marriage to Tom Shields his blessing."

Eight

✦

Careful Attention to Her Angel

As her friends judged her according to her outer life, Doris Barnes was as normal as blueberry pie. In fact, when she was in high school, she was viewed as the all-American girl. She was an excellent student, co-captain of the varsity cheerleaders, president of the junior class; and when she was a senior, she was elected Homecoming Queen.

But Doris had a secret that she kept from even her closest friends. Ever since she was five years old, she had been in steady communication with an angel.

"I remember it all began a few nights before Christmas in 1956 when we left our comfortable little town to drive to Omaha to look at the holiday lights in the big city," Doris told me. "I looked up at the night sky and said in a wistful voice, 'I want to go home.' And then I started to cry."

Her parents and her older brother misunderstood her. They thought the five-year-old meant their cozy four-bedroom home on Baker Terrace.

"I meant the stars," Doris explained. "I suddenly had a clear image that my true home was in Heaven, somewhere beyond the stars. When I tried to tell them that I meant my home in Heaven, not my home in Nebraska, my folks got all upset, fearing that I had some premonition of my impending death. I remember that the very next day they took me to see the doctor for a complete medical checkup."

Then, on Christmas Eve, shortly after she had been tucked in bed to dream of Santa coming down the chimney with gifts, the angel materialized in her room.

"The truly weird part is that Mom was just leaving the room when the being appeared. Throughout the entire time that the angel presented itself to me, Mom stood frozen, paralyzed, right next to her. I say 'her,' because the entity appeared to me to be a female. Now that I am much older, I might say rather that the angel was basically androgynous in appearance."

Doris recalled that the angel's essential message at that time was that there was a God in Heaven who loved all little children and that she had a guardian angel who was assigned to look after her.

"The beautiful being said that there were many things that she would teach me in the years to come—and that I should never be frightened by her appearances," Doris said. "She said that I would not be able to summon her at my will, but that she would come to visit me according to some kind of heavenly plan."

As would occur to most small children to ask, Doris wanted to know what her angel's name was.

"She told me that angels didn't really have names the way little boys and girls did, but she said that I could call her Zena."

It was after that first visitation that Doris began to experience a really strong sense of her true self, her soul, belonging more to some other place.

"At that age, of course, I could only express myself by telling people that Heaven was my true home. Folks in our small Nebraska town just thought that I was a very religious little girl."

The angelic being kept her word and manifested many times to Doris.

"Sometimes Zena would just appear beside my bed at night. On other occasions, she would seem to come through the walls or the ceiling.

"When I was eleven or twelve, she began to take me with her on marvelous journeys to what I could only assume—and still do—were other worlds, other dimensions, other universes. I remember clearly one time going with her right through the glass of a closed window and wondering how she was able to accomplish such a feat."

Doris told me that on a number of occasions she was provided with physical proof of her incredible voyages with her angelic guide.

"Once I returned with an acorn in my hand after we had visited some great forest in the northwest. Another time, my angel took me to see the awesome red-rock country of Sedona, Arizona, and I came back with a small red pebble that I had picked up from a hillside."

Doris attributes her ease with her classroom lessons and her homework to the "mind expansion" that she received from her angel.

"I also received lessons in humility, graciousness, and love of all things on the planet, but about the time I was turning fifteen, I began to wonder about boys and going out on dates. Zena told me that I could be 'social,' but I should not allow myself to become serious about any of the boys in my high school. She said that there was someone special for me and I would meet him in 'the fullness of time.' "

When she was sixteen, Doris began to have vivid dreams of a young man with light brown hair who walked with a slight limp.

"He seemed very pleasant, quite good-looking; and I had many dreams about meeting him and being with him. I kind of hoped that this particular guy wasn't my dream man, because at that time I was really into physical fitness and body consciousness. I was a varsity cheerleader, cheering on all those great young athletes with their terrific bodies. I knew that I would always have an active lifestyle, and I wanted someone who would be able to keep up with me."

As she entered her late teens, the angel's visitations grew much less frequent.

"I can remember seeing her only twice during my senior year of high school. I don't think I saw Zena at all during my first year in college. My sophomore year, I saw her just once.

"Although I was still certain that I 'felt' her presence and was aware of her guidance on some level of consciousness, I was kind of concerned. I knew very well that I had not outgrown my need for angelic counsel, but I also remembered Zena saying that I must never become too dependent upon her. A very important lesson in our education on Earth was to learn to be self-reliant and resourceful."

At the beginning of her junior year, Doris told me that she began for the first time to read the Bible regularly. I was quite surprised to hear this, as I assumed that the angel had taken pains to see to her religious education.

"No, Brad," Doris answered my query. "Zena saw to my *spiritual* education. She spoke always along very universal lines, never advocating the path of any particular earthly religious expression. She emphasized ethics, morality, and unconditional love.

"To love another person unconditionally is probably the hardest thing for us humans to practice. For us, love is almost always conditional. You know, 'I'll love you—if you love me back.' Even as parents we too often permit our children to infer that we love them only when they are behaving in the manner that we wish them to act."

Although the angel's appearances were less frequent, Doris said that the dreams of the handsome young man with the light brown hair had increased.

"Sometimes it almost seemed as if I were living two lives in two different dimensions. The one was the rather dull academic routine of a college student. The other was a much more romantic existence as an explorer of some sort, traveling over mountain trails, hacking through jungle growth, digging through ancient ruins—all in the company of this man my angel had said was my prearranged mate."

Since I knew her as Doris Barnes Zemke, I knew that we had to be coming to the part of her story where she met Gary and lived happily ever after.

"Not so fast, Brad," she laughed. "If only life were that easy. If only I had listened to my guardian angel."

Doris explained that toward the end of her senior year in college she had begun to go steady with a bright and attractive business major from Kankakee, Illinois.

"Ted seemed to be the right man for me. He had light brown hair, was co-captain of the men's tennis team, and he didn't have a limp. I figured that my dream lover's limp must have been symbolic of some other lesson that Zena had been trying to teach me as a fifteen-year-old, and I rationalized—against the argument of that 'still, small voice' within me—that Ted was the man that the angels had destined for me."

Doris confessed to me that Zena had manifested physically before her for the first time in two years, shortly before her wedding to Ted.

"Zena told me that I had not chosen well, but since I had chosen, I must receive the lessons of that relationship for my good and my gaining. When I argued that Ted had *seemed* to be the man that she had shown me in my dreams, Zena just gave me this cold look, like you might give a petulent child that won't listen.

"I knew that it wasn't too late to call off the wedding, but I just really felt stubborn. Like, what did an angel know about love and marriage and sex and babies anyway?"

To Doris's dismay, it turned out that her angel guide was better informed about such matters after several thousand years of experience than she was at the pseudo-sophisticated age of twenty-three.

"The first couple of years were not too bad. Ted was on the road a lot, but I found out that even then he had begun seeing other women in various cities. Although he made me fairly comfortable in the material sense—and he made two beautiful babies with me—he made my life a hell on the spiritual and psychological levels.

"After a few years, Ted came down with a very serious social disease due to his infidelities. Thank God that was before AIDS was rampant—and thank God he hadn't transmitted the illness to me. I divorced him in 1979."

In 1981, Doris and her two daughters moved to the San Francisco area. She was able to secure a good job in a bookstore, and one night she was asked by a friend to attend a lecture by Gary Zemke, who had just returned from spending two years in the Brazilian rain forests with the native people of the region.

"I was very moved by the fire and passion in this man's voice as he showed us slides of the wholesale destruction of a vital natural resource—destruction that was already beginning to blight the rain forests," Doris told me. "Afterward as luck would have it, I was among seven or eight people who accompanied him for coffee after his presentation. As we were walking to the restaurant, I could not help noticing that he walked with a slight limp."

It was then for the first time that Doris actually saw how much more accurately Gary Zemke fit the description of the soul mate that her angel guide Zena had projected in her dreams.

"Later, much later, the others had left the restaurant one by one; and it was only Gary and me alone in the booth, sipping our umpteenth cup of coffee.

"He had begun to tell me of what he considered to be his larger spiritual mission—to visit what he believed to be the most sacred power places of the world. He told me that he had felt certain ever since his earliest childhood that he was to discover some artifact of the magnitude of the Lost Ark of the Covenant that would serve to convince millions of the reality of the partnership between the worlds of the physical and the nonphysical. Until that most momentous occasion, he had decided to establish a tour business that would take spiritual seekers on odysseys of awareness to various sacred locations."

As the night drew on to a beautiful close, Gary confessed to Doris that he had been drawn to her from the moment that he had seen her enter the lecture hall. He kissed her gently before he put her in a cab, and they had agreed to meet again the next night.

"It was not, I believe, until our fourth or fifth time together, that I very discreetly asked Gary what accident or circumstances had given him the limp.

"He smiled and said that he hoped that I would not think him a nut, but he would tell me the whole story."

In brief, Gary had been hiking a narrow trail in the Andes Mountains of Peru when he had lost his footing and fell.

"It was a long drop to the next outcropping," he told Doris. "I would have been killed—surely received more than a leg broken in three places—if my fall had not been broken in a most wonderful manner."

"Yes, yes," Doris prompted him. "Go on."

"Do you believe in miracles?"

Doris assured Gary that she did.

"Well," he went on cautiously, "I actually saw my guardian angel materialize and break my fall. If it had not been for those angelic wings cushioning my body, I am certain that I would surely have been killed on those rocks."

Gary laughed nervously, never taking his eyes from Doris's face. "Can you believe an angel? I mean, that an angel, my guardian angel, actually materialized and saved my life in the Andes Mountains?"

Doris smiled at the memory. "Well, Brad," she said, concluding her story, "I reached out for Gary's hand and told him that I had absolutely no problem believing in angels manifesting to assist us in our time of trouble. I kissed him, and then asked him if he believed that angels could also serve as matchmakers?"

Doris and Gary Zemke have been married now for eleven years, fully cognizant that they were brought together to share their lives as one by the beautiful ministry of the Angels of Love.

Nine

✦

Street Angel's Mission

When Edward Neumann was five years old and playing in the backyard of his childhood home in Hartford, Connecticut, he saw a figure that he first supposed was Jesus.

"The being seemed to be standing on a small white cloud," he told me. "The cloud was suspended about five or six feet in the air, and the figure held out his arms in a kind of 'come unto me' type of gesture."

Edward remembered vividly that the entity was dressed in a white robe with a purple sash that came down across his right shoulder to drape about his waist.

"Although the being had long reddish-brown hair, he had no beard; and all the pictures that I had seen of Jesus depicted him with a beard," Edward said. "That's when I decided that the entity was not Jesus, but an angel."

Edward experienced similar visitations on six different occasions during his childhood.

"I was not conscious of any words spoken by the entity during these early visits, but I was always left feeling that I had been born to fulfill some kind of special purpose on Earth."

When Edward was twelve, the family's dog, a feisty little rat terrier named Muggs, was struck by an automobile and dealt a severe injury.

"I cried my eyes out when I found little Muggs in the backyard. He had dragged himself home and was whimpering softly. Blood trickled from between his clamped jaws, and I knew that he was dying."

When his mother came home from work and found Edward out back with the badly injured Muggs, she openly shared her son's grief; but she said that they would have to take the dog to the veterinarian's to be put to sleep just as soon as his father got home. Edward fell to his knees and began to pray for Muggs's recovery.

"I begged God over and over to let Muggs be okay again. The little dog was my constant companion, and I could not bear to think of coming home from school night after night and not finding Muggs there to greet me."

Edward remembered clearly that after nearly two hours of continuous prayer, the angelic being appeared before him.

"His mouth did not move, but I heard *inside* my head his words of instruction. He told me to put my hands on Muggs and to send thoughts of healing into his body while I prayed for his recovery."

The boy was astonished to see Muggs suddenly stand up on all fours and walk toward his food dish as if nothing had happened to him.

"Inside my head, I heard the angel tell me that part of my mission on Earth was to serve as a healer. I thanked God over and over for allowing Muggs to come back to life. Later, when Dad got home, he tried to tell me that such things often happened to dogs. They might be hit by a car, badly stunned for a while, then bounce back to consciousness and be none the worse for wear. I knew better, though. I could even see that Muggs had a kind of glow around him for the next three or four days."

Edward told his younger brother Dick how the angel had helped him heal Muggs.

"Dick was only seven, but he was still pretty much of a realist. He doubted me at first, but I told him that I could get rid of his stomachache. When he was that age, it seemed as though he was always suffering from upset stomachs and digestive problems, so I put my hand on his tummy and prayed for five or six minutes. 'Hey, man,' Dick grinned. 'It works!' From that moment on, I became Dick's official healer—and as word spread among the kids, the medicine man for most of the neighborhood."

About five or six weeks after Edward had revealed his gift of healing, the Neumann family received word of the death of Uncle Karl in Los Angeles.

"Uncle Karl was Dad's younger brother, and Dick and I just loved him. We were really torn up by the news of his death. Mom and Dad were going to fly out for the funeral, but because of the prohibitive cost, Dick and I were to stay with a neighbor lady, a widow who sometimes looked after us when our folks were out of town.

"The night after we had got word of Uncle Karl's death, we lay upstairs in our beds feeling really sad. Dick started crying and saying how he wished that we could have seen Karl just one last time. 'If only we could have been able to say good-bye and to tell him how much we loved him,' Dick kept saying over and over."

Edward began to pray with all the intensity that he had mentally exerted to heal Muggs.

"I asked my angel if we just couldn't see Uncle Karl's soul before it went to Heaven. I prayed and prayed with all my might, begging for the chance to be able to say good-bye to our beloved uncle."

After about an hour of such intense prayers, the boys began to notice a glowing ball about two feet in diameter beginning to form in a corner of their room. Within two to three minutes, they were able to distinguish very clearly the images of Edward's angelic guide and their uncle Karl.

"At first Dick hid under the covers, but I told him not to be afraid, that God had granted our wish and sent my angel to escort Uncle Karl to see us one last time. Uncle Karl smiled and waved good-bye. We told him that we loved him, and we could read his lips when he said that he loved us, too. And then the angel, the glowing ball, and Uncle Karl just disappeared.

"You know, I'm now thirty-eight years old and Dick is thirty-one; but not too long ago when he was here for a visit, he talked about that materialization of the angel and Uncle Karl and told me that whenever his faith in God or the afterlife began to waver, he just remembered that incredible manifestation and everything is all right in his personal universe."

Edward continued to receive occasional tutorial sessions with his angel guide throughout his adolescent years.

"My angel counseled me to conduct my work rather quietly while I was in high school. I would stop nosebleeds, heal kids' bumps and bruises, banish headaches and upset stomachs—low-key stuff like that."

When I met Edward in 1986, he was a full-time massage therapist, widely known as the man with a remarkable healing touch, "Mister Magic Hands."

"I knew that I must be of service to others, and this seemed to me like the best way to be able to heal subtly and quietly, just like my angel directed me. Sometimes a client will come to me for a massage, 'just to relax,' to 'remove stress.' But I'll pick up on something going wrong in his body that is really serious. After a couple sessions, my angel gives me a 'green light,' and I know that we have taken care of the more complicated problem."

In 1988, when Edward first placed his "magic" fingers on Margarete Jackson, he experienced a series of internal shocks.

"It was like tiny electrical shocks that zinged me whenever I touched her. I *knew* that this lady was someone really special—and someone who was going to be very important in my life."

Now happily married to Edward for four years, Margarete told me that she had been employed as a bank teller at the time that she met him.

"The new manager was a real jerk. He would hit on me for dates, then when I refused, he would find something in my work to complain about.

"On this particular day, I had stormed out of the bank on my lunch hour angry as a wet cat. The pompous toad had just humiliated me in front of several customers and my fellow employees on some minute and meaningless technicality. I didn't know if I should hand in my resignation, file a formal complaint, or grin and bear it. I really didn't know what I was going to do."

She bought a hot dog from a street vendor, took two bites, and tossed it in a garbage can. On top of everything else, it was beginning to rain.

Margarete remembered that a nondescript street hustler approached her with a handbill. "Check it out! It'll make you feel good. Cure what ails you," he told her as he thrust a sheet of blue paper in her hands.

She crumpled the sheet in her hand, assuming it to be an advertisement for some sordid sex show or a closing-out sale for a merchant who had been going out of business regularly for the past seventeen years.

"No, ma'am," the hustler admonished her quietly. "You really should read that sheet of paper."

Startled by his quiet authority, Margarete smoothed out the handbill and saw that it advertised the services of a massage therapist named Edward Neumann and extolled the virtues of his techniques for relieving stress and tension.

"At first the handbill intrigued me," she said. "Lord knows I needed something to relieve stress and tension—before I walked back into the bank and clobbered the jerk with the right hook that my father had taught me when I was sixteen. But could I trust someone who advertised in the streets? I mean, I had heard all about massage parlor scams for men. Perhaps this Neumann guy had come up on a variation to please frustrated women."

And then Margarete glanced up and saw that she now found herself on the street where, according to the handbill, Neumann's office was located. In fact, she was only two or three doors down from it.

An elderly woman stood outside the door of his office, stretching her arms above her head and smiling broadly.

"Oh, dearie," she said to Margarete, "that was wonderful. What a marvelous session. That Mr. Neumann is just remarkable, just plain remarkable. I feel like a new woman—and that's a fact."

Margarete paused to read the handbill again, slowly, more deliberately. It certainly seemed as though this Neumann fellow had what she needed right now. And the elderly woman didn't seem as though she would tolerate any hanky-panky.

When she looked up to ask the woman a few questions, she was surprised to see that the lady was nowhere in sight.

"I figured that she must have grabbed a cab while I was busy reading the handbill," Margarete said, "so I thought, What the heck! and decided to go inside."

Edward perceived at once that the electrical shocks that he was picking up from his new client were his angel's way of telling him that this was the special woman who had been sent to him by the Angels to enrich his life.

"And you know what, Brad?" Margarete asked me rhetorically. "We had been dating regularly for months before I found out that Edward *had never* printed any handbills to advertise his massage therapy. He said that he had always assumed—as I had done—that people would misinterpret the true nature of his services if he had utilized such a method of advertising."

Edward nodded, adding that he had relied solely on word of mouth to bring him more than enough clients to keep him extremely busy. "I had only advertised once or twice in some alternate city newspapers—and I was flooded by the response. I absolutely never would have employed street hawkers to push my business."

But both Margarete and Edward agreed that it was quite apparent that his angel had no such compunctions if such an action would serve the angelic purpose of bringing them together.

Ten

Just in Time

"Tim Martindale literally swept me off my feet," Phyllis Schneider confessed in her account of her strange experience with an angelic guide. "I was not yet twenty and very inexperienced in the ways of love. Tim was nearly nine years older than I, and he seemed to be the very epitome of masculine charm and strength."

Phyllis was even more pleased when her parents also warmed to her beau.

"Tim told Dad that he was an avid fisherman—a passion that was shared by our entire family—and soon he had become a part of our family outings at the lake."

By midsummer, Tim and Phyllis were at the "engaged-to-be-engaged" state of their courtship.

Phyllis had met Tim at a dance that had been held at a nearby resort. Since Tim lived in a city that was quite some distance from Phyllis, he had to drive a good number of miles to see her. Because of the problem of the miles that separated them, they seldom saw each other during the week.

"But after Tim had so ingratiated himself to my parents, he began to stay the weekends with us," Phyllis said.

One Thursday night before he was coming to stay with the Schneiders, Tim called to ask Phyllis if her parents would mind keeping a trunk of his personal possessions in their attic storeroom.

"That way," he explained, "I'll always have shirts and ties and a toothbrush available—and I won't have to be hauling so much stuff back and forth with me."

Such a request made good sense to the Schneiders, and permission was readily granted.

"By late summer, though, I was beginning to have vague feelings of discomfort in regard to my charming and persistent suitor," Phyllis explained.

One night as the couple parked beside the lake, she was becoming annoyed with Tim's insistence on making love.

His hands had been roaming her body with gentle insistence, his fingers gently probing and touching sensitive areas. The combination of his mouth on her own and the steady, sensual pressure of his fingers had kindled a fire within her that Phyllis knew could only be extinguished by the act of physical love.

"As old-fashioned as it might have seemed to others of my generation," she said, "I had always vowed that I would wait until I had a wedding band around my finger before I allowed any man to claim my virginity. But Tim had already unbuttoned my blouse, and the fingers of one of his hands were tugging at the hook of my bra while the fingers of the other were at the zipper of my slacks."

That was when Phyllis called a halt to the proceedings. Tim seemed just too damned experienced.

"Tim," she asked him bluntly, "have you had a lot of women before me?"

His only answer was a kind of chuckle deep in his throat that seemed to Phyllis to sound too prideful.

"Well," she persisted, "have you ever been married before?"

Tim's hands became suddenly inactive. He leaned back against the seat with a sigh of resignation. "Why do you keep asking me that? I've told you the answer to that question a hundred times. N-O. No. I have never been married. Don't you believe me?"

Phyllis shrugged away his objections. "You are nearly twenty-nine. People do get married, you know."

She could see his perfect teeth in the dim illumination from the dashboard. Tim was smiling at her. Such wonderfully white teeth, she sighed mentally. Such a handsome, tanned face. Such a great guy.

"Of course people get married," Tim teased. "That's why I want to marry you."

There was something in his voice just then. Just a slight tonal disharmony . . . just a minor variation in frequency that caused her to ask the question one more time.

"But have *you* ever been married before?"

Tim did not answer until he had shaken a cigarette from a hard pack in his coat pocket and placed it between his lips.

"Okay," he said. "I was married once before."

He touched the glowing coils of the lighter to the cigarette, exhaled a cloud of smoke.

Phyllis thought that her heart had stopped beating. "His words had been like a sword that pierced through my chest and cut my heart in two. But it started beating again with his next words."

"I was married to a pretty young blond girl . . . who died in childbirth."

"Oh, Tim," Phyllis said sincerely. "I'm sorry."

She felt at once ashamed that she had finally wrung the truth from him—and disappointed that he had not told her before about his previous marriage.

"And . . . the child?"

"Peter," he answered, expelling the name in another cloud of cigarette smoke. "He lives with my mother. He's six years old."

Phyllis swallowed hard. If they married after her birthday in December, she would be a twenty-year-old bride with a six-year-old stepson.

Oh, well. He was Tim's son, and she loved Tim.

"Peter must come live with us just as soon as we're married," she blurted out.

Tim grabbed her happily, gave her a long kiss. "Name the date," he said. "Just name the date. And Peter can come and live with us . . . right *after* our honeymoon!"

The night that she decided on December sixteenth as their wedding date, Phyllis said that she had "the most terrible kind of nightmare."

"I dreamed that I had married Tim and we had gone away to live in our own home. Then Tim began to build a cage around me, and I began to scream hysterically. But whenever I would scream too loudly, a group of nurses would appear from nowhere and tell me to be quiet or they would stick me with their long needles. And all the while Tim kept building the cage around me—until, at last, I saw that it was not a cage at all. It was a coffin!"

Even after she awakened, Phyllis knew that she was not alone in her room.

"I nearly screamed when I saw a strange figure outlined with a silver light standing at the foot of my bed," Phyllis said. "I could distinguish no features—and when I sat up to turn on the bed-lamp, the ghostly thing had vanished."

The next night turned out to be a carbon copy of the previous one.

"First, I had the strange, jumbled, frightening nightmare, then I awakened to find the eerily glowing figure at the foot of my bed. I began to fear that I might be losing my mind."

On the third night, Phyllis stated in her account of the experience, the same nightmare seized her. Tim set about building the cage that surrounded her . . . the nurses appeared to threaten her with their long needles . . . and she discovered the cage was really a coffin.

"It was at that point each night that I would awaken," she said. "And on the third night, I heard a voice calling to me. The shimmering image stood before me—only this time I could make out long, reddish brown hair flowing down to the broad shoulders of an angel, a being of light that was very commanding in appearance."

In an authoritative voice, the angel told her that she must not marry Tim.

"You will only *think* that you will be his wife, but you will be wrong."

Phyllis asked the angel what he meant by such a statement.

"He still has another wife. She is not dead. She is *not* dead."

And then suddenly there appeared with the angel the image of a tall, pretty young woman with long blond hair. Although she was dressed in some kind of shapeless gown, it was evident that she had a good figure.

It was her eyes that most disturbed Phyllis. They looked dazed, confused—almost as if she were some kind of hunted animal.

And then both the angel and the pretty young blond woman disappeared.

Sleep for Phyllis the rest of the night was an impossibility. She sat up in bed, staring until dawn at the space where the illuminated being had stood and issued its dire warning—and where the blond woman had materialized and disappeared so suddenly.

That morning over breakfast she told her mother and her fifteen-year-old sister Becky about her terrible nocturnal experiences of the past three nights. Because they had always been a religious family, Phyllis had no reluctance in describing in detail the somber warning that she had received from an angelic being.

"Look in his trunk in the attic," declared Becky, who read far too many gothic romances. "I'll bet you'll find a key to Tim's terrible secret in that trunk."

Phyllis was surprised when her mother agreed with Becky.

"I know it seems like a violation of the ethics which Dad and I have tried to instill in you girls," her mother said, "but it just may be that there might be some kind of clue to Tim's past in that trunk."

Her mother did insist that they wait until their father returned from work to investigate the contents of the trunk, however.

"When I told Dad about the appearance of the angel and the young woman and the angelic being's warning not to marry Tim, he quickly agreed with the consensus to open the trunk in the attic.

"We knew that Tim kept the key to the trunk with him, but Dad had an old friend who was an accomplished locksmith and who could be trusted to be discreet," Phyllis said.

"In one compartment of the trunk, we found an insurance policy that was still in force for a Mrs. Cindy Martindale. There was another policy on Tim which named Mrs. Martindale as the beneficiary. We all knew that no one pays premiums on policies on a deceased wife—nor does one declare a dead woman a beneficiary.

"Then Mother found a number of receipts which had been paid to a sanatorium in a nearby state. It all became very clear that Tim's wife had not died in childbirth. Rather, she had suffered a nervous breakdown after the birth of their son."

Although she feared that it would be like turning a knife in her flesh, Phyllis asked her parents to accompany her to the sanatorium so that she might verify the circumstantial evidence with firsthand investigation.

"Mom and Dad consented, and we set out on the long drive to the mental hospital.

"Dad used the pretext that we were old family friends, and we were given permission to visit Tim's wife, Cindy."

Phyllis was shocked when they entered the hospital room to find the same tall, pretty blond woman whose image that the angel had materialized in her bedroom.

"Thank God, we had somehow managed to choose a day when she was enjoying a period relatively free from trauma and delusion."

Phyllis and her parents chatted with Cindy about her husband and her son, and Phyllis was grateful that her parents had come along to bear the burden of the conversation.

"Dad told the woman that Tim had been very busy and had been working long hours, but that he sent his love.

"I could not hold back the tears when Cindy smiled and nodded. Then said very quietly, 'Tell Tim that I love him, too. But he hasn't been to see me for so long. Please . . . please tell him to come to see me. He . . . he acts like I'm dead.' "

Phyllis concluded her account by stating that her father called Tim that very night when they returned to their home.

"Dad told him to come to pick up his trunk and not to try to see me ever again. I heard Dad urge Tim to take a greater interest in the wife and son whom he was shamefully neglecting.

"Later, Dad told me that Tim had become furious with us for 'meddling in his private life,' and he had demanded who had told us of his wife in the institution. Tim knew very well that we had no common friends, and no one among his friends knew that he had been seeing me.

"Dad simply told him that an 'interested party' who had wanted to keep me from misery and shame had decided to intervene.

"I felt that Dad's way of describing the visitation of the angel in my bedroom was as good as any."

Eleven

❖

The Greatest Gift

Judith Richardson Haimes, one of the nation's leading psychic-sensitives, told me this touching story of how the Angels of Love granted Kathy Palmer's and Mike Alexander's wish for a perfect love—if only for a little while on Earth.

Kathy Palmer was a pretty girl of twenty-seven with large, dark blue eyes and a slim, but shapely, figure. She was certainly not a young woman who would blend into a crowd, but because she was so painfully shy she did not have a very interesting social life.

She caught an awful "bug" that had been going around, and it had left her weak, tired, and a little depressed. On this particular day, she was feeling very low in energy, and because her car was being repaired, she had to take the bus to work.

The job she had as a "Girl Friday" for a medical supply company did not challenge her intellectually, but it was not at all unpleasant, and the hours and the pay were good.

As she was riding the bus to work, the tall young man sitting on the aisle seat beside her seemed to be trying very hard to make conversation. As lonely as she had been recently, Kathy was still not so desperate that she would succumb to a flirtation on the bus—even if he was distinctly handsome and very well dressed.

Her attention was directed to a number of young couples who were holding hands as they walked along the street. Some couples were pushing baby carriages. They all seemed so very much in love, and Kathy felt a twinge of envy.

"Now this is something. Isn't this terrific? I love these kinds of stories," the handsome man sitting next to her was saying as he pointed a forefinger at some news item in the morning paper.

Curious, Kathy smiled and inquired about what newspaper article had so pleased him.

"Here is a family who recently became homeless," he said, his voice mounting in enthusiasm, "and then *bingo!* Overnight, they became millionaires."

"Did they win the lottery?" Kathy wondered, laughing at her anonymous companion's vicarious excitement over a desperate family's good fortune.

"You're absolutely right!" he told her, grinning at her as if she were a genius with remarkable insight. "They won the six-million-dollar lottery."

The stranger folded the newspaper on his lap. "My name is Ian, by the way."

She almost shocked herself by engaging in even a brief conversation with a total stranger. "I'm Kathy."

"You know," the man was rambling on, "if I could have just one wish, I would wish to win the lottery."

Kathy shook her head. "Money can't make everyone happy."

"Oh, really!" Ian laughed. "And what would you wish for, Kathy? What would be your one wish?"

As the bus slowed in heavy traffic, Kathy pointed out the window at a couple holding hands and looking into one another's eyes as if they were the only two people on the planet.

"See that man and woman standing there in front of the

jewelry store? That's what I want. That would be my wish. If I could have just one wish, I would ask for someone to love me like that and . . ."

Startled by her frank admission to a stranger and quite embarrassed by her forwardness, Kathy was relieved to see that the bus had reached her stop.

"This is my stop," she said as she stepped over Ian's long legs. "I must get off here."

She walked up to the door as the bus pulled to a halt. Kathy glanced back at the row of seats that she had just vacated and sought out the handsome stranger to whom she had uttered her bold confession.

His seat was empty.

Her eyes moved quickly about the bus, moving past the remaining passengers.

Ian was nowhere to be seen.

Puzzled, Kathy stepped from the bus. She hurried into her building, wondering if perhaps she might have dozed off for a moment and dreamed the entire embarrassing conversation with the stranger. After all, her bout with the illness had left her somewhat listless and low in energy. Maybe she had just dreamed about a bold conversation with a handsome stranger.

When he left for work that day, Mike Alexander felt as if his heart would break. He had never wanted to hurt Abby. After all, he had a love for her—even though he was certain that he was not *in* love with her.

Abby and Mike had grown up across the street from each other. They had gone to the same schools; they had all of the same friends; and they even shared the same profession. They were both accountants and they were employed by the same firm.

For years they had been pals, buddies, friends. But for the past year, Mike had found thoughts of another woman strongly subverting the fondness that he felt for Abby.

Perhaps he was foolish. He only saw this woman once a week when he visited the medical supply company in which she worked. Her boss, Karl Fine, was one of his regular clients; and the first time that he set his eyes on Kathy Palmer, Fine's Girl Friday, her image was freeze-framed into his brain.

Although he had never even asked Kathy for a date, he was attracted to her in a way that made his heart race just thinking about her. He knew that he could never have such feelings for Abby.

So last night, when he and Abby talked for six hours and shared their true feelings with one another, he learned that she, too, wanted to separate. She, too, had noticed that they made much better friends than lovers.

As Mike drove to work, he felt a little topsy-turvy with his emotions, but, thank God, it was Friday. The bright spot in his day would be seeing Kathy, the light of his heart—even though she had no idea how he felt.

And when the temporary at the medical supply company told him that Kathy had left early to go to the doctor, he spiraled into a dismal funk.

Feeling too depressed to go straight home after work, Mike headed for a place where he could get an order of chicken wings and a couple of beers.

A tall, dark young man came up to his table. "Hello, my name is Ian. I'll be taking your order tonight."

Before Mike could place his order for wings and beer, the talkative waiter said, "It sure was amazing about that homeless family winning the six-million-dollar lottery, wasn't it?"

Mike shrugged. "I didn't hear anything about it."

"Oh, sure," Ian said excitedly. "It was in all the papers, and it's been on the news all day. Well, I'm glad that if someone besides me had to win it was a family in such need. But boy, do I wish that I could win the lottery. If I had only one wish, that's what I would wish. I would wish to win the lottery."

Mike had to smile at the rapid-talking young waiter. "I'd like an order of wings and a beer, please."

"What would you wish for if you had only one wish?" Ian asked.

"You mean besides my chicken wings and beer?"

"I'll get those for you right away, sir. But, please, tell me what you would wish for if you had only one wish? Would you wish to win the lottery?"

Mike looked for a silent moment at the earnest young man standing before him. "Well, Ian, I guess I would wish for the woman of my dreams. And then for my beer and wings."

Ian thanked him for the order and hurried off to get the wings and beer.

Five minutes passed.

No beer. No chicken wings. No Ian.

A few minutes later, a pretty girl in a black and white uniform that looked like a cross between a scullery maid's outfit and a sailor suit came to Mike's table.

"I'm sorry, sir. We're really busy. I'm really sorry I took so long. My name is Kim, and I'll . . ."

"It's okay, Kim," Mike interrupted her spiel. "Ian has already taken my order."

"Ian?"

"Ian the waiter," Mike said a bit impatiently. "Although I think he has gone to the farm to get those chicken wings."

"We don't have a waiter named Ian working here, sir," Kim told him in a perfunctory manner. "This has been my table for the last two and a half hours now. May I take your order, please?"

Now that Abby had released Mike from any emotional obligation which he might have felt, he tossed all reluctance to the winds and called Kathy on Monday for a dinner date. He could hardly believe it when she accepted without hesitation.

Monday night's dinner date mushroomed into a dinner shared every evening for the next five days.

Kathy could not believe what a difference a week could make. It had only been that last Friday on the bus when she had told the talkative stranger her wish for true love. And now, dear God, it truly seemed as though her wish had been granted.

In less than three months, Mike and Kathy knew that they were meant to be together.

While walking on the beach at dusk one night, Mike asked her to marry him. "I want to spend the rest of my life with you."

Half-laughing, half-crying with tears of joy, Kathy answered that she accepted his proposal.

"This is my wish come true!" Mike shouted to the first stars of the evening as he took Kathy in his arms.

Over Mike's shoulder, Kathy saw a tall, handsome young man smiling at them as he passed them on the beach. There was something about him that was strangely familiar.

One year later, while sitting in Dr. Evans's office, Mrs. Kathy Alexander was filled with conflict. Both she and Mike wanted a family, but they had planned to wait a bit longer until they were a little more secure financially. But the thrill of having a baby—even unplanned—was as exciting as all the happiest moments of her life put together.

But then Dr. Evans told her that she was not pregnant.

How could that be, Kathy wanted to know. She had missed her last two cycles. She was tired all the time. She was nauseated most of the day.

Kathy felt a sense of foreboding when Dr. Evans suggested more tests.

A few days later, Mike was with her, holding her hand, when Dr. Evans told them that Kathy had very advanced ovarian cancer.

"How soon can we start treatments?" Kathy asked, trying to take control of the situation.

Dr. Evans's words seemed to ring out as if he were speaking from an echo chamber: "I am so very sorry, but my best advice to you is to accept the fact that treatment at this point would at best give you only a few weeks more . . . and they would not be very pleasant weeks. The truth of the matter is that the treatment might take up what precious little time that you have."

"How long *do* I have?" Kathy wanted to know, still trying to maintain some degree of control.

Dr. Evans said that no one could accurately predict the future, but in such advanced cases as Kathy's, one could allow six weeks to as long as three months.

After Kathy and Mike had obtained three additional "second opinions," they were ready at last to accept the inevitable.

Both Kathy and Mike were very spiritual, but neither strictly followed any religious doctrine. She was a Catholic who had not been to church in many years. She and the Church disagreed on too many points.

Mike had been brought up in a nonreligious Jewish family. They were a loving and good family, albeit unceremoniously Jewish.

Kathy and Mike believed that they were soul mates who had been blessed to have found the opportunity to become complete in the short time together in their present life experience. Since they both accepted the concept of reincarnation, Kathy and Mike reconciled themselves with the thought that they would be together again in another time.

Kathy, who wanted to die at home with her beloved Mike near, was kept comfortable. The medical supply company for which Kathy had worked had an insurance plan that provided excellent home nursing care.

Kathy's mother, Nancy Palmer, brushed a wisp of hair off her sleeping daughter's forehead as she prayed the rosary. She had let the nurse's aide go early to pick up her son at school. Nurse Brown, the R.N., was due soon.

When the doorbell rang, Nancy was surprised to see a tall, handsome young man standing there. He introduced himself as Ian Baker, a nurse's aide, who had been sent to help until Nurse Brown arrived. She had been unavoidably detained.

Together they saw that Kathy was resting comfortably. While Ian checked her pulse and started to read her chart, Nancy went to the kitchen to fix herself a small lunch. It had been hours since she had eaten, and she was beginning to get a slight headache.

Mike's entire office staff said that they would pitch in and help carry his load until he returned from his extended leave of absence to be at Kathy's side. Abby had promised him that she would personally keep close tabs on all of his most important clients.

As he drove home, he reflected upon just how much his life had changed in the past year.

As he went by the restaurant where he had once stopped for chicken wings and a beer, he remembered the tall, talkative young waiter who had got him to express his wish for the love of his life.

"I got my wish," Mike said aloud, tears stinging his eyes. "If only for too short a time."

Just at that moment, a familiar face stood out among the crowded sidewalk near the corner.

It was he—Ian or whatever his name was. The mysterious waiter who had disappeared after taking his order. There he was, a smiling face in a crowd of strangers.

The tall, dark young man waved to Mike in a familiar greeting.

Mike suddenly felt a surge of calmness and tranquility unlike anything that he had ever experienced.

There was a noise.

A flash of light.

And then it was over.

The old man never even saw Mike's car in front of him. The seventy-seven-year-old man pulled into the intersection against the light.

Someone called for an ambulance, but it was too late.

Mike Alexander was dead.

It was 3:31 P.M.

When she walked back into her daughter's room from the kitchen, Nancy Palmer at first thought something was on fire, for the room was filled with a foglike smoke.

As her eyes darted around the bedroom, she was startled to see an image of her son-in-law, Mike Alexander, standing at the bed-side reaching out for Kathy.

Then a most extraordinary thing happened: Kathy sat up in bed, reached out to Mike—and at the same instant, the "mist" that just a moment before had filled the room suddenly vanished, as if sucked out by an invisible vacuum cleaner.

Still frozen in the moment, Nancy saw Kathy's bright blue eyes half-open and glazed, her lower jaw hanging open, relaxed in death.

Nancy heard a distant ringing sound.

Her eyes met those of Ian, the nurse's aide, and then she heard an awful cry like that of a wounded animal.

It was not until the gentle hand of Nurse Brown touched her shoulder that Nancy realized that the terrible cry had been coming from her own throat.

"I rang the bell," Nurse Brown explained, "but there was no answer. Kathy is gone. I am so sorry.

"I would have been here on time, but there was a very bad accident, and traffic was held up. An elderly man struck another car after running a red light."

"Where is the aide?" Nancy asked. "Where is Ian?"

"Ian?"

"The nurse's aide. He was just here a moment ago. He was standing right beside Kathy's bed."

"Nancy," Nurse Brown said in a gentle, reassuring voice, "you were here alone when I arrived. No one was in this room except you and . . . Kathy."

As if in a dream, Nancy stood staring at the body of her sweet, loving, shy daughter. For a split second, she thought that she saw the nurse's aide, Ian, looking at her from across the room. Then he seemed to disappear. That was when she was overcome by a soft, tranquil sense of peace.

The clock at Kathy's bedside had stopped at 3:31 P.M.

Twelve

A Message of Love

According to a basic theological consensus, humans do not become angels when they die. Angels are a host of cosmic beings who were created before our own earthly species. The Bible informs us that we are "a little lower than the angels" on the rungs of the spiritual ladder, but for some reason not totally clear to us, the Angels of Love seem intent upon helping us climb up to a higher level.

While I take careful note of the above-mentioned theological points regarding the nature of our angelic guides, I have a number of cases in my research files in which the spirits of the departed have—at least for a time—maintained a loving proprietary interest in their Earth-plane love partners.

When her husband died in the fall of 1944, Dorothy Barnes of Vermont found herself beset with the many problems that a widow inherits upon the death of her mate.

Since she had two children under four years of age, Dorothy's most immediate problem had to do with finding enough money to keep them all eating. Her husband had left only a miniscule estate, as far as his insurance policies went, but he had bequeathed her a section of timberland.

"A certain gentleman from the community made me an offer which seemed fair to me," Dorothy said. "I knew that he had a reputation for pulling some rather slick deals, but I didn't think that he would try to take advantage of a young widow."

In his last days, as he had lain dying of cancer of the stomach, her husband Phil had been unable to sleep at night. In those restless and painful hours, he would lie at Dorothy's side and gently stroke her hair.

The night before she was to close the deal on the timberland, she lay in a light sleep, mentally debating the wisdom of her actions.

"I had not been sleeping long," she recalled, "when I became conscious of a hand stroking my hair. I knew then that Phil was still watching over me—and I felt prepared to handle any situation."

Dorothy awakened totally convinced that she should not sell the property.

"I found out later that just the timber on the land was worth more than the price that the man had offered me for the entire property."

The young widow struggled for over a year, trying her best to make ends meet.

After sixteen months, she was forced to the painful consideration that it might be better for all of them if she boarded her children temporarily and set out alone to get a good job in a larger city. To do so would be to increase her opportunities to make enough money so that they could all be reunited as soon as possible with fewer financial problems.

Dorothy found a young couple in a nearby town who had six or seven children already boarding with them and who seemed to be the ideal kind of temporary foster parents for her two small children. She made all necessary arrangements with the man and woman, and all that remained for her to do was to deliver her kids to them early the next morning.

"That night, as before, when I had been undecided about the sale of the land, I felt my husband's steady hand gently caressing my hair," Dorothy said.

"I awoke with the utmost certainty that I must not leave my children with that young couple. I knew that I must not go ahead with my plans to board them."

Only a few weeks later, Dorothy read in the newspaper that the couple had been arrested for ill-treating the children in their care and for feeding them spoiled food.

Four years after her husband's death, Dorothy found herself in a position wherein she was seriously considering remarriage.

"It was no secret that Bob indulged in more than a social nip, but he seemed quite able to handle his drink. Oh, I had seen him drunk on more than one occasion, but I rationalized this by saying that everyone got a little tipsy once in a while."

She had nearly made up her mind to say "yes" to Bob's entreaties, when, one night, she again felt the soft caress of her dead husband's hand.

Dorothy changed her plans, reluctantly at first. Then she experienced the knee-weakening sensation of a narrow escape. Bob's father called her to confess and to warn her that Bob was an alcoholic who had already spent one expensive session of many months' duration in a hospital.

"I later found out that Phil's seemingly ever-vigilant spirit was not really jealous or possessive of me," Dorothy wrote in her account of her experiences.

"For a time there, I thought that his presence would never allow me to marry, that his caressing hand would always materialize to find fault with any man who courted me—but such was not at all the case.

"I have now been happily married for over twenty years. The

beloved ghost of my first husband was only looking after me like a guardian angel until he could safely leave me to fend for myself."

When Michele Walinski's husband Andrew died, she left the East Coast and moved to California, selling nearly everything she owned in the process.

For more than a year she was unable to obtain any kind of steady employment. Then, finally, she decided to reactivate some long-dormant skills, and she found work as a laboratory technician in a small medical clinic.

Four years later, after she had successfully re-established herself as a highly effective technician, one of the doctors, who had recently obtained a divorce from his second wife, began to court Michele in sudden earnest.

Michele had always considered the doctor to be charming, but she had never felt entirely at ease with him. She was astonished and nonplussed when, after their third date, he asked her to marry him.

The longer they dated, the more that Michele doubted that she could ever really love the man, but he became even more persistent in his entreaties for her to marry him.

After stalling him for another two months—and after a great deal of mental debate—she at last accepted his proposal of marriage.

One night, shortly before their wedding date, Michele, unable to get to sleep, sat up in her bed reading.

"After a while, I noticed a strange radiation around the typewriter that I had left on a desk across the room," she stated in her report to me.

"I glanced about my bedroom, trying to discover what could be casting such a peculiar glow on that particular spot.

"I tried to get back to my reading, but I kept finding myself strangely attracted to that glowing blob of light.

"Then I heard the sound of typewriter keys being struck—slowly, methodically."

Michele said that she got out of bed and walked toward the desk.

"When I was only a few feet from the typewriter, I was able to see quite clearly the image of my late husband Andrew seated before the keyboard. I raised a hand as if to touch him—then he and the illumination disappeared."

She turned on the light, removed the sheet of paper from the typewriter.

"The spirit of my husband had typed these words: 'Don't marry Doctor. He will cause you heartbreak, pain, sorrow.' "

Confused, troubled by the incredible manifestation of her dead husband, Michele told her fiancé that she needed more time to think things over before she made the ultimate commitment. She asked that the wedding be postponed.

The doctor reluctantly agreed to her terms, but their relationship soon became more than a little strained.

Then, within a few months, the doctor killed himself in a fit of despondency over heavy gambling debts. Although he had somehow managed to keep it a secret from his colleagues in the clinic, the doctor had been a compulsive gambler.

The orthodox psychologist may assess Michele Walinski's account as being the fantasy of a lonely woman who feared the reestablishment of an intimate relationship with a man.

Others may suggest that the so-called spirit writing of her deceased husband was but Michele Walinski's own automatic writing in which she unconsciously typed out her inner fears.

But Michele herself will always believe that her husband's love had survived the grave and had enabled him to return to warn her of an inadvisable union with a man who would truly have caused her "heartbreak, pain, and sorrow."

Thirteen

Mirrors of Their Angels' Love

The December 27, 1993 issue of *Newsweek* magazine ran a cover story on the popular interest in angels—an interest that extended far beyond the Christmas holiday. Among the individuals cited as those who had received personal angelic encounters was Lori Jean Flory, and I read the paragraph referring to her experiences with great interest: ". . . Lori Jean Flory, 36, of Aurora, Colo., has been experiencing angels since the age of 3 . . . Usually they appear as light in motion with a vaguely human shape, and the message is always the same: 'They want us to know our pure essence is pure light and pure love.'"

Destiny will often arrange things perfectly. It was not more than a few weeks after reading this article and the reference to Ms. Flory when Lori Jean wrote to Sherry and me and initiated what has proven to be a most delightful friendship.

When I told Lori Jean about my book project retelling the accounts of angels bringing sweethearts and spouses together, she told us that she and her husband Charles had been brought together by her special angelic guide, Daephrenocles. According to Lori Jean, Daephrenocles told her, "We angels would have pulled you around until you came together—no matter how long it would take."

Early in 1980, the year after she had graduated from California Lutheran College, she was told the following during a telephone call from a psychically gifted friend named Kathy, who lived in southern California:

"Your true love is coming. He is not here yet. Right now he is involved with someone, and he is growing spiritually. He is learning specific lessons, as is the woman with whom he is currently involved. You are growing and learning lessons as well. When your true love comes, you will feel like following him wherever he goes.

"Do not run after the first man that you meet that you might think is he. If you rush a relationship, there will be a divorce. If you learn your lessons, you will meet him when you are twenty-five. If you do not learn your lessons, you will not meet him until he is fifty."

At the time that Lori Jean received the psychic impression from Kathy, she had just begun to date Jim, a man that she had met while working for a woman who ran a dating agency in Turlock, California.

"Admittedly, I still had much to learn about life and had much growing to do," Lori Jean said. "I was finding out that it was not easy supporting myself during my first year out of college.

"Jim had recently broken off with a woman to whom he had been engaged. When he got a job in San Diego, he asked me if I wanted to move down there with him. I was living at the time with two female housemates in Turlock. Jim spent two months in San Diego by himself, and then I moved down to join him."

After Lori Jean had been living with Jim for a while, her friend Kathy predicted that on December 19 she would be given a wondrous surprise from the angels.

"December 19, 1982 came and went, and I thought nothing

more of my 'wondrous surprise' from the angels. I had forgotten that there is no time or space in the spiritual realms and that the angels are often one year off in their timing."

Charitably, Lori Jean said that she and Jim grew through much karma together. They were married in September of 1982.

"As I look back, it would have been better if we had never married, but obviously we both had lessons to learn."

Lori Jean said that in June of 1983, she and Jim had moved from San Diego to the foothills of the Sierra Nevada Mountains in an effort to see if country living might not be a good change for them. It did not and Lori recalled feeling in danger from Jim's inability to control his fits of anger.

"I wish I had known then about co-dependence and dysfunction what I know now—but anyway, we moved to a beautiful area called Squaw Valley, near the entrance to Sequoia National Park. I had been used to metaphysical groups being readily accessible in San Diego. In the Fresno area, I was unable to meet anyone who had metaphysical beliefs.

"One day I phoned a woman minister back in Turlock to ask if she could suggest any like-minded individuals in the Fresno area. Even though she did not know it at the time, my relationship with Jim was coming to an end, and the angels were guiding her to direct me to my first meeting with Charles Flory, my present husband. She referred me to George Gillette, a psychic reader, and Charles, an astrologer, who were sharing an office. I called George and made an appointment with him."

On the appointed day, August 10, 1983, Lori Jean drove to Clovis, a suburb of Fresno, for her reading with George Gillette. It was a hot day, and she had her hair pulled back in a ponytail.

"I don't know why I didn't just go walking right into the office as any normal person would do, but for some reason I just opened the door a crack and kind of slowly peeked in. Charles was sitting at the front desk, and he asked if he could help me. Sometimes I am a little on the shy side, especially if I don't know someone.

"While George was finishing with a client, I told Charles how happy I was to find some people in the area who were open to metaphysical things."

One month later, her relationship with Jim had deteriorated beyond any hope of salvation. Then, one September evening, Lori had to make her decision.

"By this time, we were sleeping in separate rooms. I told Jim that I was leaving the next day and that I did not plan to return. Jim didn't believe me. Up to that point, I had been too embarrassed to tell anyone what had been going on in our marriage— especially since the wedding had been a very expensive one. But I called my father, and told him [about our troubles]. Dad told me to pack up my things right away and to come home."

Lori Jean packed up as much as she could into her car, including a kitten and two puppies, and left for her parents' home on September 10, 1983.

"As I pulled into Fresno, the brakes on my car failed. Thank goodness I wasn't going very fast and there was a mechanic right across the street.

"In spite of all the terrible things that I had been through, I still felt grateful for all the protection that the angels had given me. After all, I was still alive!"

Lori Jean lived with her parents for two weeks.

"Bless their hearts. Some of the stories I told them about my married life almost made their hair stand up on end. I thank God for their support."

A restraining order was filed against Jim, and Lori Jean worked at getting on with her life. She got a job teaching preschool in Fresno—and she turned twenty-five.

"Although my pets helped so much with my healing process, my landlady eventually said that either they had to go—or I did. At the time it nearly broke my heart to have to give them up, but now I can see that all of these 'releases' and 'clearances' were preparing more space for Charles.

"At this time, though, Charles and I were only friendly acquaintances. He had no idea of most of the things that I was going through. But I seemed to keep encountering Charles all over the place—and always unexpectedly.

"In November, I filed for divorce through a friend of Dad's, who specialized in that area of law."

In early December, Lori Jean decided to visit a local nightspot "just to watch everyone else." After she had left Jim, even grocery shopping was an adventure, as there was no longer anyone to tell her what to do and to inform her that she was doing everything wrong.

"All of a sudden, who should I see but Charles and his date. I called out his name, and when he walked over to me, my mouth just took over my mind. I took both of his hands in mine and looked at his date with a very serious expression on my face. 'Look,' I told her, 'this man is special! You had better be good to him—or *you* are going to hear from *me!*'

"She just looked at me and didn't say a thing. The two of them left, and I thought to myself, 'Oh, God, what have I said?' "

Lori Jean later found out that that was Charles's only date with that woman. He also told Lori Jean that he had tried to ditch the lady and return to find her, but Lori Jean had already left.

"When we reflect on those early days of our budding relationship, Charles will often say that he was totally amazed that someone would say something like I did about him in someone else's presence. I am even *more* amazed that I had said such a thing. It was as though the angels were speaking and not me."

Lori Jean continued to run into Charles at the grocery store, the bank, and numerous other places. She was troubled that he now seemed uncomfortable in her presence. What she did not know at that time was that Charles was attracted to her, but that he was separated from his wife Leslie and he needed to bring that chapter of his life to a close.

As Christmas approached, Lori Jean decided to write down all of her feelings about Charles.

"It took me two pages to get everything down, and then I decided to do something daring. I would call Charles and read my feelings to him over the telephone. If he rejected me, well, at least I had expressed myself and I could move on.

"The next morning I called him at his office at 10:00 A.M. and we talked for two hours. Charles did not reject me, but he did admit that he was surprised to learn how I felt about him.

"That's when I realized that the date was *December 19*. My psychic friend Kathy had said that I would receive a wondrous gift from the angels on December 19. While I had looked for the blessing in 1982, the angels had just been a year off in our time reference."

As the days went by, Lori Jean learned that Charles had been attracted to her for quite some time and that he would have pursued her more actively if it had not been for his uncertain marital situation.

"By then, Jim and I were going through the process of divorce, and Charles and Leslie, who had separated so many times, had seen their marriage crash and burn. It can never be said that either of us broke up the other's marriage. We had managed to do that individually, all by ourselves."

Shortly before Christmas, there was a knock at Lori Jean's front door. Her roommate, Thelma, was asleep, so she had to answer it.

"There was Charles on the porch with a Christmas card in his hand. I asked him to come in, and I asked him if I didn't get a Christmas kiss. He wasted not a moment of time in obliging my request.

"We went to my room and we talked . . . and kissed some more. Nothing more than that. I had a Teddy bear that looked like a little football player, and I wanted Charles to have that for Christmas.

"After a couple of hours, he said that he thought that he had better be going. As he stepped out on the porch to leave, I looked at him and said, 'I feel honored and privileged to be standing here with you.'

"Charles said that he felt the same way—and from then on we began to see much more of one another."

On January 13, 1984, Lori Jean was visiting Charles in his office. It did not take long to determine that he was very upset with Leslie. He felt that Lori Jean should leave, but suddenly she received a signal that the angels wished to speak to Charles.

"Although Charles is a professional astrologer, he had never met spirit guides or angels. The angels had me ask him to have his chair face me and to have our knees touching. Next, they instructed him to touch my fingers very lightly.

"I took the time to relax, to breathe deeply, and to lift my consciousness. Then I simply let go and allowed the words to come through.

"The angels told Charles that it was time for him to get on with his life and to stop allowing himself to be abused and manipulated. It was time to feel good about his work and to tolerate no longer those who made fun of him.

"They went on to tell him that it was purely time to begin loving himself and to stop the suffering that he had been feeling. He was to free himself from the pain that he had endured that dated back before Leslie, to his first wife Kathy.

"The angels did not tell him what to do, they simply made suggestions to stop the suffering that he had been feeling for so long.

"The angelic energies were peaceful and harmonious, and when I opened my eyes and looked at Charles's face, I could see that his troubled expression had turned to one of peace. Although I had been receiving the angelic vibrations since I was three years old, this was the first formal reading that I had ever given to anyone."

Charles asked her to remain in her chair and not to go anywhere. He left his office door open and went to the receptionist's desk to make a telephone call. No one was in the office except for his partner, George Gillette, and Lori Jean.

"Charles called Leslie and quite clearly and decisively told her that he wanted a divorce—and that this time he was not going to change his mind.

"He came back into the office with a relieved look on his face. He announced that he was going for lunch, and he asked if I wanted to go with him.

"So that was our first date. Charles loves English fish and chips, so we went out to have lunch. I was a little nervous, as it had been awhile since I had been on any kind of positive, loving date. I didn't quite know what to say or do or how to act—but it was fun! Charles still thanks the angels for that day of release."

Not long after that day, Lori Jean informed Charles that she felt he was going to be her second husband.

"Does that bother you?" she asked him.

"No," he said. "It certainly does not."

From then on, the two spent every day together.

"We literally could not get enough of each other. We jokingly complained that our bodies were getting in the way of our being as close as we really wanted to be. On the soul level, you see, we remembered merging our energies in the spirit state."

Then came the glorious day when Lori Jean visited Charles's office and was astonished when he unexpectedly got down on one knee and said: "I, Charles, love and serve you."

Lori Jean immediately followed suit and did the same thing for him.

"I have a box full of everything sentimental that we have ever given each other," Lori Jean said. "Once Charles gave me a card in which he had drawn two stick figures with a line connecting their hearts. He wrote that this connection between us would be like a rubber band that could stretch to any length—and that we would always be connected.

"One night after going to a meditation group, Charles dropped me off at Thelma's house; and before I got out of the car, he started to cry. He told me that nothing was wrong. They were happy tears because we were together."

The end of January, they went looking for an apartment and moved in together. They were in tune with one another from the very beginning. When they were out shopping separately, they would often come home to discover that they had brought each other the same gift.

They moved to Colorado together in October of 1984, and they were married in a Unity Church on July 28, 1985.

"My angel guide Daephrenocles says that Charles and I are like two white horses prancing together. He says that we are like 10 x 10 and not 1 + 1. We are doing our spiritual work together, and we work as a team.

"After more than ten years together, we are still very much in love. The words in our house are 'us, ours, and we,' not 'I, me, and you.' "

On June 18, 1994, Lori Jean and Charles were in the process of moving to a new home in Colorado at an even higher elevation, but she wrote to inform us that she had received confirmation that their recently acquired property was surrounded by a force-field of light.

"When I am relaxed," she said, "I see beyond the physical reality. I see the frequencies, energies, vibrations around us, and they are always of a high nature."

Years ago, Lori Jean learned that her angel guide Daephreno-cles' personal symbol was a cross of light. As a Light Being from the eighth dimension, she has seen him manifest tiny crosses of light as a signal to the nature spirits that their property is off limits to them, as far as damage from nature is concerned.

"I have seen hail revert back to rain in moments when I have prayed that the flowers we love not be damaged. Charles and I hold nature to be sacred. Sadly, I have often seen our neighbors' property sustain damage from weather—yet ours has received none. They shake their heads and wonder why."

On this particular day in June, a tornado siren awakened Lori Jean from an afternoon nap.

"I immediately asked for protection, and I saw a brilliant flash of light at the foot of the bed.

"I looked out over our property, and I saw hundreds of clear, see-through etheric crosses of white light *everywhere*. Then I beheld the transparent light bodies of Higher Beings around the place.

"The wind became a breeze. The thunder calmed to silence. A gentle rain began to fall through breaking clouds. The threat of a tornado was no more. We were safe."

Fourteen

The Universal Language of the Soul

I have known Joshua Shapiro for many years, but I had not had the opportunity to meet Vera, his bride of six months, until Sherry and I joined Joshua on the lecture platform in Chicago in January of 1992.

Vera proved to be a very charming lady, and it was immediately apparent to Sherry and me that these two lightworkers had most certainly been brought together by the Angels of Love. The Shapiros agreed—and explained that since Vera was a native of Brazil, spirit had led Joshua on quite an odyssey in order to find his destiny.

Joshua pointed out that their story really began in 1989 when he was living in Pacifica, California, working for the city of Berkeley as a computer programmer.

"At the time, I was involved with a number of women," Joshua said, "but there wasn't anyone who was special. I was following my Aries nature in being independent and not being tied down."

In January or February of 1989, Joshua met Carmen Balehistero, a Brazilian channel for the entity of St. Germain. Ms. Balehistero had expressed an interest in the bizarre archaeological artifacts known as the "crystal skulls," and since Joshua was co-author with Sandra Bowen and Nick Nocerino of a book entitled *Mysteries of the Crystal Skulls,* the two found that they had a great deal to discuss.

It was during the course of that meeting that Carmen informed Joshua that she and her family were in charge of a spiritual group called Pax Universal that organized metaphysical conferences in Brazil. Joshua accepted her invitation to be a speaker at a conference in São Paulo in June of 1990.

Vera explained that 1989 had been a year of great changes in her life. A native of Brazil who had lived all of her life in São Paulo, the largest city in that country, she went to Peru for the first time in July of 1989 as part of a metaphysical tour led by her spiritual teacher Luiz Gasparetto, a famous psychic. In Vera's opinion, the experiences which she underwent in Peru changed her life completely.

"While we visited the ancient mountain city of Machu Picchu in Peru," Vera said, "Gasparetto channeled an entity named Chuma, who said that she had been a high priestess of the Inca. She gave us the true history of Machu Picchu as well as specific information about some of the people in our group."

When she returned to Brazil, Vera herself received a message from the entity Chuma.

"She told me that I should quit my nice-paying job as manager of a large bank. Chuma said that I should begin organizing tours to Peru that would provide individuals with the opportunity for spiritual experiences at the various powerful energy vortexes that exist in that country."

Vera was cautious. "I was very confused about this inner message from Chuma. I am a Virgo. I don't just make changes in my life on a whim. I felt a great deal of fear about making such a dramatic change to do work that I had never done before."

Vera told us that she asked the spirit teacher for signs that would clearly demonstrate to her that such work was truly to be her life's path.

"I did receive several proofs, but the most powerful and convincing one came through Gasparetto when he was in the trance state and channeling artwork from some of the great masters.

"I prayed inwardly and told Chuma that if one of the artists who channeled through Gasparetto should paint her face, then I would absolutely believe in her message."

After the session was completed, the psychic's assistant showed the observers all the many paintings that various entities had channeled through Gasparetto.

"In one of the pictures was the face of a high priestess that I immediately recognized as Chuma," Vera recalled. "It was the same face that I saw in meditation when she communicated with me.

"I walked closer to the painting and I saw that Chuma's name was written on the canvas. The work had been signed by Toulouse-Lautrec. My heart began to beat very fast, and from that day on I have never questioned Chuma's messages. I quit my job at the bank; and thirty days later, I was on board an airplane to Peru with my first tour group."

Joshua remembered that in April of 1989 he had developed an unexplainable compulsion to go to Peru.

"Although I couldn't explain why I had to go to Peru, I have learned over the years to trust the inner voice."

He met with Peter Schneider, president of Peru Mystic Tours in Lima, while he was visiting in San Francisco.

"Peter has a strong interest in the UFO phenomenon, and he had attended a UFO sharing group which I had hosted in my home. He said that he could help me with his agency, and even said that I could stay in his home in Lima."

In December of 1989, Joshua visited Machu Picchu, Cuzco, and Lake Titicaca.

"I was especially drawn to Lake Titicaca as I had heard reports of a secret brotherhood in the area. While there, I had a spiritual reading from a shaman who lived on the Island of Amantani. He used coca leaves in his reading. He would throw them in the air and chant in what seemed to be a combination of Spanish and Quecha, the native language of the Inca. Depending upon where and how the leaves landed, the shaman would gain information about myself or the question I had asked."

When Joshua asked if he would ever be married, the medicine man answered, "Yes, to a Peruvian woman."

Intrigued by such a prediction, Joshua's thoughts moved back in time to a conference that he had attended earlier that year. He had found himself gazing at a Hispanic woman, and his inner voice had told him that one day he would be involved with such a woman.

Joshua recalled that the shaman's prophecy had sent a feeling "like electricity" running through his body.

"But what this meant at the time, I really didn't know; for I had never been involved with a Hispanic woman before."

Vera's first tour to mystical Peru had been a great success—but then she was forced to deal with the reality of the rainy season. She really could not offer tours during the period of December to March.

"This caused me to become very depressed," she told us. "I began to question again if offering tours to Peru was really the right thing for me to do since I didn't have any other source of income at that time."

An elderly teacher from a sacred spiritual society guided her through a special ritual in which she placed a tall mirror against a wall and sat before it with a white candle in her hands. The teacher told her to focus her entire attention on the light.

"After I went into a trance state, I didn't see myself any longer in the mirror. I saw a strange, but familiar, young woman about twenty years old. She was dressed in old Peruvian clothes, and she had long dark hair and was very pretty. I heard the smiling woman tell me that everything in my life would be all right. The feelings that I received from her were strength, confidence, freedom, happiness, and peace."

When the teacher who was guiding Vera through the experience asked the pretty young woman in the mirror what she meant when she said everything would be all right, Vera began to perceive different images above the woman's head.

"It was like watching a movie of a past time in Machu Picchu. I knew that the woman was me in a past life when I lived in the ancient city as an Inca.

"I saw her sitting on a large stone in Machu Picchu. A man approached her and they began to hug and to kiss. I knew the woman was me, but I did not recognize the face of the man.

"Then the movie changed. The man was crying, saying that he had to leave. She was understanding of his need to go, but she asked, 'What about our child?' And the only thing that I could understand from the man was that he felt he had no choice other than to leave the relationship."

As Vera watched these images, she talked out loud to share everything with her teacher-guide.

"He helped me to ask the questions, to better understand their situation. They seemed to ignore me—even though I was certain that they were aware of me.

"My teacher advised me to return to the face of the woman and the mirror, and it felt like we were linked together for hours. I was in utter joy, experiencing her essence and all her feelings and emotions.

"Naturally there was a part of me that was concerned that I was remaining too long in trance, but it was so wonderful to be with this other part of me that I couldn't let her go. My friend and teacher understood and told me to take my time. So I stayed at the mirror until she disappeared.

"Once the ritual was over, I rejoiced in the wonderfulness of the experience, but I still didn't feel that I had any real answers—so my depression was still inside of me."

Ten days after he returned from Peru in December of 1989, Joshua had an opportunity to move to Las Vegas to work with friends to create a non-profit New Age foundation.

On May 3, 1990, he was walking down a main street in Las Vegas, heading for a restaurant at lunchtime, when he heard a loud screech directly behind him.

"My last remembrance was everything blacking out, from bottom to top. The next thing I remember is waking up in a hospital, strapped down to a bed. I found out that it was two days later.

"I was asked if I could recall the truck that had struck me. At first I thought the doctor was joking, but then I was informed that a van had jumped the sidewalk curb and had struck me. I had a scrape on my left ankle, but no broken bones. I felt very weak and had little energy, but I never really experienced being hit by the van. To this day, I believe that some higher intelligence took my spirit out of my body and traveled with me to inner dimensions. I have a distinct feeling that I attended some kind of important meeting, but I have no clear memory of this time.

"I flew to Colorado about two weeks after the accident, and it seemed to me that I had been on some kind of flying vehicle during the two days that I was in a coma."

By the end of May, Joshua was able to get around with little difficulty; and he continued with his plans to leave to speak at the Brazilian metaphysical conference in June.

He missed his plane in Los Angeles, because no one had informed him that he needed a visa to travel to Brazil. He rescheduled his first presentation for two days later, and when he arrived in São Paulo, he was overwhelmed by the interest that he received from the local media. Then he learned that he would be speaking to an audience of three thousand people.

"The first day I spoke about UFOs and the second about the crystal skulls," Joshua said. "I really fell in love with Brazil and its people. I felt very comfortable being with them."

About the middle of December 1989, Vera sought out the services of a highly recommended psychic, in an effort to gain more insights into her uncertain life.

"I remember sitting in the woman's living room when she opened the door, walked directly over to me, smiled, and hugged me, saying, 'Oh, I can see that you finally discovered your mission in this lifetime!'

"I felt very strange—and I wondered what she was talking about."

Vera accompanied the psychic into her "special room" where the woman used a deck of regular playing cards to accomplish her consultations.

"She told me that I was finally reconnecting with my past and that I should trust the choice that I had made. She said that my mission in this lifetime was to take people to Peru to assist them in recognizing their Inca lifetimes. I was very impressed with this woman because her words were so accurate without my saying one word or asking one question."

Vera finally asked the psychic how she could know all those things that she was telling her.

The psychic smiled and replied: "When I look at you, I see the priestess that you were in Peru. You are a very special soul. You have a mission to accomplish. You should not worry, because the universe will take care of everything for you. Continue to conduct your tours. You have made the correct choice. Be peaceful about it."

And then the woman's consultation went an entirely different direction.

"I know that you are very happy being single and that you don't want to get married," she told Vera. "But I need to tell you that in the first six months of the next year [1990], you are going to meet your soul mate."

The psychic went on, telling the astonished Vera that everything between her and this man would happen so fast that she would not have time to think about it. Everything was being arranged in the higher dimensions between Vera and this man, whose name she believed to be Ricardo.

"By the time that you finally become conscious of what you are doing," the psychic explained to Vera, "you will be married to this man and living in another country."

Vera was totally frustrated. "There is no way in hell that I will leave my country to marry someone!"

Then she remembered that the psychic had teased her and said, "He is such a wonderful man that if you don't want him, give him *my* phone number!"

A few months later, Vera found herself taking a workshop on crystals conducted by Carmen Balehistero. During one of the classes, the topic suddenly changed to that of crystal skulls.

"When I heard those words, 'crystal skulls,' my heart jumped," Vera said. "Somehow I could no longer pay attention to anything else Carmen was saying for the rest of the class. I had thought that I knew everything there was to know about crystals—and now, suddenly, I was hearing about something new."

Later, after the class, Vera inquired further about the strange new topic.

Carmen told her that the mystery of crystal skulls was a subject area that would be covered at her next metaphysical conference.

"I met a man in San Francisco who is knowledgeable about the crystal skulls," Carmen said. "I hope to bring him here to lecture on the subject."

Vera told us that she could not stop thinking about crystal skulls and this man that Carmen hoped to bring to Brazil.

"After the workshop, I saw Carmen three or four times before the conference, and she finally told me that the man had confirmed that he would be coming to Brazil to speak about the crystal skulls," Vera said. "She added that I should watch television in the next few days because she would be showing a video that she had on the subject."

Vera was seated excitedly before her television set on the Saturday night when the program would show the video on crystal skulls.

"I became hypnotized by the magic of the crystal skulls," she remembered. "The different poses of the skulls in tandem with the background music was very powerful. As if I were in a trance, I could see flashes of my past lives—pyramids, Mayans, Atlantis, UFOs.

"However, this video did not contain any verbal information, so it only made me all the more excited to meet this man from the United States who would be bringing all this information to Brazil."

The Third International Metaphysical Conference sponsored by Pax Universal was held from June 29 to July 1, 1990. Vera was a volunteer at the conference, but she managed to be in the front row when Joshua Shapiro gave his presentation on crystal skulls.

"I was totally fascinated with all the information that Joshua shared—just as everyone else in the room was," Vera said. "The room was very quiet, as people had to wait for Carmen to translate his English into Portuguese.

"During Joshua's presentation something very interesting happened to me. I was sitting next to a blind man and all of a sudden an extraterrestrial entity appeared in front of me. The entity came close to my ear and said, 'Vera, do you remember the library that Chuma mentioned when you were in Peru? The library *is* a crystal skull!'

"And I said, 'Oh, now I understand!' When I was in Peru, Chuma told us that when the human beings were ready, they would find a library in Machu Picchu that will reveal the science of life—the past, the present, and the future.

"I had not understood the entity Chuma at the time, but now I perceived that the information of the great library was in the crystal skull and would not be damaged because crystal is a hard substance that could remain buried and unharmed in the ground of Machu Picchu for a long time.

"The blind man sitting next to me leaned over and whispered, 'What is Shapiro talking about? A library in Machu Picchu?'

"And then I laughed, because he couldn't *see* the entity that had spoken to me, but he had *heard* him! The blind man was confused, because he couldn't tell if Joshua was saying this or someone else—the entity—was speaking."

Vera remembered that when Joshua concluded his presentation, he commented that if anyone had had any kind of an experience during his presentation about the crystal skull to please come forward to speak to him about it.

"I thought at the time that I should share this information about the library with him, but I didn't know any English, so I decided to forget it.

"I knew that there was to be a party on the last day of the conference. Joshua would be likely to be there. Perhaps if the situation arose, I might be able to mention it to him there."

Joshua remembered having a wonderful time at the party for the conference speakers and organizers. Although he did not speak Portuguese, there were enough Brazilians there who spoke good English.

"A woman named Dulce told me that she had a friend who wanted to speak with me about an experience that she had during my presentation at the conference," he said. "But for some reason I didn't seem to be able to get over to speak to the woman until the party was ending.

"I went up to Dulce, learned that her friend's name was Vera.

We all agreed that the hour was getting late, so courtesy dictated that I be polite and express a hope that we might have an opportunity to talk before I needed to return to the United States."

In retrospect, Joshua told us, he has since wondered why he didn't feel an immediate connection with Vera.

"And Vera has since told me that although she was fascinated with the information that I shared about the crystal skull, she didn't really like my spontaneous and somewhat lighthearted lecture style."

The next day, a Monday, Joshua and the other speakers from the United States went to the home of a famous Brazilian television producer to be interviewed regarding their special areas of expertise. Vera was also there, still wishing to tell him about her experience during his presentation on the crystal skulls.

"Pepe, Vera's tour guide in Peru, had been one of the speakers at the conference, so he was able to translate for us while we drove to the producer's home. I saw that a healer who had offered to 'balance' Vera's energy had only made her dizzy and confused, so while we were waiting in the producer's garden to be interviewed, I offered to help restore her psychic equilibrium."

After Joshua had finished restoring Vera's energy to a better balance, he felt strongly that he had known her before in a previous life experience.

"Her energy was very familiar. Somehow, a special connection was established between us—or perhaps we were reactivating a connection from our past. I felt that we had been married before, and I told her this."

When it came time for Joshua's interview, Vera also recorded it on his video camera.

"Later, I remember that we held hands all the way back to the hotel."

Joshua joined Vera, her roommate, and Pepe for dinner; and afterwards, he and Vera went down to her car in the garage to talk privately. Also, it was Vera's assignment as a conference volunteer to see to it that Joshua got back to his hotel that night.

"Well," Joshua smiled, "one thing led to another, and I never returned to my hotel room that night."

Vera attended the after-conference party with the expectation of being able to speak to Joshua about her experience during his presentation on the crystal skulls. However, her friend Dulce made three unsuccessful attempts to bring Joshua over to their table, so Vera had grown discouraged.

"Joshua was too busy talking with other people at the party. Carmen, the conference organizer left the party, then came back to speak with me. She asked me if I would be able to bring Pepe, my Peruvian guide, to be part of a television interview that was scheduled for the next day. I told her that I would be happy to help out."

Vera and Dulce were at the front door of the restaurant preparing to leave when Joshua finally came over to Dulce to ask about her friend.

"It was too late to talk with him; so I told Dulce to forget it, and we left."

To Vera's surprise, Joshua and some of the other speakers from the United States were waiting at the hotel for transportation to the producer's home. She asked Pepe to translate for her, and she was at last able to tell Joshua about her mystical experience during his presentation and about an earlier UFO encounter.

"I feel very strongly that something, some energy or force, made Carmen return to the party to ask that favor of me. If she hadn't come back to ask me to accompany the speakers who were to be interviewed that next day, I would not have had an opportunity to be with Joshua. Maybe an angel guided her."

At this time, Vera told us, she did not feel any special connection with Joshua nor any attraction to him as a man.

"When the healer had made me feel strange and dizzy, I was

unsure whether I should accept Joshua's help. But I felt so bad that I gave him permission to work with me.

"I held his hands, closed my eyes, started to breathe—and I immediately left my body.

"I went back to the time in which I was the Inca woman in Machu Picchu. The same man was speaking to me and crying. Somehow I knew that the man who was with me in that Inca life was Joshua.

"When I returned to full consciousness, Joshua was asking me if I was okay. After I said that I was, he told me that he felt that we had known each other before. I thought, 'Oh, no, maybe he, too, went into a trance and saw that Inca time with me.'

"And when he said, 'You were my wife in a past life,' I thought for certain that he must have seen everything!

"Then he smiled in a funny way and said, 'You are going to marry me again in this lifetime!'

"I thought, 'Oh, my God! Americans are crazy! Forget it! No way!' "

Later, Vera recalled, the "magic" started to happen. Pepe, who had been translating for them, wasn't around anymore—and she and Joshua continued to speak to one another although neither understood the other's native tongue.

As they grew friendlier, the hours literally seemed to melt away.

"Joshua and I talked and talked until very late. We shared things about ourselves in a magical way. I would be saying something to him, and before I even completed my thought, he was completing it for me. And the same thing was happening for him. I knew what he was going to say and could complete his sentences.

"I still don't understand how two people who could not speak the other's language could do this. My only guess is that at this time the language of love was already speaking through us."

* * *

Joshua was supposed to stay in Brazil until the end of the week as he had a private lecture scheduled for the Pax Universal Center. A problem developed with the hotel in which Joshua was staying, so Carmen asked Vera if he might stay in her apartment until he returned to the United States. He immediately bought a Portuguese-English, English-Portuguese dictionary for each of them.

"I could not believe that I was speaking of marriage. I had been married once before. I wasn't certain that I would ever repeat the experience," Joshua recalled.

"One day when I was with Vera and a few friends in her apartment, I felt that our connection in the past life in Peru was so strong that I started crying. Normally, I don't get this emotional, but I was overcome with a joy of meeting her again. My tears were not of sadness, but of joy.

"When it was time for me to return to the United States, I knew that I had met a very special person, and I definitely planned to stay in touch with her."

After the "magic" had occurred between them, Vera was struck with the sad reality that Joshua would only be staying a few more days in Brazil.

"We really wanted to be together as much as possible," she said. "We had four days, and I wanted to make them last as if they were four years.

"When he left, Joshua told me that he felt for certain that we would be married. Even though our connection was *very strong*, I could not imagine how this could happen."

However, two days after Joshua had returned to the States, Vera's telephone rang—and there was the "crazy" American trying to speak Portuguese using the dictionary that he had bought in Brazil.

"I couldn't believe it! I knew that he would write to me, but there he was, live, on the telephone, speaking to me. I felt so bad that I couldn't speak English. When we had been together, we could feel what the other person was trying to say. We could read our thoughts and feelings through our eyes and gestures. But on the phone, it was impossible. I told Joshua to call in the morning. I had begun to take some English classes, and my teacher would be there to translate."

Back in the States, Joshua felt that he finally understood what the shaman had meant in Lake Titicaca when he had told him that he would marry a Peruvian woman. Even though Vera was Brazilian, she had told him that Machu Picchu in Peru was her true spiritual home.

It was indeed fortunate for Joshua and Vera that she had a friend who was teaching English and who could translate for them on the telephone.

"Vera was willing to help pay for my trip back to Brazil by organizing some lectures there for me. In addition, she was taking another group to Peru, and she invited me to go, free of charge. I charged my airfare on my credit card, and I was able to return to Brazil at the end of August, just before she took her group to Peru."

By the time that Joshua returned to Brazil in August, Vera said that she was more comfortable with the idea of marrying him.

In July, she had taken a tour group to Machu Picchu, and she had gone off by herself to do a meditation on Huyna Picchu, the mountain that overlooks the ancient Peruvian city.

"I placed a picture of Joshua on the ground, and I asked God and my guides to please help me to understand what the relationship with Joshua meant to my life. I needed to know what to do, because things were becoming very serious between our letters and our telephone conversations.

"As I was looking at the picture of Joshua, a butterfly flew over it—then stopped to rest on top of it. Incredibly, the butterfly stayed on his picture for fifteen minutes.

"I don't know how to explain this, but I felt that I was having a telepathic conversation with the butterfly. I was able to feel peace and confidence. And for the first time since I met Joshua, I felt secure in our relationship.

"The butterfly somehow was able to help me to release all my fears, doubts, and questions.

"I felt that the butterfly was like an angel who helped me to see the answers clearly.

"After this experience with the butterfly, I didn't hesitate to open my heart completely to Joshua.

"And before he left Brazil the second time, I accepted his invitation to come to the United States and marry him. And the psychic had been correct about my future husband being named 'Ricardo.' Although his spiritual name is Joshua, his birth name was 'Richard.' "

The September 1990 trip to Peru was really a time of celebration for Joshua and Vera as they had the opportunity to be together in the places where they had spent one of their most powerful past lifetimes. Joshua found that he was able to do a great deal of healing work and to channel energy to some of the people who were in their tour group. He could almost hear the spirit of the ancient Inca whispering to him.

"Our special memory of the trip was that we went back to the exact spot where Vera had conducted her meditation with the butterfly on Huyna Picchu, and we did a meditation together.

"Then, further up, near the top of the mountain, in the Temple of the Moon we conducted our own sacred spiritual marriage and promised to work together to do God's work."

Joshua explained that it took about three months for U.S. Immigration to approve a fiancée visa for Vera, and then another five months for the American Consulate in São Paulo to approve it. In July of 1991, Vera arrived in the United States.

"On September 7, almost exactly one year from the day that we performed our spiritual marriage in Machu Picchu, we were married near Chicago in a simple ceremony by a minister of the Church of Religious Science in one of the local parks.

Fifteen

❖

The Wonderful Union of Twin Flames

I have known Moi-RA and RA-Ja Dove for many years now, and the all-prevailing impression that I have always received from them is that of love. They speak freely of their guidance from otherworldly and multidimensional beings, and they seem completely dedicated to their avowed goal of serving as beaconlights of peace, love, and light on Earth.

Although a superficial glance might initially focus upon the physical contrasts between a ruggedly built American man and a diminutive lady from the Philippines who is a few Earth-years older than he, the challenge is to comprehend that such mundane matters as appearance, age, and ethnicity have no bearing on the truth or the power of a spiritual message.

Moi-RA was born into a spiritualist family who lived in a small province near Manila in the Philippines. Her mother died when Moi-RA was only two, leaving her with her father, whom she grew later to consider the greatest philosopher she has ever known.

When she was four, Moi-RA heard her father tell her uncle,

"This child of mine is an old soul. She is going to do something important for the world."

At that same age, Moi-RA's eldest sister took her to seances at the Spiritualist Center that had been founded by her uncle, Juan Ortega, the originator of the world famous trained Philippine Psychic Surgeons.

"I would sleep at the beginning of the sessions," Moi-RA said, "but I would wake up automatically when my uncle would deliver spirit messages. I clearly remember being so interested in those messages, especially when he talked about the angels and outer space. Later, I discovered the same wisdom in the Theosophical Society of which I became a member at the age of sixteen."

Moi-RA kept to herself and seldom played with other children. "I loved to read stories about Buck Rogers in outer space from the comics section of the newspaper," she recalled. "I read books until sundown every day. My father would look for me all over the house—and then find me hiding behind walls in a window overhang where I could watch the ocean and read to my heart's content."

An amazing spiritual experience occurred to Moi-RA during her teen years.

"It was during one full moon of May which is called the *Wesak* Festival, the time when the Buddha comes back to give his blessings to the Earth. According to tradition, the masters and teachers of humanity meet in the Wesak Valley during this time. I saw myself in a vision sitting on the top steps of an amphitheater that had been hewn from the ground. I felt a continuous stream of tiny droplets of cool refreshing mist enveloping my entire being, bringing a feeling of healing and a blessed calm of contentment and peace.

"Then I beheld the masters and the teachers arriving one by one, wearing flowing robes. I saw them form a six-pointed star on the grounds while the Buddha appeared in the night sky above the amphitheater, giving his blessings to the world.

"As a member of the Esoteric Group in the Theosophical Society I was supposed to 'tune in to' this festival each year; but that year, in my vision, I actually attended it.

"Later in life, I made the practice become a physical reality by actually pilgrimaging to the Wesak Valley to worship in the holiness and to imbibe the wisdom of the Buddha."

All the time she spent reading certainly produced valuable academic dividends for the young woman. She became a superior student, pursuing advanced work after her college graduation and becoming a university professor of Ethics and the Religions of the Far East, as well as a Dean of Women and a guidance counselor.

In spite of her academic degrees, Moi-RA clung to her childhood belief that each person is led immediately to wed his or her soul mate.

"I married a man who quickly disproved my hypothesis, but I had four children by him. When I had the fourth, I nearly died. The anesthesiologist had sought to stop the operation because my pulse had touched bottom—but then quickly picked up again. The child, a girl, died six hours later. When I woke up, I knew what had happened even before the nurse told me."

Later, she was told that the surgery had taken nearly three hours. Amazingly, she had not required a blood transfusion even after fifty surgical clips had been used to stop the profuse bleeding. After her uterus was removed, it was found to have been torn in many places due to the unborn child's fingernails, for the baby had been a month overdue.

In her anguish, Moi-RA asked Higher Intelligence why she had been brought back to life.

"The answer I received was that I was supposed to do something for the world before I left it for good. I replied that I was ready."

While she was recovering from the surgery, Moi-RA had a vision while she was sitting under a bridge, watching the flow of the water.

"Suddenly, I felt the presence of a great being who put his hand on my crown chakra and whispered with a gentle, soothing voice, *'Do not worry, my child, we will always be with you.'*

"My head was bowed, looking at his feet, feeling the wonderful energy protectively enveloping my whole being. I was so much in awe of his greatness that I dared not look at his face. To see his feet was enough for my soul.

"I felt the blessedness of the healing energy that I was supposed to transmit to humanity.

"This vision guided my life from that moment onward. It led me to the United States. It showed me that I would later meet someone who would do the mission with me."

Moi-RA came to the United States in 1977 after she had taught philosophy and psychology at the University of the City of Manila for ten years. She planned to teach at the University of California in Berkeley and complete her doctoral dissertation there. She had told her children that they would return to the Philippines after five years on American soil.

As fate would have it, by 1981, her first husband had passed away and her children had all found themselves suitable mates.

Moi-RA now devoted herself to her duties as a president of a Theosophical Lodge, and she had begun to content herself that such was to be her mission in her present lifetime. Although she had been given a number of readings by clairvoyants that predicted her remarrying, Moi-RA firmly stated that she would never again marry.

But then came the day when she met RA-Ja—and her protestations of remaining single faded away into nothingness.

"When I first met RA-Ja and peered deeply into his light-filled blue eyes, I knew he was the other pea in the pod. I knew that we had finally come together and that we would now be ready for anything. My energy—the energy—was complete. RA-Ja is the most loving being that I have ever known."

RA-Ja said that although it had occurred nearly twenty years ago, he could remember the day well. He had just completed a workshop on Naturopathic Health Principles when a kind lady in the audience came forward to present him with a book entitled *Revelation: The Divine Fire* by *Brad Steiger.*

"You are one of the men and women that this book is about," she told him. "While you were lecturing, I could see angels and starships around you."

As RA-Ja examined the book, he received a jolt of spiritual recognition. He had been told in his visions and meditations that one day the Arch-Angels would guide him in establishing a Spiritual Angel Garden and that they would build a new Earth from that garden.

"This was the first time I had ever seen in print accounts of others doing similar kinds of things. The entire book was filled with angelic and extraterrestrial lore. Somehow, I heard a little voice say that this marked a point in the evolution of Earth. And soon after that, my angel guides told me that it was time for a graduation for me. I was to begin a new leg of my mission on Earth."

After working for over a decade as a naturopathic physician, teaching in medical universities and hospitals, working with medical doctors, chiropractors, and having maintained his own clinics in remote and exotic spa centers of the globe, RA-Ja Dove was now led by his guides to give up his naturopathic work and head for Oaxaca and the Yucatan.

He was staying at an ashram when he had an out-of-body experience in which the Holy One revealed to him that he must journey to Palenque's ancient ceremonial site and visit the Temple of Inscriptions.

RA-Ja donated all of his medical equipment to the ashram. He also gave away his automobile and bought a bicycle. He would undertake the long journey to the central American jungles as a wandering holy man, taking nothing with him beyond his immediate necessities.

Trusting completely in the angels to protect him, RA-Ja embarked on the pilgrimage that took him to the interior of Mexico, all the way down to Oaxaca, Yucatan, taking time to visit numerous Mayan temples and pyramids.

While in Oaxaca, at Monte Alban in tomb number seven, he experienced another remarkable out-of-body experience in which he seemed to see himself attired in a pharaoh's headdress. He saw himself working with the priests of the One God to establish peace on the land and goodness for the people.

Later, in Tulum, a beautiful ancient Mayan temple complex, RA-Ja joined a group that had gathered one evening to list to the prophecies of a reputable local seeress.

"The seeress explained that I would go back to the United States and meet my twin flame," RA-Ja said. "She said that the woman had been with me in previous lifetimes and that we would find completion in the Aquarian cycle.

"No," I said. "I have been married, and I am not interested in bonding at this time. I believe that I have been called by God to do my spiritual work alone.

" 'Nonetheless,' explained the seeress. 'What I see, will be.' "

Upon his return to the United States, RA-Ja became severely ill.

"My skin became yellow like parchment paper. I knew that I must have yellow jaundice—or worse, hepatitis.

"After two weeks of suffering, I decided to seek medical assistance, and I received the official diagnosis of a severe case of hepatitis. No cure was known, so it was up to my body's defenses. If it could withstand the disease, I would recover. If not, the end was near!"

RA-Ja visited native elder healers and herbalists and put his own knowledge to work to heal himself. But to no avail.

"I felt that the forces of evil were trying to put a stop to the great mission that had been handed to me. They sought to put a halt to it before I had really been able to get it off the ground.

"I wondered how my Angelic Order could assign me a mission and invest so much into my training, just to let it fail before it began.

"I knew some stories of how some great missions had been subverted by the evil forces—yet somehow I felt a deep sense of winning within me. I knew that I would not fail, but at the same time I didn't know how I would win. I knew that the Holy Spirit was the only force left that could heal me."

According to RA-Ja the miracle occurred when he was on a bus in Tucson, Arizona, reading *Gods of Aquarius: UFOs and the Transformation of Man* by Brad Steiger. Chapter Eight, "Healing with UFO Energy" told of a man in Denmark who had been cured of a severe case of hepatitis by the low overflight of a UFO.

"This was it! I knew that my Angelic Order was having me read a story exactly like my own because they wanted to help me. I looked up at the sky and said, 'Isn't it true, my beloved ones? You are having me read these words because you wish to cure me of my disease?' And they whispered ever so softly, *'Yes, it is true!'* "

And then, according to RA-Ja, it happened.

"I was healed instantly. I could feel a new surge of energy enter my being. I knew that as I got off the bus, I would be able to walk wherever I wished without getting tired."

Within days, RA-Ja received a message from the Space Brothers that since he was now totally healed, he was to travel to Sounion, Greece, the Temple of Poseidon, for the next stage of his Earth mission.

While RA-Ja focused and meditated at a secluded beach in Greece, he was surprised when Buddha appeared to him in a very vivid vision. The Buddha told him that he was going to assist his mission by giving him something special. The Buddha further guided RA-Ja to take up a temporary job as a naturopathic physician, nutrition consultant, and a psychiatric counselor.

And then he was back in the United States, hoping that he might find open and receptive minds for the information that he knew it was his mission to share. He felt strongly that the lodges of the Theosophists would present him with a solid network across the country; but he discovered that while the Theosophical Society may have been the harbinger of the New Way at the turn of the century, it seemed to have crystalized its teaching and become resistant to innovative discussions.

But one of their members was listening. And in terms of RA-Ja's mission, she was the most important.

"There she was, an elected Federation president of several Theosophical Lodges. My sweety-hearty, the pink rose of the Philippines, the wise and varicolored lustrous pearl of the Orient, Swami Moi-RA."

RA-Ja realized then why the Buddha had appeared to him in Greece.

"He was bringing me to one of his own kin, an Oriental lady, who certainly lived his core principles. All at once I realized that the seeress in Tulum had been correct. I would be able to work together with this woman. When Buddha said that he was going to help the mission, he had meant that he was bringing my lovely Moi-RA to me. He was adding the other half that would allow the mission to go forth publicly.

"We immediately became co-founders of The Aquarian Perspectives Interplanetary Mission, and we began spreading the word in April of 1985—one year after the impetus for commencing the earth-based portion of the mission was issued in Palenque."

Their wedding ceremony took place on Mount Shasta on April 6, 1985.

"Ah, yes," RA-Ja reflected. "Love beckoned and I responded

immediately and without hesitation. We stayed on a honeymoon for three years; and to this day we are as happy as we were twelve hundred billion years ago—when we were created together, male and female, as one."

The Doves,' angel guides told them that it was necessary for them to travel around the world, as Jesus did, to see the suffering of the world and the plight of the masses on planet Earth.

They have now pilgrimaged completely around the world, stopping at every major spiritual place and power vortex on the planet.

One of the most common questions the Doves are asked is, "How do you know when you meet your Twin Flame?"

"Once the soul has attained the Grand Union," the Doves answer, "it never forgets. It may take many lesser romances before the Grand Union takes place. But these lesser affairs are but karmic episodes on Love's Grand Path. Every true romance, not infatuation or lust, is the tuning fork of the Twin Flames. There may be a dozen soul mates, but only one Twin Flame!

"When your Twin Flame enters your life, biological age matters not; neither race, color, creed, or cultural origin can keep the inevitable marriage from occurring. The angel seed recognizes and responds."

In Angel Love, as differentiated from earthly love, only the eyes reveal the secret.

"Angel Love is sired from the Soul," state the Doves. "Sex finds its manifestation last. Infatuation or lust are physical and transitory, and they bind those who so indulge to the lower rungs of the spiritual ladder.

"When you have found true love, be ready to give up all and follow your heart's call—for Love speaks but once!

"The love that I feel for RA-Ja is a limitless, unselfish love,"

Moi-RA said. "It is a love that soars through emotions and thoughts, unharmed, unhindered, ever-flowing, joyfully giving, forward-looking, never-ending, ever-present, not expecting anything in return.

"My love for him is never an addiction, for I give him freedom to be himself, to go at his own pace, to manifest his angelhood. I see the beauty of his soul, the focus of commitment, and the courage of action every moment of the day.

"I feel that I am always with him wherever we are. One thing I notice is the difference in energy when we are apart. It is not complete. But there need not be any sadness, only a lull in inspiration.

"There are not enough words to define my love for RA-Ja; yet I truly believe that if I can show the world that *unconditional love* is possible, then this fallen planet can be redeemed in its full glory. This, I believe, is my true mission: *To live Love!*"

Receiving Unconditional Angelic Love

One basic lesson that I hope you have received from reading this book is that when you give unconditional angelic love, its energy can never be depleted—for you will also receive it anew from the Angels of Love in a higher dimension. You can never receive imbalance, hatred, envy, or jealousy when you are filled with angelic love. You can never be touched by negative vibrations when you are filled with the energy of the Angels of Love.

Neither can you fill yourself with such love and hold it within your being. You must pour it out upon the world or it will stagnate.

If you bottle up love within you, you will find that it simply cannot keep. It will soon sour. Love must be given so that you may receive it afresh.

Even now as you read these words, feel unconditional, non-judgmental, angelic love pouring into your body, mind, and spirit.

Feel this angelic love entering your Crown Chakra and filling up your entire physical vessel.

Be aware of it filling your feet, your ankles, your legs, your hips, your stomach, chest, and back. Feel it entering your arms. Sense it moving up your spine. Know that it has entered your neck, your shoulders, your head.

Understand that you are now filled to the crown of your head.

Be aware that you are vibrating, glowing with unconditional love.

Now visualize that there is a golden pyramid above your head, directly over your Crown Chakra.

Understand that this pyramid collects vibrations of love from the angels, then channels it directly into your Crown Chakra. Be aware with all your essence that you have now banished negativity and that your psyche and your physical body are now balanced.

Visualize someone whom you love. See a golden beam of angelic love and light from your Heart Chakra streaking across space and touching that loved one at his or her Heart Chakra. Feel strongly the link-up between the two of you.

Now imagine that you are sending the angelic love and light that the two of you have shared around the world. Visualize that you will touch all those men and women who are depressed, who are feeling unloved, who are feeling imbalanced. See all those who are imprisoned by negativity being able to reach out and make contact with the beautiful energy of angelic love that you are transmitting around the planet.

Feel yourself pouring out unconditional, angelic love and light from your Heart Chakra.

See it streaming all over the Earth.

Know that it is touching the lonely, the despondent, the bitter, the angry, the negative.

Know that it is uplifting their spirits.

Know that it is helping to raise their consciousness.

Know that it is balancing their energies.

Be aware that you are giving and receiving anew the unconditional love vibrations from the Angels of Love. Feel the energy, the strength, the angelic-vibration within the love frequency. Know that the more love that you pour forth from your Heart Chakra, the more love you will receive from the Angels of Love through your Crown Chakra. The more angelic love you transmit, the more you will be energized by the Angels of Love.

Practice this broadcasting of the angelic love vibration on a regular basis, and no negativity can ever pervade your physical being, can ever harm your mind, can ever injure your soul. If you truly fill yourself with unconditional love from the Angels of Love, negativity will never again be able to touch your life.

Give and receive love, and you will immediately become a positive conduit for the Angels of Love, sharing in unparalleled glory and awesome power.

Sixteen

Their Love Was Meant to Be

Lois East told me that she was certain that she and her husband Clay were "truly brought together by the Angels." Lois is a fine artist, who, since 1963, has had the honor of seeing her paintings and sculpture featured in numerous books and national art magazines.

Regarding her unique work with the Angels of Love, she explained that she enters a meditative state, then focuses upon the vibrations of the subject's own angel and renders an interpretation of them in pastels and oils.

Lois and her husband met in 1977 while visiting a meditation class being given by Paul Solomon. Clay said he would not normally have enrolled in the class, since it meant driving diagonally completely across Denver every night for a week. But he felt a strong urging that he take the class. There were no doubts about it. Lois was brought to the class one night as a guest by a friend of hers.

Later, they were told in a reading by Louis Gitner of the Louis Foundation that they had been together many lives before and that they had special work to do. They then realized that angelic influences must have brought them together, working through intuition and through a friend of Lois.

"In the beginning, we were friends, and we spent time together in metaphysical and spiritual classes and various groups. Through these classes and the books we read, our awareness was opened to the Angels and to the truths beyond the physical realm. As our spiritual unfolding grew, we began to see with ever-increasing clarity how our lives were gently guided by the angelic realm."

Lois had moved to the area west of Denver, Colorado, in 1960, and she gained a fine reputation for her paintings of Western landscapes and Native-American life. An art major in college and a former teacher of fine art, she was soon motivated to capture the Angels of Love on her canvas and paper. In 1976, she began studying metaphysics in classes taught by Rev. Allen Miller, and she learned to unfold spiritually.

"In meditation focus, I am able to bring through images and messages from the angels and master teachers for people all over the world who write to me at our post office box number with their birth data and questions. I always say a prayer when I begin, and ask to be a clear channel for the Angels of Light. The paintings of these angels are sent in a heavy mailing tube, and the messages are mailed on tape."

"Clay is very supportive of these endeavors, and many times he reads the questions to me as I am bringing through the messages and the answers. He is a very special and caring partner. It is wonderful to be able to do this work together and to reach out and help others through the paintings and the messages."

Clay is a native of Colorado, a retired engineer, who had hosted a study group of the Manly P. Hall books in his home for many years prior to his meeting Lois.

"In the early 1980s, Clay and I were told that we would be freer in our lives in many areas in the years to come. His first wife had multiple sclerosis for many years, before she passed away; and I had been married for more than twenty years to an architect. When we met, I was concentrating on my fine art career of painting people and landscapes. Although Clay had studied many of the ancient metaphysical teachings, my previous spiritual work had pretty much been limited to having taught Sunday School when my two children, Tara and Craig, were young. I had also illustrated childrens' Bible books."

Lois and Clay were married in December, 1983.

"We feel that marriage in the highest sense is not only gazing into each other's eyes, but also in gazing together in the same direction.

"And we are very blessed by being in conscious communication with the angels. In meditation, I bring through messages from my spiritual helpers, Ra and Sha-Lin, as well as words from individuals' angels."

In her paintings, Lois most often depicts the angels in colors of light lavender, gold, pink, peach, white, light blue, and magenta.

"These are all light and beautiful colors that join the abstract lightness of watercolors and pastels with the hazy translucency of the angelic forms. I fashion paintings that bring forth that which I see in meditation and prayer—the Light dimensions.

"When we meditate," Lois said, "we are focused into the Light. We are never alone."

Lois and Clay have plans to reproduce many of the angelic images which she has received on prints and greeting cards.

"I feel that I have been given this talent by God, and I have chosen this direction in my career with the help of the angels. It is now time to share these angelic images with thousands of people who also love the angels."

According to Lois, an angelic entity named Aranaea told her that within the Angelic realm, beautiful entities express the greatest love in the Angelic Kingdom of Light. The activities of these honored beings never cease.

They are attracted to the seeking many.

They see the need; they feel the thoughts; they shower love; they envision the perfection within the human embodiment.

Therefore, as you know, the mind is the builder. Many choices are within the minds of many who are seeking health of the body.

It is beneficial to seek the Angels. They want only to shower healing, to teach and to share love.

They want only to love.

Seventeen

❖

Patience and Faith

Fay Marvin Clark of Perry, Iowa, was a highly valued mentor of mine during my formative years as an author and researcher in the mid-1960s. Although I had been exploring the unknown ever since I was a child and had begun publishing when I was fifteen, it was reassuring to me to meet a wise and cheerful silver-haired gentleman, who had begun his own paranormal explorations before I had been born. And it only enhanced our friendship that in those days, Fay was a dead ringer for Claude Rains, an actor that I had very much admired as a youth.

When Fay passed away on October 23, 1991, he was married to Marvel, a charming lady whom I had met many years before they had become man and wife. I knew intuitively that she and Fay had been guided to be as one by the Angels of Love, and I knew that their relationship of many years had undergone numerous transitions that must have required patience, unconditional love, and genuine acts of caring.

"I miss Fay so much," Marvel told me, "but I have many indications of his presence and his continued love. I love him more than any person I have ever known, and I am sure that our angelic guides or some higher power helped to arrange our meeting in this lifetime."

Marvel said that their meeting had not occurred at the best of timing for either of them, for they were each married to another at the time. Of less consequence was their difference in age. She was thirty-one; he was fifty-six.

"But just knowing each other was wonderful—and when we finally did get our eleven wonderful years together, it was like Heaven on Earth for both of us. I *know* that Fay and I were destined to meet."

Through a somewhat extended process, Marvel had become aware of Fay's Hiawatha Publishing Company in Hiawatha, Iowa, and she learned that he had been involved in metaphysical research for many years with his first wife, Adeline.

Marvel herself had pursued her own psychic and spiritual studies in Perry, Iowa, since about 1954.

"I had discovered the Edgar Cayce readings, and I had communicated with the Association for Research and Enlightenment (A.R.E.) at Virginia Beach, Virginia. By such correspondence, I had placed my name on their mailing list, and since Fay was on the Board of Trustees for the A.R.E., he was able to acquire use of the list. Although he only used that mailing list for one six-month period sometime in 1962, I received a catalog from his Hiawatha Book Store. I placed the catalog in a drawer, and I didn't run across it again for a year or so."

When the catalog resurfaced, Marvel glanced at the list of books and made a mental note to herself to one day drive to Hiawatha and visit the book store.

And then *something* or *someone* caused her to sit down and dash off a quick note, asking what hours it would be possible to visit the Hiawatha Book Store.

"In three days I had a nice reply from Fay, saying that he *knew* from my letter that I was someone that he very much wanted to meet."

After a series of short correspondences that continued back and forth for many weeks, Marvel finally walked into the Hiawatha Book Store on August 16, 1963.

"That meeting was to change my life forever.

"Fay had a showcase of beautiful gemstones just inside his door, and we spent the first two hours looking at and talking about the various stones. All my life I have loved gemstones, and I had studied a lot about them. I even had a good-sized collection of my own."

As they were engrossed in an examination of the various attractive and fascinating stones, Fay paused in his conversation, looked deep into Marvel's eyes, and said: "This has not been the first time that we have met. I have known you before—many times."

Then he went right on with his explanation of a particular stone before Marvel had a chance to say anything in response and as if he had said nothing at all out of the ordinary.

"Of course I wouldn't have known what to say anyway. Later, as I came to know Fay, I knew that he would *never* say *anything* like that to *anyone*—even if he *did* have such thoughts.

"I am still certain to this day that those words came out spontaneously—as though he had no control over what he had said.

"Many months later, we talked briefly about the incident. He agreed that he would not under normal circumstances have said such a thing to anyone, but he did remember having said those words to me; and he went on to say that when I had first walked in the door to the store, he had the most powerful sense of *knowing* me.

"On the way home that evening of August 16, 1963, all I could remember were Fay's eyes. I seemed to know them, and a deep bond of love was there instantly. From that day on, Fay was the 'Light of my life.' "

Marvel was married at the time with two little daughters.

"I was very busy and involved with my family, my music career, and my spiritual studies. I had no intention then of obtaining a divorce. Such thoughts never entered my mind.

"Then, early in 1968, my husband left me and my little girls. We divorced several months later."

It was not until the fall of 1968 while she was working for Fay at his publishing company in Perry, Iowa, that the two of them finally shared the deep love that they had felt for one another since their first meeting five years earlier.

"We were on cloud nine, but there were other responsibilities, and it was not the right time for us to be together—and it would be twelve more years before the 'right timing' came for us."

Adeline had passed away in 1961; and in 1965, Fay married Mary Luther, a close friend of Marvel's.

"In fact, they had even met at my home when I hosted a metaphysical meeting."

Mary passed away in May of 1979, and Fay and Marvel were married on September 6, 1980.

"We had eleven wonderful years together until his death from a heart attack in October of 1991. Each day reconfirmed the deep love and caring that we felt for each other.

"Fay was twenty-five years older than I, but this made no difference in the joy we had in sharing our lives over the thirty years that we knew each other.

"I am certain that our love continues on the other side. Love is forever!"

Eighteen

❖

Beautiful Tapestry of the Spirit

For many years now, John Harricharan, the award-winning author of *When You Can Walk on Water, Take the Boat* and *Morning Has Been All Night Coming,* has been one of my closest friends. Since I knew that John and his lovely wife Mardai had been brought together by the Angels of Love, I asked him to share the touching story of their loving relationship for the readers of this book.

John's forefathers had traveled from India to work on the farms of British Guiana, the only British colony on the northern coast of South America. In the small fishing and farming village where he was born, Muslims, Hindus, and Christian converts lived together in peace and relative prosperity.

His parents were Hindus, but the Harricharans had many Muslim and Christian friends. The people of various religious faiths cooperated with one another and tolerated the multitude of beliefs that had become normal in such a diverse society. During religious holidays, the villagers would all visit the different churches, noting more similarities than differences in beliefs.

"About the age of eleven," John told me, "I started attending the Christian churches, as well as our own Hindu temple. Later on, I became a Christian; and my father, a liberal Hindu, encouraged my church-going and even attended with me on a number of occasions. At the same time, I still visited the Hindu temple."

John was baptized and confirmed into the Lutheran denomination of Christianity.

Village life revolved around sowing and reaping, between the dry season and the wet season. And in the evenings, the younger boys would listen to the elders tell stories of their youth.

"We would sit by a wood fire, the flames fanned by the trade winds of the Atlantic, totally entranced by the tales of guardian angels, friendly ghosts, and unseen influences that had made their presence felt. I grew up believing, as Shakespeare's Hamlet did, that 'There are more things in heaven and earth, Horatio, than are dreamt of in your philosophy.' "

High school was not mandatory. It was an honor. And some of the village children were fortunate enough to attend high school in the city while the others went to work on the farms with friends and relatives.

John's father had been unable to finish fourth grade when he was a boy, but later in life, he believed so strongly that he should educate his children that John was one of the fortunate ones to attend high school.

"I have always felt a guiding hand in my affairs in life. Even my earliest memories reflected a wonderful world of friendly beings who were willing to help me. It was as if an angel sat on my shoulder and whispered to me when I wasn't sure which way to go or what to do."

It was during his second year in high school that an incident occurred which was to have a major effect on John's entire life.

"To attend high school in those days, one had to pay certain tuition fees. Because of some financial problems in the family, my fees were not paid in time; and I was asked to leave school.

"When I returned home and told my dad what had happened, I could see the sadness in his eyes and hear it in his voice. He had worked very hard to earn the money for my school fees—and now there was confusion."

John's father, a simple farmer from the village, always seemed to listen to an inner voice. After a moment of quiet, he looked at his son and said, "There is a man of importance who lives in the city, not too far from where your school is.

"I hear that he is very kind and that he helps many people. He is also a pastor of a Lutheran church, and so may be inclined to help us—especially since you attend services every week. We will talk to him about our problem, and then we'll see what else to do."

Early the next morning, John and his father set out on the long trip to the city.

"We caught the bus at 5:30 A.M.," John remembered. "We reached the ferry at 7:00, and finally arrived in the city at 9:00 A.M. We asked directions, and we eventually arrived at the home of the Lutheran pastor."

John was only twelve or thirteen, but he recalled vividly the sense of excitement as if something extraordinary were about to happen.

His father rang the doorbell. John could tell that he was nervous and worried.

What if this man couldn't—or wouldn't—help them? What if they were forced to return to the village without any hope?

If that were so, John would never be able to finish high school, and all of his days would be spent working in the village fields as his father was doing—and as his father before him had done.

Such thoughts were crossing John's mind when the door opened and a maid, dressed in a white uniform, asked their business.

"We are here to speak to the master of the house," John's father said solemnly. "We would be most grateful for a few moments of his time."

"Do you have an appointment?" the maid asked haughtily.

"My son and I . . . we did not realize that an appointment was necessary."

"The master is very busy. You'll have to make an appointment and return another day. He just can't see everyone who turns up on his doorstep."

John's heart fell as he heard those ominous words of dismissal.

His father, however, held his head high and told the imperious maid that they would wait until her master could see them.

Before the maid could say another word, John remembered, they heard footsteps, and a regal-looking man came through the door. The maid held the door open for him as he looked at the father and son with kindly, but questioning, eyes.

"I was just leaving," the pastor said, "but I do have a few moments. What can I do for you?"

John's father, sensing that time was precious, did not hesitate. "We need your help, sir."

"Come with me, then. Let's sit in my office, and you can tell me what you need."

The two nervous villagers followed the pastor up the stairs and into his office. He motioned for them to sit while he sat behind a giant desk that occupied one corner of the room.

After John's father had introduced them, he quickly explained why they had come into the city to see him.

The pastor listened intently and took some notes. After he had asked a few questions, he smiled and told them to go home.

"Don't worry anymore about this," he advised them with calm assurance. "I know the principal of the school. I will take care of this whole business of fees. I'll also make sure that it never happens again . . ."

The pastor was unable to finish his sentence, because at that moment there was a loud bang on the door.

The door flew open as a little girl, pedaling furiously on a tricycle, rushed into the pastor's office. She could not have been more than five or six years old.

The pastor smiled and said, "That's my daughter, Mardai."

The girl turned and headed out the door, running over John's foot with her tricycle in the process.

She turned around, smiled up at John. "Sorry."

And then she was gone.

"As I stood there," John recalled, "a strange, sweet sadness came over—and a still, small voice whispered in my ear: *'You'll marry her one day.'*

"I quickly regained my composure as my dad thanked the good man for his help before we left his home.

"But that was how I met Mardai, the one who, years later, was to become my wife. It was as if my guardian angel had orchestrated the entire affair so that I could get a preview of coming events. She was only six, and I was thirteen when this initial meeting occurred."

The problems at high school were solved, just as the Lutheran pastor had promised. The years went by, and every once in a while, John would recall the time when his father and he had visited the kind pastor in the city. It appeared unlikely that he would ever see the clergyman and his daughter again. They were from the city, and they socialized with the highest levels of society— while John was from a small country village of fishermen and farmers.

But, as John phrases it, "The angels of God looked down on this country boy and smiled!"

John graduated from high school, and the world seemed to be full of opportunities.

Word came to the village that the church at the outskirts of town would be expanded and that a very famous pastor would temporarily stay in the parsonage until the expansion plans would be accomplished. John was surprised when he found out that the new pastor was the same one whom his dad and he had visited years earlier.

"I discreetly inquired as to whether his family would stay there with him. I was disappointed when I was told that they would visit only on weekends. I was also informed that he had only one child, the daughter whom I had first seen on the tricycle."

The day finally came when John saw Mardai again.

"This time she was not a little girl, but a young lady with all her hopes and dreams shining brightly. Again, that strange other-worldly feeling came over me as I looked at her. Again, the voice whispered in my heart and soul, *She is the one you'll marry. She will be your wife and help you do the things that you came here to do.*

"The angels seemed to have a way with words. It seemed so ridiculous—and yet, there was a ring of truth to it."

The time came for John to leave the shores of that little colony on the northern coast of South America to further his education. With the help of Mardai's father, he was able to enter a university in the United States with a full scholarship.

"University life was very different from life in the little village. In time, I graduated with honors and went on to graduate school.

"I had my share of girlfriends, but all through the years, I would think of Mardai. I wrote poems about her, and I dreamed about seeing her again."

One day, years later, John received a letter from Mardai's father. The family had relocated to Canada to begin a new life after leaving behind all the political problems and the near civil war that had shaken Guiana. The pastor told John that they would be spending the summer with relatives in New York City and that he would like John to visit them and to have dinner with them as soon as it would be possible for him to do so.

"The threads of time weave strange patterns in the fabric of life, and so it was, through strange coincidences and synchronicities, I found myself in New York City. By this time, I had begun working for a Fortune 500 company, and my future seemed bright. All I can say is that the Angels of Love and Mercy had smiled upon me again!"

Not long after John had reunited with Mardai and her family in New York City, they moved to a small town in Pennsylvania. As destiny would dictate the scenario, John soon relocated from the city to a small town across the river in New Jersey. In such close proximity, he would visit Mardai and her family every once in a while. And the more he stopped by, the better friends he became with Mardai.

"Some things seemed to be destined. They make no sense if we try to reason them out. If we do attempt to unravel their mystery, we only serve to confuse ourselves even further.

"Thus it was that Mardai and I were brought together across oceans and countries and time. No longer the little girl, she had grown into a beautiful, charming young woman.

"The words of the Angel of Love were finally fulfilled. Mardai and I became engaged; and a year later, we were married. She was only nineteen, and I was all of twenty-six. Our marriage was one of those special unions that only seemed to have been made possible with the help of other dimensional friends. A few years later, our first child, Malika, was adopted, followed by her brother, Jonathan, four years later."

Mardai encouraged John to write and to publish his award-winning allegorical work, *When You Can Walk on Water, Take the Boat,* a book which creatively portrays the subtle interaction of other dimensional beings in the flow of human experience.

"She always believed in me—even when I didn't believe in myself. Sometimes I thought that she wasn't brought to me by an angel of love, but that she herself was an Angel of Love."

Mardai and John spent many happy years together. She stayed by his side through all his trials and tribulations, never complaining, always encouraging, and always having a kind word for others.

But the Angels of Love had not told John what the rest of the story would be like.

"One day, unexpectedly, Mardai was diagnosed with cancer. She fought a valiant battle, but she finally left the Earth plane to continue her angelic work on other, perhaps brighter, shores.

"It's been a few years since she has been gone, but sometimes it feels like yesterday. I often wish that I could share my thoughts with her.

"On quiet evenings, I sit on my back porch in our home in Marietta, Georgia, feeling the wind blow through my hair. I look up to the skies and see the twinkling stars far, far away. If I let my mind wander, I can almost hear Mardai singing a song of joy and love as she used to do years ago.

"Perhaps, once upon a time, there walked on Earth an Angel of Love named Mardai. Perhaps she had intended to stay with me for only a little while before she went back to join her other angel friends. And yet I cannot help feeling that the ties that bind us span eternity itself."

Nineteen

✦

The Greatest Lesson of the Heart

Sometime in the mid-1970s, I made the acquaintance of two healers who had begun to gain a growing national reputation for quietly channeling what they considered to be otherworldly energy to accomplish physical healings. What struck me as delightfully ironic was that Lorraine and Victor Darr conducted their healing ministry in Rochester, Minnesota, the home of the august Mayo Clinic, a mighty bulwark of conventional medicine.

Neither of these two soft-spoken people made any kind of extravagant claims for their ability to channel healing energy, and they expressed amazement whenever folks flew in from California, New Jersey, or one of the Canadian provinces to consult with them. It was apparent to me that this shy, unassuming couple sought only to serve their fellow humans in the best way that they could.

It was on September 2, 1974, that Lorraine began to receive automatic writing—at first from a spirit entity who claimed to be her grandmother, then later from various elevated beings.

Often Lorraine would enter a state of light trance and permit the entities to write through her and channel various instructions, advice, and criticisms that she and Vic might then use in their healing ministry.

Vic and Lorraine treated all manner of ailments, and they began to receive "patients" from as far away as Europe. Some people swore that they were able to see a white-colored energy flow emanate from Vic's hands.

An exceedingly down-to-earth kind of fellow, Vic never spoke of psychic phenomena, mysticism, or his ability to become a co-creator with multidimensional beings. He was appreciative of these Light Beings' assistance in his work, but he really attributed all blessings to self-awareness. When people became totally aware of themselves and their potentialities, he argued, then they automatically became citizens of other dimensions of being.

Vic had also heeded the Master Healer's admonition, "Physician, heal thyself." He was a former steelworker who had been injured in a factory and had been left partially paralyzed. By that time, he was already active in his healing ministry, and while he lay in a hospital bed, people came from miles around to receive healings from him.

The irony of the entire situation struck him with powerful impact one night. He spent two and one-half hours working on himself, during which time he admits that he sweated a great deal. Within a day and a half, he walked out of the hospital.

He had also once worn a hearing aid and had been told by doctors that his damaged sense of hearing was beyond help. Again, by working on himself, Vic was able to discard his hearing aid.

I stayed in touch with the Darrs throughout the years. Victor made his transition to the Great Mystery in 1993; but now, twenty years after our first meeting, I have asked Lorraine to describe the lifetime in which these two light workers lived under the guidance of angelic spirit beings.

*   *   *

The tale began, Lorraine said in answer to my query, on a summer's day with a group of young women gathered together in a dormitory room on the campus of what was then known as Teachers College of Iowa during the 1949 summer session.

"None of us had teaching jobs for fall, so we opened the Sunday paper to the want ads. My way of scanning and assessing ads was quite different from my friends'. I held a pencil raised above the paper and moved it in a spiral toward the listings saying, 'Where the pencil lands, I will apply for a position.'

"I was accepted to teach third and fourth grade at Hartford, Iowa, a small town twenty miles southeast of Des Moines, and that was where I would begin a life adventure of more than forty years. That was where Victor Darr lived—the person the angels were guiding me to meet."

Victor had served as a military policeman in Japan during the early days of the occupation, and he had lived in Hartford with his family ever since he had been discharged from the army. He had two younger brothers in high school, and his youngest brother was in third grade.

Many times after she had begun her teaching duties, Lorraine asked herself what she was doing there in that little town of two hundred people where nothing seemed to happen.

One Friday night in February, six months after she had arrived in Hartford, she and a friend, the instrumental music teacher, went to the tiny cafe to visit with people from the local community.

Lorraine learned later that someone had dared Vic to ask the "new teacher" to dance. Never one to pass up a dare, he punched in a tune on the jukebox and asked her to dance.

"I did not realize then that the universal Powers That Be had accomplished the task of bringing two teachers together to begin an adventure like no other," Lorraine said.

"Vic felt from the start that we were to be together—whereas I took about four weeks to know and to accept that we would be married."

Brad Steiger, author and lecturer, and Sherry Hansen Steiger, lecturer, author, and ordained Protestant minister, have traveled to many of the world's sacred sites on their shared journey of the spirit.

In a true miracle of love, an angelic being temporarily entered the person of Dr. Mary Meadows to bring Brad and Sherry together. Today, the Steigers refer to Dr. Meadows, who currently operates a spiritual retreat and health resort in Rockport, Texas, as their Cupid Unaware.

In this series of remarkable photographs, Sherry Hansen Steiger draws down the Light while she meditates on a ledge overlooking one of the vortex areas in Sedona, Arizona. In the final picture, she has literally become one with the miraculous energy of love and light.

Jon Marc and Anastasia Hammer found each other through the powerful spirit of love, guided by their Angel of Love, Jeshua.

Judith Richardson Haimes, one of the nation's foremost psychic sensitives, and her husband, Dr. Allen Nelson Haimes, freely acknowledge the divine support that they have received throughout the years. Judith has shared the account in which a handsome angel guide brought two lovers together to share their perfect love in heaven.

Author of *The Wisdom Teachings of Archangel Michael*, Lori Jean Flory has received angelic messages since she was a small child. She has never doubted the guidance of her angel guides nor did she question them when they led her to her marriage with Charles Flory in July, 1985.

When they first met in Brazil, Joshua did not know any Portuguese nor did Vera speak any English. But through the miracle of love, the two fully recognized that their destiny was to be with one another.

RA-Ja Dove, left, and his destin[y] love, Moi-RA on their wedding [day?] in 1985.

The Doves conduct world[wide] seminars from their Taos, [New] Mexico, headquarters, al[so] emphasizing the miracles of lo[ve to] be found all aroun[d].

RA-Ja Dove invokes high spir[itual] energies of love and light near their ashram.

Lois East, a fine artist whose work has received national attention and published widely, now almost exclusively devotes her talent to painting portraits of the beautiful angels that she envisions. She and her husband Clay proudly admit that they were brought together by the angels.

Brad Steiger poses with John Harricharan, consultant to CEOs of major corporations and the award-winning author of such books as *When You Can Walk on Water, Take the Boat*. John first met Mardai, his wife-to-be when she was six and he was thirteen.

Ever since she was a teenager, Tara Buckland had a precise mental image of the man that she would marry and just how old she would be when she wed. She knew her husband would be English, a writer or artist, and that there would be a marked age difference between them. For over seventeen years now, she has been married to Ray Buckland, the noted English author and teacher.

The internationally acclaimed psychic-sensitive Clarisa Bernhardt had endured a number of tragedies of the heart and was beginning to despair that she would ever find true happiness. That was when the Angels of Love intervened and brought a wonderful man named Norman into her life. Clarisa and Norman are pictured here on their Canadian estate. One of their favorite racing horses, Pegasus Princess, can be seen in the background.

Stan Kalson, internationally known authority in the field of holistic health, learned from a friend's vision that a special woman would soon appear to serve as a helpmate in his work and in his life. When he developed a strong rapport with Lee Lagé immediately after their first meeting, she confessed that his image had appeared to her in meditation. They knew that they were destined to be together.

When Dr. Lawrence Kennedy and Sandra Sitzmann first met, they went together like oil and water. Now, many years later, they have accomplished both a lasting love and a number of breakthroughs in their exciting and important research into the destiny of humanity.

Patrick Flanagan and Gael Crystal Flanagan view their story of destined love as a modern-day fairy tale. After being married in the Great Pyramid in Egypt, these "twin flames" chose to live in virtual seclusion, devoting their energies to the creation of scientific products and services to better humankind.

When her mother wanted to introduce her to an actor friend, Lisa's practical attorney's instincts told her to avoid meeting another Hollywood "flake." However, this particular actor turned out to be John Hodson, a remarkable man who soon proved himself to be the Knight in Shining Armor that she had always yearned for.

David and Barbara Jungclaus have been led through many peaks and valleys in their spiritual evolution, but they have never lost their trust in Angelic Beings to see them through every challenge.

In show business since she was eleven, Laura Wesson thought she was immune to smooth-talking men with come-on lines. So she was more than skeptical of the fellow she'd just met who proclaimed his destined love for her and said that they had a past-life connection. Although she tried her best to resist, she learned that miracles of love cannot be denied. Today, Laura and Dan Clausing conduct spiritual retreats on their Evening Star Ranch in Washington.

To celebrate their love, Brad and Sherry were married first in Sedona, Arizona, in August, 1987 during the Harmonic Convergence and again, with their children present, on September 30, in Phoenix. Both ceremonies were performed by Brad's long-time friend, Rev. Jon Terrance Diegel.

By the time school ended in May, they had rented an apartment. Their marriage took place on June 11, 1950.

"Basically, our married life unfolded in eleven-year cycles. The first eleven in and around Hartford, where our five children began their schooling. The second eleven commenced in 1961 when Spirit pushed us to move to New Hampton, Iowa, which was my birthplace. Vic joined the crew in a car dealership and auto repair business that my father had built from scratch. This was a difficult move because Vic and the children really didn't want to leave Hartford. I just 'felt' we needed to move.

"But whether the whole family wanted to move or not, the angels had brought us there to undergo some very big changes."

A little more than a week after their move to New Hampton, Lorraine's mother was diagnosed as having a very fast-spreading type of cancer. She died thirteen months after surgery. Lorraine's father passed away in his sleep eighteen months later.

Lorraine taught for another five and a half years, then left public school teaching forever due to ill health.

It was at this time that Vic began studying the healing arts of reflexology and zone therapy in his spare time. He found that both methods, which deal with pressure points on the feet, were great aids to assisting people to heal themselves.

This was also the period of time when Vic hurt his back at work, and the Darrs interpreted his "being released from work by an accident," as a sign that they should now expand their healing work.

In 1972, at the onset of their third eleven-year cycle, they chose to move to Rochester, Minnesota, ten blocks from the Mayo Clinic, to establish their healing ministry.

"After twenty-three years of living with Vic, he had shared very little with me about his paranormal abilities. I had observed that he always seemed to 'know' what the children were going to do, but he appeared reluctant to reveal too much of his inner self.

"I was not yet fully aware of my own inner abilities, because of all the emotional lessons in which I was so deeply enmeshed.

"So there we were, placed by Spirit in an orthodox healing city, prepared to expand our lives, thoughts, and abilities by working on peoples' feet. I often wonder if the angels and guiding spirits smile or laugh *at* or *with* us Earth humans as we learn and grow.

"Our third eleven-year cycle—from 1972 to 1983—was by far the most momentous time of change in our journey. Here we were grandparents and starting forth on a new path. We had always been workaholics, so our guides filled us with energy and pushed us along."

After the move to Rochester, Minnesota, Lorraine is convinced that there were many aspects to their newly begun activities which were clearly apparent to all who knew them.

"First, the angels and Spirit broke down Victor's walls and helped him to feel secure enough to use a whole new set of 'tools' to expand his consciousness as much as possible each day. His initial work on the feet became the foundation upon which he built to include body energy balancing, harmonizing physical body systems, and allowing healing energies to flow through his hands, heart, and thoughts."

Victor came to be known as "the man with the magic fingers." Lorraine received channeling that informed them that a medical doctor and a chiropractor in Spirit would work through his hands and guide his thoughts. He accepted their help, and they would often move his hands differently from what he had intended so that he might discover a previously undiscovered aspect of the patient's problem.

Also, in 1974, Lorraine began her work with automatic writing.

"At first I had much fear about such things. Spirit first had a grandmother of mine speak to me and answer questions. It was much less frightening to me to be able to speak to her.

"Then Spirit used many different entities who wrote through me, giving information and teachings.

"After four months of such writing to break down my fears, my guiding spirit added direct voice channeling in which I would speak in voices not my own. This was terrifying to me at first, but I soon grew to accept the phenomenon with greater willingness on my part."

Lorraine also began to practice "journaling" at this time.

"I would write down all of my feelings and emotions regarding this new life. I found this process to be very cleansing, and it helped to bring clarity to my mind. The journaling and the voice channeling were the major links to my Higher Self.

"Spirit gave instructions, information, support, and a great deal of energy for both Victor and myself through my voice and written channeling. Our awareness was growing and expanding at a furious rate."

The paranormal and healing abilities of Vic and Lorraine continued to develop at a very rapid pace during their years in Rochester. Lorraine said that she sometimes felt as though she were on a fast-moving train that made very few stops.

"There were times when I felt as though I had been blind and was just learning how to see. Thankfully, the spirit helpers were always there to help me put the pieces together. I spent a great deal of time in prayer and meditation."

The Darrs remained in Rochester for nearly six years. They traveled and worked in parts of Illinois, Wisconsin, Iowa, and Minnesota, sharing their healing and teaching abilities with individuals and with groups.

"From mid-1979 through 1982, Victor and I were like a mobile healing unit that was sent here and there to encounter new situations and to help people.

"The angels had helped me to learn how to 'read' people's

physical body systems. I could read their auras and discover their individual energy systems.

"Neither Vic nor myself had ever had any human teachers to guide us and to direct the explosive manner in which doorways to other worlds had opened for us. All of our steps—both hesitantly and confidently—were taken only with the guidance of our spirit helpers. We had to learn to trust, trust, trust our spirit teachers through all of our earthly learnings."

In November of 1982, Vic and Lorraine moved to Lake Forest, Illinois, where Spirit guided them to live with a woman for five to six months. During that time, their host organized a trip to Egypt with the Darrs.

"What we could not know was that that fateful trip to Egypt would close the doors on our working together as a couple and open new vistas for our individual pathways in the future. After thirty-three years together, we would now begin to walk alone."

Lorraine remembered that the act of visiting certain places in Egypt was like "going home." And always for her there was the sense of timelessness.

Angelic beings had given Vic a design that enabled him to create from brass welding rods a work that resembled a flower and which he called a flow-er. Their popularity soon placed them in private homes and in metaphysical and healing centers all over the United States. In Egypt, Vic intuitively carried one of the smallest of the pieces into many tombs, temples, and even the king's chamber of the great pyramid.

On their first night in Cairo, Lorraine beheld the great pyramid illuminated with floodlights. Shocked, she uttered, "That's not how we left it!"

She was the only one of the ten people on the tour who was not allowed to crawl up inside the great pyramid to meditate in the king's chamber.

"A large hand on my head turned me out of the line to go back outside," she said. "As I sat on a block near the entrance to the pyramid, I cried and asked why I had not been allowed to experience the chamber like everyone else.

"The answer came immediately: 'You did not come to Egypt to go inside *anything* but *yourself!*'

"That was hard for me to accept, yet I had to comply."

After they returned from Egypt, Lorraine and Vic moved to Spring Green, Wisconsin, and presented Crystal Conferences there and other places. The following year on her birthday, April 3, 1984, they moved to Westby, Wisconsin.

"By June of that year, Vic and I were on our separate pathways, each of us growing enormously toward the attainment of linking the full understandings of Heaven and Earth to become radiant lights. Vic moved to Franklin, North Carolina, in the Smoky Mountains. I stayed on a farm in Westby for five years, then began to spend time between the Midwest and Arizona."

In June of 1990, Victor suffered a stroke and spent two weeks in a coma. After six months in a hospital, he came home to be cared for by his second wife, Nancy.

The angels took a hand again when Nancy asked Lorraine if she could please come to look after Vic for a week while she took a vacation to stave off exhaustion. Lorraine consented to come to North Carolina to take care of her ex-husband.

"After I was back home in Tucson, I spent much time in prayer, listening and learning more of trust. Spirit and the angels kept saying to me, 'You are to take care of Victor!'

"I finally consented—part of me *knowing* it was right to do . . . and part of me saying, 'Why are you doing this? It's crazy!' "

In June of 1991, Victor flew into Des Moines from North Carolina. Lorraine had driven from Tucson to pick him up and to begin a new life together.

"Our new life lasted one year and eight months. We had both

changed a great deal—yet the Soul love and personal regard for one another had never changed.

"The divine guidance in our relationship created the space and the time to enjoy each other and to complete the purposeful times on Earth that we had worked together. We released each other on all spiritual levels of interaction. It was good for both of us.

"The actual closing came about two days after I had a heart attack, lying on a hospital bed. On the morning of February 23, 1993, Victor's soul-spirit disconnected the lifeline to his body.

"The essence of Victor was standing by the Earth body when Jesus came to him, asking if he was ready to go.

"Victor said, yes, so in the early light of dawn, he began his next life phase in spirit.

"I was also beginning anew, lying in a hospital bed, agreeing to by-pass surgery, knowing that Spirit would carry me on where I needed to be, all owing, trusting. This is what life is as the love of One lives fully in all hearts."

Lorraine told me that Victor has communicated with her from the other side on a number of occasions.

On July 5, 1994, she received this message from Spirit regarding the Angels of Love:

"Angels appear to humans in whatever form the receiving human holds in his or her thoughts at the time.

"The greater *Love* of Being is a force that has many forms to use as the situation requires. *Love* denotes Soul-Spirit sense. *Love* is of human sense. *Love* of Being is a force we are to learn again to use.

"Angels give us images and thoughts from the knowingness to guide and prepare us each day. They often appear at critical moments to ease our learnings and to leave us 'wondering' and 'knowing.'

"Thank the *Love* of God for Angels!"

$\mathcal{T}$wenty

$$\maltese$$

Reaffirming a Telepathic Link with Your Beloved

Telepathy as you no doubt understand, simply means that one can, through the mind, make contact with another.

When you first experiment with telepathy, you may find to your surprise that you will soon hear from someone whom you have had in mind a great deal—almost as if the person knew that you wanted to hear from him or her.

If you deliberately set out to "reach" someone by your mental telephone, you may encounter a delay in receiving an actual *physical* response. This should not discourage you, for you will be able to know that your telepathic message reached its destination if you felt a *mental* response at the time.

If you are visualizing the recipient of your telepathic message clearly and you suddenly feel a small tingle in your arm or solar plexus, you will *know* that your message has been received on some level of that individual's consciousness. You don't have to imagine this response, for it will be real enough.

Before attempting to make telepathic transfer with your loved one, it is best to sit quietly for a few moments.

Take three comfortably deep breaths. This will give added power to the broadcasting station of your psyche.

Visualize the vastness of space.

Contemplate the meaninglessness of time.

See yourself as a circle that grows and grows until it occupies the Earth, the galaxy.

See yourself blending into a Oneness with the Living God, All-That-Is.

Now visualize the loved one whom you wish to contact. See him (or her . . . use whichever pronoun is appropriate) plainly. Feel his presence.

In your mind, speak to him as if he were sitting there before you. Do not speak to him aloud. Speak to him mentally.

Take three comfortably deep breaths, revving up your broadcasting power.

Mentally relay the message that you wish your loved one to receive from you.

Once you have transmitted the message, ask him to call you or to get somehow in touch with you on the physical level.

RECEIVING IMPRESSIONS OF YOUR LOVER'S TRUE FEELINGS

If your loved one has not yet made the commitment of love that you have been hoping to receive, you may wish to find out telepathically how the loved one in question truly feels about you. Here is how you may make your mind a receiving set for your lover's thoughts and feelings.

Sit quietly and breathe slowly in comfortably deep breaths.

Picture in your mind your loved one sitting or standing there before you. Don't beat around the bush. Get right to the bottom line. Ask him (her) point-blank: *"Do you really love me?"*

If you receive a very warm and gentle impulse or tingle, you will immediately become aware of the fact that the loved one in question really loves you.

If you receive a cool impulse, the loved one may not truly love you and may even be deceitful in dealing with you.

TRANSMITTING HEALING
THOUGHTS TO LOVED ONES
WHO ARE ILL OR INJURED

It is possible to send healing energy to those loved ones who are ill or injured and who may be separated from you by some distance. You must understand, of course, that it is not you who can heal, but your unselfish act of tuning in to the Infinite Mind of All-That-Is that does so.

The *most vital point* in telepathically healing or helping another is this: You must actually *see* the desired condition and *know* that it will be accomplished.

When you send healing thoughts to your loved one who is ill, you must visualize your loved one as being *completely* healed.

You must *not* permit yourself to visualize him as he is at the present time.

You must *not* see him in the throes of his illness or the misery of his accident.

You must actually see him in *the desired state of health* and in your heart and mind *know* that it will be so.

If you should happen to be concerned about a loved one who has a very bad habit or dependency that needs correcting, you may also send mental pictures to that person of his hating the habit or the dependency so much that he, of his own free choice, will give it up.

When you visualize your loved one who is plagued with the bad habit or dependency, he, too, must be seen as *triumphant* over the problem.

You must visualize him as having *completely forsaken* the habit or dependency.

Only by seeing the habit or dependency as *totally negated* will the problem be discontinued.

If you have learned that a loved one has become bereaved, you may telepathically send him a comforting thought that the Divine Will has been done and that It will soon send solace.

In all the above instances, always remember the cardinal rule: *You must actually see the desired conditions and know that it will be so.*

Twenty-one

✥

Manifesting a Vision of Love

In order to achieve the utmost success with this exercise, be certain to place yourself in a very restful, meditative state. It would be very helpful to play some romantic classical or New Age music in the background. Just be certain that whatever musical accompaniment you select does not contain any lyrics to distract you.

You may study the following procedure so that you can retain the essence of its steps in order to guide yourself to the vision. Or you may prerecord your voice, giving yourself step-by-step instructions from your cassette recorder.

Once you have attained a comfortable state of relaxation, proceed on the path to attain your vision of love:

Visualize yourself surrounded by a violet light. Feel the warmth of the light from the Angels of Love beginning to stimulate your Crown Chakra.

Become one with the feeling of being loved unconditionally by the Angels of Love—beings of light who have always loved you. Sense the presence of an angelic intelligence that you have always known was near to you ever since you were a child.

Be aware of a sensation of warmth in both your Heart Chakra and your Crown Chakra.

Be aware of a ray of light connecting your individual spirit essence to the higher vibration of the Angels of Love.

Visualize that the violet light has now acquired a tinge of pink. See it begin to swirl around you, moving faster and faster until it begins to acquire a form and a substance.

Visualize now the shape of a body . . . hair . . . a beautiful smile on a loving face.

Become especially aware of the eyes.

Feel the love, the unconditional love, that flows out to you from those beautiful eyes.

You have an inner knowing that your guide has come to take you to a special dimension where you will be able to receive a clear image of the one who will be *your life partner!*

You will be able to receive a clear image of the one who will be your partner in love. (If you are already with your life partner, substitute the command: *You will be able to receive a clearer understanding of the true nature of your love relationship. You will be able to comprehend a clearer understanding of your connection to the Angels of Love.)*

Whatever it is that you most need to know about your love relationship for your fullest good and gaining will be revealed to you in this holy place.

Your angel guide stretches forth a loving hand. Take that hand in your own.

Feel angelic love flowing through you. Feel the vibration of an angelic being who has always loved you.

Feel the vibration of love from one who has loved you with pure, heavenly, unconditional love.

Feel the vibration of love from one who has come to take you to a special place where a *profound vision of love awaits you!*

See a violet mist clouding up around you as you begin to move through time and space with your angelic guide.

Feel yourself moving through time and space.

At the count of five, you will be in the holy dimension of angelic love. One . . . two . . . three . . . four . . . five!

See yourself now in this holy dimension of love and light.

You may be seeing yourself in a beautiful garden that lies before a majestic temple.

You may be seeing yourself in a magical place in a lovely forest.

You may be seeing yourself high in some mountain retreat.

There is now a vibration in the air as if bells are chiming.

At that sound, that signal, a wise teacher comes to meet you. *(The teacher may be either male or female in form, whichever you prefer.)*

Look deeply into the eyes of the beloved teacher.

Become totally aware of this teacher. See the teacher's clothes . . . body . . . face . . . mouth . . .

Your angelic guide has once again materialized beside you, and you are walking together behind the teacher.

You are now walking in a tunnel. The teacher is taking you to a secret place.

Experience your emotions as you walk silently between your angel guide and your spirit teacher. Feel deeply your expectations.

Be keenly aware of any aromas . . . sounds . . . sights.

Now you are in a great room.

Look around you slowly.

See statues . . . paintings . . . works of art arranged around the secret room. Each object has been designed to honor the mission of the Angels of Love.

Now the teacher is showing you a great crystal that is supported on a golden tripod.

The teacher says that the great crystal is a powerful transmitter for the Angels of Love.

When you are permitted to lean forward and gaze into the crystal, you will be allowed to see the vision of love for which you have come to this holy dimension of awareness and unconditional love.

The teacher says that you will only see that which is meant for you to see for your utmost good and gaining.

You will see only what is necessary for you to see for your present level of understanding.

You will see a beautiful vision of love that will be completely individualized for you and for your particular needs at this moment in your spiritual evolution.

Your teacher tells you to get ready. Prepare yourself mentally for your vision.

Step forward to the crystal.

Lean forward . . . and see your vision of love *now!*

(Allow three or four minutes for the vision to manifest.)

Now with the beautiful images of the glorious vision of love clearly fixed in your memory, return to full wakefulness at the count of five. At the count of five, you will awaken feeling better than you have in weeks and weeks, in months and months. You will feel positive energy in body, mind, and spirit—and you will be filled with unconditional love from the Angels of Love.

One . . . coming awake. Two, more and more awake. Three, opening your eyes. Four, waking up and feeling wonderful. *Five* . . . wide awake and feeling great!

When you have returned to full consciousness after the vision of love has been induced, attempt to hold the images in your mind as long as you can. It is important that you hold the thought-forms as long as possible so that you can impress the energy of angelic love upon your Earth plane reality.

The vision images of love and light will open your heart and mind so completely that they will soon condense into the patterns which you are visualizing.

Sometimes after a particularly profound and moving vision of love, you may feel a compulsion to share the essential message of your vision—especially with your love partner. Do so. In such a case, each time you share the vision of love with another, you will receive even more details of the vision and more insight into their specific meaning.

You will clearly know when a vision has been intended only as an individualized instruction strictly for you and should not be described to another.

Twenty-two

❖

The Healing Colors of the Angels of Love

Since this guided visualization deals with color and with repetitious progressions, it is easy to memorize, so that you can place yourself in a state of deep relaxation. As with the other exercises in this book, you may wish to have a like-minded loved one read the process to you and guide you through the visualization. Or, as before, you may prefer to record a cassette of your own voice ahead of time and thereby serve as your own guide through the experience.

Once again I recommend that you play a recording of the proper music to suggest a mood of lifting yourself away from your mundane environment. Any music that you find inspirational will do—as long as it does not contain any lyrics to distract you from the goal of the exercise.

Sit in a chair, lie on your bed, lean against a wall—whatever position is most comfortable for you. As always when performing these exercises, select a time when you are certain not to be disturbed.

* * *

Visualize that at your feet lies a blanket the color of rose. The color of rose stimulates your natural body warmth and induces relaxation and sleep. It can also provide you with a sense of well-being and a marvelous feeling of being loved.

Now you see that the blanket is really a kind of auric cover, a rose-colored auric cover that has been created by the Angels of Love.

Visualize an Angel of Love slowly moving the blanketlike aura of rose up over your body.

Feel the Angel of Love moving the blanket of rose over your feet . . . relaxing them. Over your legs . . . relaxing them. Over your stomach . . . easing all tensions. Over your chest, your arms, your neck . . . relaxing them, relaxing them.

Now see the Angel of Love fashioning a hood of the rose-colored auric energy. Visualize the angel bringing the rose-colored aura over your head. *Feel* the color of rose permeating your psyche and activating your ability to become one with the Angels of Love.

The color green serves as a disinfectant, a cleanser. It also influences the proper building of muscle and tissue.

Visualize an Angel of Love pulling a green, blanketlike aura over your body. Feel it moving over your feet, cleansing them. Feel it moving over your legs, healing them of all pain. Feel it moving over your stomach, ridding it of all discomfort and irritation.

Feel the color of green moving over your chest, your arms, your neck—cleansing them, healing them.

Now see the Angel of Love fashioning a hood of the green-colored auric energy. Visualize the angel bringing the green-colored aura over your head. *Feel* the color of green permeating your psyche and activating your ability to become one with the Angels of Love.

* * *

Gold has been recognized as a great strengthener of the nervous system. Visualizing the color of gold can aid your digestion and help you to become calm.

Visualize now that an Angel of Love is pulling a soft, beautiful golden aura slowly over your body. Feel it moving over your feet, calming your entire body. Feel the color of gold moving over your legs, relaxing them. Feel it moving over your stomach, soothing any nervous condition.

Feel the color of gold moving over your chest, your arms, your neck—strengthening them, calming them.

Now see the Angel of Love fashioning a hood of the gold-colored auric energy. Visualize the angel bringing the gold-colored aura over your head. *Feel* the color of gold permeating your psyche and strengthening your body-brain network so that it will serve as a better conduit for the Angels of Love.

Research has determined that red-orange strengthens and cleanses the lungs. Yogis and other masters have long understood that proper meditation can best be achieved through proper techniques of breathing through clean lungs.

Visualize before you a little red-orange-colored cloud of pure oxygen.

Take a comfortably deep breath and visualize some of that little red-orange cloud moving into your lungs.

Imagine it traveling through your lungs, cleansing them, purifying them, taking away particles of impurities.

Now visualize yourself *exhaling* that red-orange cloud of oxygen from your lungs. See how soiled with impurities it is.

Take another comfortably deep breath. Visualize as you inhale that you are taking a little more of that little red-orange cloud into your lungs.

Imagine it traveling through your lungs, purifying them of the negative effects of exhaust fumes, cigarette smoke, and other pollution.

Exhale the impurities—then breathe again of the purifying, cleansing red-orange cloud.

Research has demonstrated that the color yellow-orange has the ability to aid oxygen in moving into every organ and gland of the human body, purifying them, cleansing them.

Imagine before you now a yellow-orange cloud of pure oxygen.

Take a comfortably deep breath and inhale the cleansing, purifying yellow-orange cloud into your lungs.

Feel the yellow-orange cloud moving through your body. Feel it cleansing and purifying every gland.

If you have *any* area of weakness or disease *anywhere* in your body, *feel* the yellow-orange energy bathing it in cleansing, healing vibrations.

As you exhale all impurities and inhale again the pure yellow-orange cloud of oxygen, visualize the cleansing and healing process throughout your body.

As you exhale and inhale, see your body becoming pure and clean.

Blue is the color of psychic ability, the color that increases visionary potential.

Visualize the Angel of Love moving a blue blanketlike aura over your body. Feel it moving over your feet, relaxing them. Feel the auric cover of blue moving over your legs, soothing them. Feel it moving over your stomach, easing all tensions.

Feel the vibration of blue moving over your chest, your arms, your neck—soothing them, relaxing them.

Visualize the angel fashioning a hood of the blue-colored auric energy. *Feel* the color of blue permeating your psyche, activating your ability to develop such gifts of the Angels of Love as prophecy, healing, telepathy, and clairvoyance.

*   *   *

Violet is the color of the highest vibration.

Visualize the Angel of Love pulling a violet, blanketlike aura over your body.

Feel it moving over your feet, relaxing them. Feel the color of violet moving over your legs, relaxing them, soothing them. Feel it moving over your stomach, removing all tensions.

Feel the vibration of violet moving over your chest, your arms, your neck—tranquilizing them, relaxing them.

Now visualize the Angel of Love fashioning a hood of the violet-colored auric energy. *Feel* the color of violet permeating your psyche, activating your ability to become one with the Angels of Love.

Feel the color of violet attuning your psyche to the highest heavenly vibration.

Feel the color of violet connecting your psyche to the Source of All-That-Is.

Feel the color of violet permitting you to become one with the Light and the Angels of Love.

Using the Violet Light
from the Angels of Love
to Transform Any Negativity
That You May Have Sown

Numerous teachers have said that the violet light that issues from the Source of All-That-Is and the Angels of Love constitutes the highest vibratory level.

There are moments on the Earth plane when, in the course of our day-to-day existence, we may clumsily and thoughtlessly transgress against others. Summoning the violet light from the Angels of Love can assist you in balancing your account. It can help you to *transform* the negativity that you may have sown.

Certain masters have likened the violet light to a cosmic eraser. When you learn to use it often and properly, you may "erase" all elements from your personal vibrations that are not of the Light and of Love.

Other teachers have said that the violet light from the Angels of Love may be used to dissolve disease, to alleviate suffering, and to cure illness.

Disease, suffering, and illness are, after all, manifestations of chaos and discord. Suffusing them with the violet light of love may alter them and raise their vibratory levels to points of transformation.

You may wish to use the violet light of the Angels of Love in a kind of daily ritual of transformation.

Call for the violet light and ask that your angelic guide connect you to the energy of the Angels of Love.

Visualize the violet light moving over you in a wave of warmth.

See it touching every part of your body.

Feel it interacting with each cell.

Say inwardly or aloud to your angelic guide:

"Beloved angel guide, assist me in calling upon the highest of energies and the Source of All-That-Is. Activate the energy of the Angels of Love within me so that I may receive the power and love of the Oneness.

"Provoke the law of harmony for myself who has strayed from the Light and transgressed against another.

"Permit the violet light to move around me and through me. Allow the transforming energy of angelic love to purify and to elevate all impure desires, incorrect concepts, anger, greed, wrongdoings, and improper actions.

"Keep the light of the Angels of Love bright within me.

"Replace all chaotic vibrations around me and *in* me with pure energy, the power of Love, and the harmony of the Divine Plan."

Twenty-three

The Search for
the Divine Soul Mate

Some years ago while visiting the Chicago psychic-sensitive Teddy O'Hearn, I asked her if Spirit had given her any teachings concerning the idea of the search for the divine soul mate. Her guidance provided the following message:

"Mark this well, there is a great tapestry being woven as each of us entwines our lives with the other in our journey through the Earthwalk.

"This tapestry is, at one and the same time, a record of the past, as well as a means for each thread—each person—to evolve and to reach that perfection in an evolution which will free the individual from Earth's tapestry—and the further necessity of returning to its travail. Woven into this tapestry are ugliness, horror, agony, suffering, and tears, as well as beauty, joy, a measure of fulfillment, and happiness. As in all of nature, nothing is ever lost.

"Only by experiencing the depths of what is inherent in the lowest can we reach the heights of the mystical ecstasy—the union with God and our divinely ordained other half, our soul mate—which transcends beyond imagination anything possible in earthly experience.

"Regardless of the name one bears in any one Earth lifetime, each of us has the eternal 'I' which carries either the male or the female connotation of the androgynous being which we all were in the beginning, before Adam and Eve.

"The separation of the sexes came at that point in time depicted by the Bible's symbolic story of Adam, wherein God made the androgynous Adam two—male and female, plus and minus, negative and positive, Adam and Eve.

"At this time, Earth's beings evolved into self-consciousness. This was not a fall from Grace, but a further step in human evolution in order that the male and female counterparts of each entity might experience and learn and eventually be reunited when they had evolved through the testing of Earth experience and attained the point at which each had earned the right to a reunion with his divine other half.

"This is the true soul mate, the only 'other' that each of us can look forward to meeting one day. It is with the soul mate that we will share complete fulfillment, a fulfillment beyond anything which we may ever know in any relationship on Earth.

"Our conscious mind may have long since forgotten its soul mate, but the soul memory that we have of our divine 'other half' filters through, though dimly, to our consciousness and leads us to a constant yearning and searching for complete and loving fulfillment which may continue life after life. It is this search which provides us with the means whereby we learn that love is not possession, that love is not self-serving, that love is not tyrannical or cruel, that love is not sex alone in any of its ramifications.

"We learn by trial and error through many loves and many lives—often encountering the same soul mates over and over again. All of these mates are soul mates by reason of the mutual learning process which takes place, but they must not be confused with the 'divine' soul mate—both halves of which are seldom encountered in the physical Earth plane. Each of these earthly soul mate relationships must be transmitted, from disharmony into harmony, into true universal love.

"We must learn real love through giving and receiving, of dealing with imitations and misconceptions of the real thing in order to achieve a complete education in love which will make us fit for the reunion with the divine soul mate.

"Thus our searching and learning process may take us through many lifetimes in which we encounter many of the same 'loves' over and over again, sometimes as parents, as sisters, as brothers, as children, as friends, as enemies, as business associates, as teachers, as students, as well as lovers and husbands and wives.

"Our relationship with any one other individual is a learning experience and a perfection of the many facets of love. When we have learned and earned the right, we will begin to realize that love is indeed universal, rather than personal—that love, tempered by wisdom, is the tool we have to carry with us in our release from our earthly lives.

"When we progress to the next step on the ladder and achieve the reunion and the fulfillment of self in the personal love of our divine soul mate, the two of us—as One—will go on into the fulfillment of ourselves in the work of God."

Twenty-four

❖

My Wife, My Best Friend

Although we've actually spent very little time together, I've always had a pleasant mental association with Raymond Buckland that I know has to extend far beyond his English gentleman's good manners, his sense of humor, and the pixie-like twinkle in his eyes. We have always kept in touch wherever our journeys have taken us.

Although we had had some correspondence after his move to America in 1962, I don't believe we actually met until late 1975, when we were both speakers at an event sponsored by Carl and Sandra Weschcke of Llewellyn Publications in Saint Paul, Minnesota. Ray is best known to the metaphysical world as the individual primarily responsible for the introduction of contemporary witchcraft into the United States. The author of *A Pocket Guide to the Supernatural, Buckland's Complete Book of Witchcraft,* and *Witchcraft from the Inside,* he also founded a new variation of the old religion Seax-Wicca, a more open and democratic expression, and became a leading spokesperson for It to the general public.

A *poshrat,* or half-blooded gypsy, the London-born Buckland left the Church of England around age twelve to explore Spiritualism and metaphysics. A veteran of the Royal Air Force, Ray was educated at King's College School in London and received a doctorate in anthropology from Brantridge Forest College, Sussex. His spiritual search led him to study witchcraft, and in 1964, he received initiation into the craft by Gerald Gardner's High Priestess, Lady Olwen.

When I mentioned in correspondence that I was writing a book about destined lovers, Ray replied that his wife, Tara, had known for many years exactly the type of man she would marry, the age difference between them, his profession, etc.—and it all added up to Ray Buckland.

Here is Ray's account of their destined love match:

On the rebound from a failed marriage, I married a charming young lady with whom I had very little in common. We stayed together for a number of years, but slowly drifted farther and farther apart.

In addition to my writing, I did a certain amount of teaching and often traveled around the country, giving lectures and leading workshops. In February 1982 I was invited to give a weekend of workshops in Cleveland for the fledgling Association for Consciousness Exploration, then known as the Chameleon Club. As part of the package, and to promote the workshops, ACE president Jeff Rosenbaum arranged for me to appear on the television talk show *The Morning Exchange,* hosted by Fred Griffith on WEWS-TV.

Tara Cochran had read some of my books and had even, a year or two prior to this, written a fan letter to me, though I did not remember that then. She and a friend heard that I was going to be on television and watched the show together.

"I fell in love with him, seeing him on screen," Tara later told a friend.

She did admit to me some months later that she wondered about the earring I wore. She was delighted to learn the only reason I wore one was due to my Romany heritage. (A gypsy boy is given two gold earrings. When he grows up and finds "the one woman of his life" he gives her the right earring, which she usually wears on a fine chain around her neck.)

Seeing the impact that I'd had on Tara, this friend admitted that she knew Jeff Rosenbaum, who was instrumental in bringing me to Cleveland, and told me he was hosting a welcoming party at his house that evening. She and Tara were determined to attend.

I had had a long, hard day, and I tried to relax at the party. No sooner did I manage to disentangle myself from one person than another would buttonhole me. They were all charming people, but I knew I had a very full weekend ahead of me and wanted a little time to myself.

Two young ladies arrived. One hailed Jeff and then introduced her friend Tara. In turn they were introduced to me. I was immediately attracted to Tara. She was slim and attractive, with long blonde hair. She was intelligent and had a good sense of humor. Somehow, we seemed to find ourselves sitting alone together, eagerly exchanging our life stories. Tara had recently broken up with her boyfriend and had sworn off men for "at least two years," she said. With my two failed marriages, I was definitely not looking for any new involvements.

Before we knew it, it was past midnight and people were leaving. Tara and I were still ensconced in a corner, oblivious to everything around us. Eventually Jeff came and broke into the talk. Finally Tara left, reluctantly, but promised to be at my workshops the following morning.

I had difficulty starting the first workshop because Tara didn't show up at the start and I just couldn't get her out of my mind. But she arrived, slipping in unobtrusively, noticed solely by me. I felt a glow of happiness as our eyes met. She had been unavoidably delayed and was as anxious to get there as I was to have her there.

The weekend went all too quickly, with Tara and me spending all our spare time together. On Monday morning she came to see me off at the airport.

We wrote to one another every single day and ran up astronomical telephone bills. Whenever I had to fly across country to give a lecture I would arrange to be routed through Cleveland. For a Canadian booking, I flew to Cleveland and then Tara and I drove her car to Toronto and back. It was a wonderful trip. We even made a point of stopping overnight at Niagara Falls and buying tacky souvenirs, as though it were a honeymoon trip!

By September I was separated from my wife and Tara had moved down to be with me in Virginia. We rented a house outside Charlottesville and started to plan what we wanted to do with our lives. We married and moved to San Diego in August. There we lived happily for over eight years before moving to Ohio.

Tara and I have been married for over twelve years. We have only become closer over those years. We are each other's best friend. Even though we both work at home, we never tire of each other's company, never get on each other's nerves. Rather, we miss one another tremendously anytime we do have to be apart, no matter for how short a time.

Over the years, Tara has developed into a writer and a fine teacher in her own right. She has told me that she had known from her young teens just how old she would be when she got married and exactly the sort of person who would be her husband. She knew he would be English, that there would be a marked age difference (I am twenty-one years older than she is), and that he would be a writer or artist.

We now live on a small Midwestern farm where we lavish love on a variety of animals (lambs, sheep, a goat, some chickens, and a variety of pet snakes) and spend innumerable hours walking in the woods. It seems it was destiny that we should find one another just when we each had almost given up all hope of happiness.

Twenty-five

Led by His Dreams to Love

Whenever I think of lovers who fulfilled their destiny through dreams, I remember a colorful individual I met at an awareness seminar I conducted in New York City in the fall of 1984. Dom Spicuzza was a robust Italian American who laughed easily and seemed satisfied with his life. Most of all, he was contented with his dream lover who came true.

As Dom tells the story, he had never been out of the Bronx when Uncle Sam shipped him to Vietnam in 1969.

"I went right from the old neighborhood to boot camp and on to Nam before I could even learn how to spell Vietcong," Dom said. "Half my buddies were draft protesters, hippies, and peaceniks who accused me of being a baby butcher and a war-monger—at the same time that the sergeants in basic training were trying to transform me into a killing machine."

Strangely enough, Dom said, the only thing that gave him any stability in those awful days of chaos and conflict was a repetitive dream of a pretty young woman who lived in an idyllic country set-ting.

"She looked like a milkmaid in a dairy commercial on television," he said. "Every time I dreamt of her, I would feel like the guy in that old country song yearning for the green, green grass of home. And yet *my* home was subways, crowded streets, and a crammed apartment with a widowed father and four brothers."

Although the teeming streets and concrete canyons may have comprised the physical reality of Dom Spicuzza's home in the Bronx, throughout his troubled adolescent years, he had been pacified by a dream of walking through a picturesque covered bridge on a bright spring day in a rural area.

"I would feel real peace and happiness as I strolled beside a creek," he said. "Eventually, I would come to an old stone farmhouse. I was always dimly aware of someone walking beside me, though I could never make out who it was. I would enter the home and find myself in a neat country kitchen where a young girl with light brown hair would be stirring something in a big bowl."

According to Dom, the girl would always look up at him with great love and warmth in her large green eyes. The best part of the dream came when she walked right into his outstretched arms.

"It was like we had known each other for years," he said. "In my dream I would always call her by name—though I could never seem to remember it when I awakened. We would hug each other and hold each other like we never wanted to let go."

The dream became a kind of talisman for Dom.

"It got me through some pretty rough times," he remembered. "As a kid, I was always kind of shy around girls, and I went through a really bad scene with blackheads and pimples. But whenever a girl avoided me or gave me the cold shoulder, it didn't hurt me quite as much as it could have as I knew that somewhere this fantastic dream girl was waiting for me."

After the adolescent blights had left him, Dom dated a number of different girls and even went steady for a while.

"But at the weirdest and sometimes most awkward moments, I would start daydreaming about that beautiful lady in her country kitchen who I knew was waiting for me somewhere."

While Dom was in Vietnam, he had a particularly memorable dream:

I had been drinking way too much while on R & R with some buddies. There was a lot of dope being smoked in Nam. I stayed away from that scene, but I managed to get really bombed out of my skull on beer and bourbon. I was trying my best to sleep my way out of a hangover when I saw my country girl so clearly and so three dimensionally that I would have sworn on all things I deem holy that she was right there with me in that two-bit hotel.

Dom said that his dream girl was shaking her finger at him and glaring at him in disgust.

She really looked upset with me, and I actually heard her talking. I mean, her words rang in my head to the point of pain. "Listen, you big, dumb lug," she scolded me, "I'm not going to wait for you forever. And I won't wait at *all* if you behave in such a disgusting manner. Look at you! You look and smell like a pig! And what if you get drunk on patrol and the enemy soldiers kill you because of your carelessness?"

Dom swore that he'd clean up his act after the vivid visionary experience, and he made a determined effort to tone down his party-time rest and relaxation activities.

Through the unfathomable process of job assignments often associated with the military, Dom, who had barely known how to drive when he'd entered the service, found himself assigned to a motor pool.

"I think Pop had a car when we were kids, but who needs a car in the city? They're usually more trouble than they're worth," Dom explained.

"But Pop always brought us boys up to try to make the best of any situation, so I made up my mind to learn as much as possible about the mechanical aspects of the vehicles in my charge. I also focused on becoming a really good driver."

Upon his discharge in 1971, Dom got a job with a trucking firm that transported produce from the farming regions of upstate New York to the grocery stores in the Big Apple.

"I've since learned through reading metaphysical books and taking workshops like yours, Brad, that there are no coincidences in life," he said. "But one day I got lost and found myself suddenly on a country road that started looking very familiar. Pretty soon I knew I recognized it from my dreams, and I knew that right around the next bend I would see the old covered bridge, the creek, and the stone farmhouse. And I started to pray that I would also see *her* in real life!"

Within the next few moments, Dom was truly seeing it all— exactly as he had in his dreams so many times before.

"There was the stone farmhouse right in front of me. All I had to do was to turn down the lane. I knew *she* was there, in that house, waiting for me!"

Or was she?

What if she had decided not to wait for him any longer and had gotten married to someone else?

He was twenty-four years old. He had been having those dreams of his country girl since he was eleven or twelve.

"I knew better than to just stride boldly into the kitchen, the way I did in my dreams," Dom said. "I didn't want to be arrested for breaking and entering . . . or to be shot by a protective father—or worse, a jealous husband. I prayed that I had not found her after all these years only to find her married to someone else."

When he pulled his truck into the graveled farmyard, Dom was surprised to see a man from the vegetable market come out of the farmhouse to investigate.

Dom knew the man only as "Hugh," and he didn't know if the farmer would even recognize him.

"Hey, Big City Boy," the farmer teased him. "You lost or something?"

Hugh was about his age, Dom reckoned, maybe a few years older. Was he his dream girl's husband?

Dom admitted that he was lost, then asked if he might use the farmer's telephone to call his boss and explain why he'd be late.

As Hugh walked beside him to the stone farmhouse, Dom remembered how in his dreams there had always been someone near him as he'd entered the home. Someone whose features he could never quite distinguish.

"I was so nervous that I could hardly breathe," Dom recalled. "In the next instant, I was inside the warm kitchen and I was staring at the back of a girl with light brown hair who was stirring something in a large mixing bowl. *Everything was just as it had been in all those dreams!*"

When the young woman turned to acknowledge the presence of a stranger in the house, Dom beheld the beautiful features of the girl of his dreams.

Suddenly, he remembered her name.

"Linda!" He nearly shouted his joy and amazement.

The large green eyes blinked, and the full red lips worked at a quizzical smile in a manner that had become familiar to Dom over the previous twelve years.

Hugh edged between them. His large fists had bunched, and the farmer didn't look nearly so hospitable as he had a few minutes before.

"How is it that you know my sister's name?" Hugh wanted to know. "Have you ever met her before?"

"At the sound of the word 'sister,' a one-thousand-voice choir of angels sang a chorus of 'Hallelujah.'" Dom laughed at the memory. "If Hugh had said 'wife,' I probably would have gotten right back in my truck and driven it off the nearest cliff."

To answer Hugh's direct inquiry, Dom smiled and responded truthfully, "Only in my dreams."

When the young farmer frowned and narrowed his eyes, Dom said, "Linda means 'pretty' in Spanish. Your sister certainly is pretty, right? I guess it was just a coincidence that Linda is also her name."

Dom's open smile and his quick-witted compliment won him an invitation to dinner.

"That was all the opening I needed," Dom said. "After another visit to the farmstead, Linda accepted my invitation to dinner. After another couple of dates, I told her how she had been my dream girl for the past dozen years. She didn't laugh at me or think I was putting her on. I'll never forget the way she just kind of smiled knowingly when I told her about my dreams.

"Now I drive the truck from the country to the city, instead of the other way around," he said, concluding his account of his dream lover come true. "Linda and I have a small truck garden next to Hugh's farm. This countryside has the green, green grass of my true home, and it has the green, green eyes of my true love."

Twenty-six

◈

Dreams of a Past-Life Lover

I had to ask Maureen Conners to repeat herself.

"I'm serious, Brad." The vivacious brunette laughed at my disbelief. "I first dreamed about the man who would be my husband in my present life when I was five or six years old. I swear it!"

"But you didn't actually *know* him when you were five or six years old?" I asked, wanting to get the jumble of facts as straight in my mind as possible.

"Oh, no." Maureen shook her head vigorously. "We didn't meet on the physical plane until we were in graduate school."

I had to pursue one last point for clarification. "But you knew that he had also been your husband in a past-life experience."

Maureen gave me an enthusiastic "thumbs up" and a broad smile of approval. "Now you've got it, Brad."

I had been conducting a workshop in past-life awareness in Scottsdale, Arizona, and during the dinner break, Maureen Conners had asked if she might join me to describe her unique situation, in which she had literally grown up with her past-life lover.

Maureen was a tall, slender woman in her late thirties with attractive streaks of gray in her dark hair. Quite dark-complexioned and tanned, she had brown eyes that seemed to glow with enthusiasm as she told me of her destined love match with her husband, Todd.

She began by telling me how, as a very young girl, she would always dream of the same place, a lovely cottage near a sandy stretch of beach.

"I'm certain that it must have been someplace on Cape Cod in Massachusetts," she said. "We visited the Cape a couple of summers ago. I feel that I could have found the exact area if we'd had more time."

The focal point of each dream, Maureen explained, was a blond-haired, blue-eyed man who she knew was her husband.

"And he was always standing before an easel, looking out toward the sea, painting something that had caught his attention in the magnificent expanse of ocean," she said. "From time to time, he would look away from the sea and smile at me with such love, such warmth, that I would be quite overcome with a terrible sense of longing."

I didn't mean to break the spell of her memory, but I had to chuckle over the intensity of such emotions. "Somewhat precocious for a six-year-old, wouldn't you say?"

Maureen nodded. She had taken no offense at my interruption. "I suppose such feelings *were* rather precocious. But, I can still feel the depth of those awful feelings of a lost love.

"When I was older and told my friends about my dreams, they would always start to laugh at this point. After all, I grew up in Kansas, far away from any ocean. And I have always been dark complexioned, with brown eyes. So the cynics have always gotten on my case about childish fantasies of a terrain and a mate that would be the opposite of my native environment and my general appearance."

As is the case with most people who profess past-life memories, Maureen had grown accustomed to the arguments of the skeptical mind. But the dreams of the man who she knew was her past-life husband persisted all through high school.

"I would dream about him at least once a month," she said. "Sometimes we would no longer be by the ocean, but in an apartment in some large city, probably New York, maybe Boston. Sometimes I would be posing for him in long, elegant dresses."

I asked Maureen how she appeared in these dreams.

"Quite different from my present-life appearance. I'm nearly five-ten in this life. In that life, I was about five-two or -three. I was bustier and a strawberry blonde, with almost porcelain skin. I looked like a pretty little china doll."

Popular in high school, Maureen was dating rather seriously when she graduated in 1972. "But I knew that a permanent relationship with any male other than my past-life husband would be out of the question," she said.

"What made you think he had even been incarnated during the same time sequence?" I asked.

She shrugged. "I just knew it. I had faith in my dreams."

"I guess you must have believed that faith has the power to move mountains or find past-life loves."

Maureen pursed her lips and sat for a moment or two in reflective silence. "I just always knew that one day I would find him again and that our great love would be rekindled."

I suggested that she had to have great inner resolve to be able to be sustained by a belief.

Maureen agreed. "I always believed with every fiber of my being that this man from the past would also be my destiny in my future. I knew he was out there somewhere."

A child of the sixties, Maureen admitted that she had longed to participate in significant peace marches in high school. However, teenaged hippies were something of a rarity in small Kansas towns—especially if they came from good middle-class families and had to be home by midnight. Her protests primarily consisted of wearing leather vests with Native American beadwork and worn jeans with the knees gone. Maureen developed a social conscience and went to college planning to enter either law or social work.

Dreams of her perfect past-life mate also went with her to college, but it wasn't until her first year of graduate school that she actually met him.

"Never will I forget that fateful day," Maureen said. "Never will I forget the culmination of all my dreams of yearning and desire."

It happened on a beautiful October afternoon in 1976. Maureen and the present embodiment of her past-life love nearly collided with one another in the stacks at the Northwestern University library.

"It was incredible," she said. "He looked exactly as he had appeared in my dreams. I suddenly somehow knew his present-life name as well. It was Todd.

"My heart was beating so fast that I really thought I would faint. I said his name, and I am sure that the sound came out like the croaking of a big bird."

Maureen recalled Todd's mouth had dropped open when she'd called him by name.

"He stood there gaping at the stranger who had just appeared before him and who'd dropped all the books she'd had in her arms." She giggled.

Todd frowned and asked how she knew his name.

"I've seen you . . . around campus," Maureen managed to tell him.

Todd studied her thoughtfully. "I don't know your name, but I think . . . I know you from *somewhere*."

"I'm Maureen. Maureen Martinson."

He smiled. "All right, Maureen. Do we have a class together? You do look familiar to me."

She was encouraged by the tiny ripple of recognition in Todd's memory.

"But then I remembered that although he looked just the same as in my dreams, I looked *nothing at all* like I had in my past-life memories," Maureen said.

Todd continued to work on the mystery. "Did we go to school

together? I mean, way back in elementary school, or something? My family moved around quite a bit. Could it have been long ago, maybe?"

Maureen told him that it was long ago and far away.

"Let me buy you a cup of coffee," she said. "I mean, I nearly knocked you over. Come on. We can talk about it."

As they walked to a nearby coffee shop, Todd told Maureen that he was about to become engaged.

"My heart sank," she admitted. "I mean, I felt like it exploded, then sank. But I had come too far and waited far too long to let anything come between us, now that I had actually met him in the flesh. And I certainly wasn't going to let something like another woman take him away from me. At least, not without a damn good fight!"

Maureen said that she did not immediately come right out and tell Todd about their past-life relationship and her dreams about their union.

"I think I waited until he was at least on his third cup of coffee," she said. "Thank God, he didn't laugh at me. I really think that I would have punched him out if he had laughed."

Maureen knows that for a while Todd thought he'd met a "Dorothy" from Kansas who probably knew the Wizard of Oz and even had his unlisted telephone number in Emerald City.

"But he heard me out," she said. "He sat there and listened to me and heard all about the dreams about 'us' that had haunted me since childhood. Then he asked me to a movie that night.

"I really think that at the beginning of our relationship Todd thought I had managed to come up with the most original line he had ever heard to pick someone up, but it wasn't too long before memories of what seemed to be our past life together began to come into his own consciousness. Just before he kissed me for the first time, he looked deep into my eyes and said, 'Somehow, I know that I *do* know you.' "

Although Todd was working on his master's degree in education, he confessed that he had always liked to paint as a hobby.

"It wasn't until we had been seeing each other for several weeks that he showed me one of his paintings," Maureen said. "It still gives me goosebumps thinking about it. The first time I saw it, I nearly flipped out. It was of a stretch of beach and a small cottage. In front of the cottage stood a woman with strawberry blond hair and fair, white, almost porcelain skin. Todd could not explain why he had painted the scene, but he said that he had found himself in the strangest state of anticipation ever since he had completed the work. It was as if he had been waiting for destiny to tell him what was about to occur in his life. That was why he had heard me out that first night. On some deeper level of inner knowing, he had sensed that his life was about to change."

Maureen leaned back and glanced at her wristwatch. "Oh, goodness. I hope I haven't made you late for your next lecture."

I still had a few minutes. That evening I was giving a demonstration in group regression. "So both you and Todd are convinced that you came together because of the past-life dreams of your childhood?"

Maureen smiled. "Yes, although after nine years of marriage and two beautiful daughters, I guess it really doesn't matter all that much how we came together."

A caseworker for the welfare department in a large Midwestern city, Maureen continued to exercise her concern for social issues. Todd taught American literature on the secondary level and painted in every spare moment. He most enjoyed doing portraits of his three lovely ladies.

As a postscript to our discussion, Maureen added, "Each morning I begin the day by asking my two girls, ages six and four, if they had any good dreams while they slept. I don't push it, but I'm curious to see if any of this can be transmitted genetically. I'm curious to see if either of them might begin to have dreams of her past lives—and her future husband."

Twenty-seven

Being Together Out-of-the-Body

Michele Kaplanak's husband, Ed, is a construction worker who once, due to the scarcity of local employment, was forced to take a job on a large dam project more than three hundred miles from their home.

"It was the longest six months I've ever spent," Michele said. "Ed could get home only on weekends. He would not arrive until after midnight on Friday, and he would have to be back on the road right after the noon meal on Sunday. For those six months, we lived only on Saturdays."

She remembered one dreary fall day when she was particularly lonely. The clouds hung low in the sky and drizzled on the leaves at sporadic intervals.

"It was the kind of day to share with someone you love," she said. "It was the kind of day to cuddle by an open fireplace."

She felt lonely and depressed, but she pulled on a heavy sweater and sat in her chilly house, pasting premium stamps in books.

"That night my bed felt as cold and damp and lonely as a grave," Michele said. "My only consolation was that it was

Thursday night, and Ed would be home that next evening. I lay shivering between the sheets, cursing the job situation that had taken my husband so far away from me."

Then she thought she felt a slight pressure on Ed's side of the bed.

"I turned over and saw nothing, but it seemed to me that I could feel a kind of warmth coming from Ed's pillow."

She ran her hand along the inside of the sheets.

"For a crazy minute there, I feared that I might be losing my grip on reality," Michele said. "Ed's side of the bed most definitely felt warm, like he had been sleeping there and had just gotten up."

Michele lay on her side of the bed for a few moments longer, then, once again, she slid her hand over the sheet.

"There could be no mistaking it! The bed on Ed's side was as warm as toast," she reported.

It had been a lonely day for Michele. She had no interest in attempting to theorize *why* that side of the bed should be so warm when no one was sleeping there.

"Without another moment's hesitation, I slid over into the blessed pocket of warmth and comfort and fell fast asleep almost at once."

Michele really did not think of the strange incident again until three days later, when she and her husband were eating their farewell Sunday meal. Ed's response to her curious story was hardly what she had expected.

"He stared at me for a few moments in complete silence, as if uncertain how next to proceed. Then he spoke to me in slow, measured sentences and told me a most amazing story."

That Thursday night, Ed Kaplanak had been lying in the construction workers' bunkhouse, trying to come to terms with his loneliness.

"I really felt like chucking it all that night," he told Michele. "Job or no job, I just wanted to come home to you right then."

That night, as he lay there surrounded by his snoring bunk-mates, Ed's entire being seemed suffused with personal anguish. He wanted so much to be in his own clean bed, to be able to feel Michele sleeping next to him.

"I decided to experiment," he told Michele. "I wanted to see if it were possible to will myself home over those three hundred miles. I rested my hands behind my head and summoned every ounce of concentration that I had inside my brain. I thought of nothing but you and home. I kept telling myself that it was possible to project my spirit to you. I have always believed that we were destined to be together and that all things would be possible for us—even this.

"There was a kind of rushing sensation, and I stood beside our bed, looking down at you. You were just lying there, looking kind of sad, not yet sleeping. I slipped into bed beside you, and you moved your hand over me. A few minutes later, you did it again. I thought that you knew I was there, because you rolled over and snuggled up next to me. I put my arm around you, and we both went right to sleep."

Michele stated in her report of the incident that although Ed awakened back in the bunkhouse and she awakened alone in their bed back home, they will always wonder if Ed really did come home that night—or if their deep love enabled them to share a vivid dream so that they could experience a moment of comfort when they were both longing so terribly for one another.

A growing number of scientific researchers are becoming increasingly convinced that experiences similar to Michele and Ed Kaplanak's may truly be much more than exceptionally vivid dreams. The phenomenon of leaving one's body to manifest in spirit to float to the ceiling, to travel to another room—or in some cases, to another city or country—is known as astral travel or out-of-body experience.

Dr. Charles Tart, a psychologist and lecturer at the University of California at Berkeley, has noted that accounts of out-of-body experience (OBE) can be found throughout history.

"You can go into Egyptian tombs and see diagrams on the walls of how it is supposed to be done," Dr. Tart said. "Greek mystic religions apparently had techniques to induce this experience that were the crux of their initiation ceremonies. [OBE] seems to be an altered state of consciousness . . .

"In the Western world, we've rejected these states; we deny they exist, when in fact, we should be asking, 'Is ESP an evolutionary factor just coming in or just dying out?' In other cultures—all Asia, almost—the altered states of consciousness are acknowledged and used."

Of the over 20,000 men and women who have responded to the "Steiger Questionnaire of Mystical, Paranormal, and UFO Experiences," 74 percent reported having undergone out-of-body experiences.

Psychic researcher Frederic W. H. Meyers saw out-of-body experience as the manifestation of that which is deepest and most unitary in the whole being of the human entity. Dr. Meyers considered OBE, of all vital phenomena, the most significant, "the one definite act which . . . a person might perform equally well before and after bodily death."

The numerous accounts of spontaneous out-of-body experience and the carefully conducted experiments in controlled mind projection seem to demonstrate that the human psyche has the ability to circumvent the physical limitations of time and space. Although our physical bodies may have to exist in a material world where the confining strictures of mass, energy, space, and time shape our environment, it appears that an ethereal, spiritual part of ourselves, our Essential Selves, are fully capable of traveling free of our physical bodies.

* * *

Perla Margulies told me of the time when she and her husband, Cody, had resided in an eastern seacoast colony of painters, artists, poets, writers, and visionaries.

"That was back in the early 1970s. We were both in our mid-twenties and not yet married," she explained. "I had decided that I didn't want to be an elementary schoolteacher any longer. I wanted to be a painter. Cody had decided that he didn't want to be an accountant any longer. He wanted to be a singer.

"We met in Miami, Florida; and after a couple of months of seeing each other nearly every night, we had begun living together. We were completely convinced that we had been destined to meet in Miami . . . he from Wyoming, me from Oklahoma. Cody supported us by singing in different clubs and lounges, but we knew that it was our ultimate destiny to move on to bigger and better things. However, by the time we'd decided to move up north and try life in the artists' colony, I was pregnant."

Although they were both tuned into metaphysics and the paranormal, they approached the field of inquiry with very different ideals.

"I began to practice cosmic motherhood toward my unborn baby," Perla said. "I had really gotten into certain aspects of the Goddess movement, especially honoring the Earth Mother and walking a life path of love and balance. I also very much believed that my thoughts and my meditations would influence the character and the personality of the developing soul-entity within my womb. I shopped primarily at health food and natural produce stores; I meditated daily; and I tried to live a spiritual life as completely as possible."

Cody, on the other hand, found it difficult to follow a disciplined path. "Like so many other 'metafizzlers,' he wanted a quick fix," Perla explained. "He used to argue that he could find spirituality nice and easy by smoking dope. I warned him that he was following the path of illusion."

Perla became upset when she saw Cody beginning to experiment with certain occult practices that she had always considered to be negative and exploitive of other people.

"To make matters worse," she said, "Cody was unable to hide his fascination for a certain young woman, barely twenty, believed by some to be the High Priestess of a coven of self-styled witches."

Perla did not claim to be an expert on the old religion of Wicca, but it seemed apparent to her that the loosely organized coven that met under the young witch's direction had begun, perhaps ignorantly, toying with the dark side of the occult mysteries.

"So at this point," Perla said, "while I was seeking spiritual development and Cody sought kicks, we were still unmarried—and I was still very pregnant. Nearly every night Cody left to perform a gig at a local bar or lounge while I stayed home alone and watched my girlish figure become transformed into a blimp."

Cody usually stayed out well past the bar's closing time, so Perla was painfully aware that he was avoiding both her and his responsibility.

"What of our destiny together?" I would remind him. "We had such wonderful plans. Were we deceiving one another?"

Cody would then take her in his arms and beg for her understanding. "I just need some time. I'm going through a lot of heavy stuff right now. Of course you are my destiny, lovebug," he told her.

"Finally, when I was in my seventh month of pregnancy, Cody proposed marriage," Perla said. "I wept openly with joy and relief. I had resigned myself to being left alone to face motherhood."

However, it was soon sadly apparent that the mere vocalization of his commitment to the pregnant Perla had done little to domesticate the father-to-be.

"In spite of numerous tearful sessions, I could not convince Cody to stay at home during the day and to come directly home after his last set of the evening," Perla recalled. "I begged him to give me the crucial support and love I so desperately needed."

Perla began losing sleep, worried by her acute awareness that a woman in her advanced state of pregnancy would present little competition to the slim and lovely young things who frequented the bars and lounges where Cody sang.

"One evening, I was having a particularly difficult time coping with my ruptured reality," Perla said. "In an effort to divert my raw nerves and my damaged emotions, I began to sketch. My troubles with Cody had got me behind on a deadline for some artwork that I was doing for a local advertising agency, so I decided to try to catch up—since I knew sleep would be out of the question."

Perla found to her puzzlement that her pencils seemed to have a life of their own. A line here. Another there. A bit of shading.

"To my utter astonishment, the sheet of paper began to fill up with the face of an attractive young girl. I knew that I had never seen her before, but I also *knew* that the features before me comprised an exact rendering of a real person."

Perla slumped back in her chair as she began to receive impressions about the young woman whose portrait she had just sketched.

"She was barely eighteen. She had recently graduated from high school and was feeling very worldly out on the town with some friends. Cody, singing love songs in a cheap bar, had seemed the very epitome of sophistication in her innocent and limited worldview."

Then, as Perla stared at the portrait, something very, very strange occurred. "The paper became a swirling, fuzzy mass of images. I shook my head to clear it of its sudden weird feeling of lightness. I felt as though my entire consciousness was suddenly scrunched up somewhere near the top of my skull—*and then I was out of my body, floating up near the ceiling, looking down at my pregnant physical self.*

"I felt as though the real me, my spirit body, was being tugged and pulled. Colors and lights passed before my spiritual eyes. And then I was soaring through the night sky, moving, it seemed, toward the stars."

The next thing Perla saw was Cody.

"I was in the back seat of our car. Cody was driving with someone I could not see clearly. I could, however, see all too clearly that it was a woman."

Cody drove up to a motel and got out of the car. Perla strained to see who his companion was.

"The car door opened, and the girl whose picture I had just drawn stepped out.

"Although I loathed watching my lover's infidelity, something, some force, seemed to hold me near Cody and his pickup. Like an unseen voyeur, I entered the motel room and watched."

Perhaps, Perla has since worked it out in her mind, the force that held her in that motel room intended to remove all doubts about Cody's unfaithfulness and prompt her to act in a manner that would once and for all end her humiliation.

"With the last cries and sighs of their passion, my spirit self was drawn back to our apartment," Perla said. "When the colors and lights stopped swirling around me, I was once again sitting at my drawing board and staring at the portrait of the young woman whom Cody had been with."

Cody returned to their apartment at daybreak. Perla was still awake, still weeping, when the memory of seeing her lover in another's arms became too much to contain.

"I wasted no time in confronting him with his infidelity," Perla said. "When he denied any knowledge of what I was talking about, I flashed the portrait in his face. He blanched visibly and tried to regain his composure, but his eyes could not keep from straying toward the portrait."

About an hour later, the doorbell rang. Since Cody was angrily hunched over on his side of the bed, still vehemently denying everything, Perla got up to answer the door.

The sight of their caller almost made Perla recoil against the doorframe. There, wearing a simpering expression, was the girl.

"Is Cody home?"

Perla made an expansive sweep of her arm and indicated a shocked, open-mouthed Cody hunched on the edge of the bed.

"I noted with grim satisfaction that the girl had become suddenly very subdued," Perla remembered. "She was intelligent enough to assess the role that I—very obviously pregnant and red-eyed from weeping—played in Cody's life. Without another word, she turned from the door of our apartment and ran away."

Cody got up and splashed some bourbon in a glass. "You knew, didn't you? You really knew. Somehow you saw it all tonight, didn't you?"

Perla lowered her eyes and began to weep again. "Some energy, perhaps my spirit guide, first took control of my hand and sketched her portrait. Then, somehow, I was taken out of my body and brought to the motel room where the two of you made love."

Cody's eyes brimmed with tears. "I've been a real creep! A total bastard! I've forgotten my vow to you. I've dishonored the destiny that we used to see so clearly.

"At this point, after the way I've behaved, the unforgivable things I've done, I realize that my words and my promises will mean nothing to you. Marry me right now, and I swear by all things bright and beautiful and holy that I'll be a changed man. I'll be a good husband and father."

Today Perla is a successful commercial artist and Cody has published a number of country songs that have enjoyed a modest popularity. They have two children.

"Perhaps the most amazing part of our story," Perla said, "is that I still agreed to marry Cody—and that nearly twenty years later, we're still together. A little part of me will probably always wonder if Cody married me because he truly *did* come to believe in our destiny together—or if he figured he had better be good because my out-of-body eyes would always be upon him."

* * *

Closely linked to out-of-body journeys of the spirit are instances that may be *unconscious* projections of the etheric body.
In these instances, men and women have been confronted by the
apparitions of loved ones who still solidly reside within their
fleshly shells. In other words, we are talking about "ghosts" of the
living.

One evening, Brian Denomme had worked late. It was nearly
midnight before he returned home. There were few lights left on
in the house, but as he opened the door, he thought he caught a
glimpse of Debbie, his wife of four months, hiding in a corner of
the front room.

Believing that his playful wife wanted to tease him, Brian pretended not to see her, hoping to surprise her at her own game. He
walked straight ahead for a few steps, then suddenly whirled
around toward the spot where she crouched behind a piece of
furniture.

Debbie managed to evade him, and she danced lightly out of
reach of his arms.

Brian pursued her around the room, but she always moved
just ahead of his grasp.

At last he darted forward and laughingly cornered her by the
wall. He gave a shout of triumph, but as he was about to throw his
arms around her, he heard a peculiar sound, like the report of a
faraway rifle—and Debbie vanished before his astonished eyes.

He stepped back from the wall, his head literally throbbing as
he tried to understand just what had happened.

"Brian, honey, is that you? Are you finally home?" It was
Debbie's voice, coming from the bedroom.

But how could she be in the bedroom when she had just been
running around, teasing him, in the living room?

"What was all that noise?" Debbie wanted to know. "What on
earth are you doing out there?"

Brian found his wife in bed, where she insisted she had been all the time, having grown weary of waiting up for him.

The bizarre incident troubled Brian Denomme for three years until I explained ghostly doubles of the living to him after one of my lectures on psychic phenomena.

Jayne Langstaff saw her husband's astral double one night as he lay sleeping beside her.

"I was sleeping very restlessly that night," she remembered. "We had gone to bed too early, about ten o'clock; and now here it was only a little past midnight and I had awakened. As I turned my head toward Peter, I saw a most remarkable sight. His astral body, or soul, was rising out of his physical body. It was transparent, and it had a soft silver glow to it. While I watched, it sat up beside him for a moment, then it got up and walked toward the bathroom door."

Jayne knew that she was wide awake, but she didn't know for certain what was happening.

"I was kind of frightened," she admitted. "I mean, I didn't know if Peter had died and I was seeing his soul leaving me. I guess I was somewhat reassured when it headed toward the bathroom. I figured if Peter had died, his soul would head for someplace other than our bathroom."

At last she called out to the figure, asking Peter where he was going.

"It paid no attention to me. The physical Peter lay sleeping peacefully beside me. The astral body of my husband stood before the bathroom door, as if undecided whether or not to leave the bedroom.

"I was able to get a good look at Peter's astral body as it walked across the room. It was identical to his physical body— same reddish-colored hair, same pajamas, everything. Except, as I said, his astral body had a soft, silver glow around it, and it was transparent."

Jayne closed her eyes for a few moments and prayed that all was well with her husband.

"When I opened my eyes again, Peter's soul-body had returned to his physical body, and he lay sleeping restfully beside me."

In her account of the experience, Jayne Langstaff said that the incident convinced her that it is possible for the human soul to exist outside the body while the physical shell is asleep or in a deep trance. She also stated that the experience had provided her with personal proof that the human soul goes on living after the death of the physical body.

Twenty-eight

❖

Destined Love Sent from Another Dimension

In June 1983, Greg Lovering was called back to the family home in Carmel, California, to be at the bedside of his dying mother.

"Dad had passed on five years before," Greg said. "I had just sold my interest in an East Coast advertising agency, so I was able to spend the last two weeks of Mother's life at her side.

"After the reading of the will and a number of family business matters were completed, I decided to take some personal time to 'find myself.' I didn't have to hurry back to work, because I had sold my business. The money I had made on that transaction, plus the inheritance from my mother, made it possible for me to embark on a journey of self-discovery.

"And there was no question that I was greatly in need of some time to reevaluate my life. I was thirty-five years old, and I could already chalk up two marriages, two divorces, and a recent broken engagement. Although I had made a lot of money, I had lost even more. In the process of building and destroying two fortunes, I had managed to acquire ulcers, a spastic colon, and, from time to time, a very good imitation of a nervous breakdown."

Greg decided to drift around the area, rediscovering the

scenic beauty of the Monterey Peninsula, visiting the lush vine-yards, and frequenting the bustling fishermen's docks. He hoped to lose a morose spirit among the carefree people who visited these popular tourist attractions.

"I first saw Sofia Evangelista at one of those quaint outdoor cafés in Carmel," Greg said. "She was sitting alone, sipping pen-sively at her cup of tea. I was almost overcome with her elegance, her beauty, her poise. I could not believe that this dark-haired god-dess could be alone. And although every man's eyes were on her, it seemed as though no one had the temerity to approach her."

No one, that is, except for Greg.

"When I asked if I might share her table, she looked up at me and smiled as if she had been sitting there just waiting for me to join her. Truly, it was as if we were already together and I had just returned to our table after using the telephone.

"Within minutes, I knew not only her name, but her age (twenty-nine), place of birth (La Jolla), and occupation (freelance photographer). We talked without pause over a splendid lobster dinner, continued our nonstop conversation over drinks, and were in the process of sharing our innermost secrets when our waiter begged our forgiveness and understanding, but the man-ager was insisting that the café really must close."

By that time Greg knew that he was in love as he had never been before.

"When we went back to my hotel room, I told Sofia that I felt our meeting had been destined, that everything that had ever hap-pened to me—the good, the bad, the ghastly, the magnificent—had only been a prelude to the wonderful moment when I first saw her.

"Sofia agreed that we had been destined to meet. She said that it was as if she had been waiting for me to appear all her life."

Sofia became Greg's reason for living. She was in the area pho-tographing scenic layouts for a national magazine. Day and night for two weeks they were with each other constantly.

"Never had I loved so intensely," Greg stated in his account. "Never before had I felt so completely that a woman loved me to the very fiber of my soul."

When Sofia sadly informed him that she had to return to New York soon with her photographs, Greg convinced her to send the pictures by Express Mail and to spend another week with him.

"I would have married her then," he said, "but she told me that she had been given the assignment for which she had yearned her entire career. A magazine with an international circulation was sending her to the Amazon rain forest to do a photo piece on the plight of the native people in the path of progress."

Since Greg had no work-related responsibilities at that time, he suggested that they get married, then travel to the Amazon on their honeymoon. He could be her willing pack-bearer and tote all her film rolls and extra lenses.

"Sofia told me that this assignment was something that she must do alone, on her own," he said. "She reminded me that I had told her that I was embarked on my own journey of self-discovery when I met her. This voyage to the Amazon, she said, would be a kind of vision quest for her."

Sofia warned Greg that she could be gone for as long as three months.

"I groaned that such a period of time seemed like an eternity to me, now that I had found her," Greg said. "I told her that I doubted I could stand being apart from her for so long.

"She became very serious, placed a forefinger on my lips to silence them, then told me that on the level of soul communion, we would always be together. 'My darling,' she said, 'we are two halves of a whole. We have been one since before time began. We shall be one forever.' "

Sofia promised to telephone whenever she could and to write as often as possible.

"She phoned me just as soon as her plane landed in Rio de Janiero. I received another call from somewhere in the interior about three days later. After a month, I got a hastily written letter from her. Then . . . nothing. "

After Greg had heard nothing more from Sofia for six weeks, he called the magazine that had given her the assignment in the hopes that they might provide him with some additional information regarding Sofia's welfare.

"Some snide and pompous twit told me that they could not give out information about any of their reporters or photographers," Greg said, still bristling at the insulting behavior. "Finally, some officious-sounding person came on the phone and said that she, to the best of her knowledge, had never heard of a Sofia Evangelista."

Greg was both outraged and confused. A friend in the publishing business reminded him how often publication staffs experienced turnover of personnel, so he might indeed have gotten connected with some editor who had never heard of Sofia. On the other hand, she also advised Greg that editorial staffs were very protective of their writers and photographers. After all, he could have been some nut trying to stalk Sofia while she was on assignment.

Greg plunged into a period of dark and brooding gloom.

"I leased an apartment in San Francisco, and I began spending long hours with a number of newly acquired friends. I simply did not wish to be alone. I didn't know if my dear Sofia was alive or dead. I kept torturing myself with the thought that just as I'd met the love of my life while on *my* journey of self-discovery, maybe Sofia'd met the love of *her* life while on her vision quest in the Amazon."

Five months passed. Two days before Christmas, Greg sat with two close friends discussing philosophy, part of his mind, as always, on Sofia. A knock sounded at his door, and when he answered it, he was astounded to see his beloved Sofia.

"She seemed even more lovely than before—serene, elegant, and amused by my obvious state of surprise and confusion. She was dressed almost completely in white, a color that accented her dark beauty. She wore gold high-heeled shoes, and a gold necklace, and as before, she allowed her magnificent black hair to fall to her shoulders."

The two lovers rushed to each other's arms, embracing wildly, dancing about the room in joyful spins and swirls. Greg's friends soon left them alone, after having been completely captivated by Sofia's charm and gentle personality.

"We talked endlessly," Greg said, "but each time I asked her how she'd been, why she hadn't communicated with me, or how she'd found my apartment, Sofia would say, 'Hush now, my darling. Be quiet. I'm here now, and that's all that's important.'"

When they went to bed that night, Greg held his dear Sofia tightly, as if fearful she might suddenly vanish.

Once, much later that night, he reached out for her and was reassured by her presence.

Sofia lay propped on an elbow, her dark, somber eyes gazing at him with love and kindness. When she asked him why he slept so restlessly, Greg answered her frankly: "Because I am afraid that you are going to vanish again. I am afraid that you will somehow vaporize . . . just disappear."

Sofia laughed at his fears and told him to go back to sleep.

"Yet that next morning, when I woke," Greg said, "my darling Sofia was gone!"

The bed where she had slept was still warm. The pillow still held the shape of her head. But Sofia was nowhere to be seen.

"It seemed impossible that she had been able to get out of bed and leave the apartment without awakening me," Greg said. "Especially since I had been sleeping so fitfully with my fear of losing her once again."

Greg found a note on the nightstand. It was in Sofia's handwriting and bore only the briefest of messages—the name of a coffee shop, and these words: *a surprise for you.*

Greg's heart lightened. Somehow, Sofia had managed to

leave his apartment, but she had indicated where she would meet him.

"When I entered the coffee shop, I immediately spotted Sofia, sitting at a table in the back with a handsome young man," Greg said. "I felt lightheaded and my knees almost buckled. If her surprise was to introduce me to the man with whom she had fallen in love during her five months in the Amazon, I knew I would never be able to bear it."

Greg tried his best to calm himself, but he heard his voice quavering when he stood at the table. "Sofia, I . . . I am here for my surprise. I hope it will be one I will like."

She looked up at him with no sign of recognition. "I beg your pardon, sir?"

The young man was immediately wary, defensive, and protective. "Do you know this man, Sis?"

Sis? Thank God, the handsome young man was Sofia's brother!

"Sofia," Greg wanted to know, "why are you looking at me so strangely?"

The beautiful woman smiled as the scene began to make sense to her. "Oh, you have mistaken me for my cousin Sofia. Our mothers were sisters. People say that Sofia and I look enough alike to be twins. I am Gloria Perez."

This was moving a bit too fast for Greg, and he asked permission to sit down.

"I'm sorry," Gloria said. "You appear shocked. Did you know Sofia well?"

Why was the question asked in the past tense? "What do you mean, *did* I know her?"

"He doesn't know," she said to her brother. Then, redirecting her attention to Greg, she told him in a soft, gentle voice, "Our dear Sofia died last June after a long illness."

Greg asked for a glass of water, and then, cautiously at first, began to tell Gloria and her brother Ray the entire story.

Although they were obviously shocked at his claim that he had spent the night before with Sofia, he showed them the note that had directed him to them that morning, and they silently agreed to hear him out.

"Is it possible for other people to share someone's hallucination?" Greg challenged them. "My two friends saw Sofia last night. They'll tell you that I'm not making all of this up. Sofia has been with me many times. To me she was warm, real, full of love and life."

Greg arranged for Gloria and Ray to hear the testimonies of his two friends, who were astonished to learn that they had met a ghost. "We each saw her with our own two eyes," they swore.

As they entered Greg's apartment building, he played a hunch that his maintenance man might have seen Sofia.

"Gil," he asked him, "did you happen to notice any of my guests last night?"

The man laughed at what seemed a nonsensical question. "D'ya mean the two gents, or this pretty young lady standing beside you? That was some terrific white dress you had on, miss, if you don't mind my saying so."

Gloria blanched at the man's comment. "Do you mean to say that you saw *me* here last night?"

Gil became flustered, then angry at Greg. "Don't get me involved in nothin', man. So who's this other guy? Her angry husband, I suppose."

"Relax, man," Ray told him. "I'm her brother. And I'm not angry. I'm just thinking what a wonderful Christmas present Sofia has given all of us."

Gloria's eyes misted over and she nodded her agreement. "You're right, Ray. She's just shown all of us that life goes on. That we do survive the grave."

Greg concluded his remarkable account on the positive note that Sofia's Christmas present extended beyond the season.

"I spent Christmas Eve with the Perez family, and after a couple of dinner dates, Gloria and I began seeing each other seriously. We took things very cautiously, and we were married in August of 1985.

"I would never be so callow as to compare individuals, but Gloria seemed to embody all the wonderful attributes with which Sofia had so charmed me. Plus, she has the added attraction that she never disappears."

Who—or *what*—was Sofia Evangelista?

Was she a restless spirit who had been cut short in her own Earth life and who sought to live vicariously through her cousin?

Was she an angelic being who assumed the physical appearance of the deceased Sofia in order to bring Greg together with his true destiny, Gloria?

Could she have been the soul-entity of one of Greg's past-life loves, manifesting in spirit form to bring him together with Gloria, another past-life lover to whom he owed a karmic debt?

Or, as one metaphysician theorized, could Sofia have been a personified projection of Greg's own psyche—literally, his "other half," his feminine self—that manifested for the sole purpose of guiding him to Gloria, his destined love?

Of the over 20,000 respondents to our "Steiger Questionnaire of Mystical, Paranormal, and UFO Experiences," 48 percent are convinced that they have seen a ghost; 42 percent state that they have perceived the spirit of a departed loved one; and 60 percent claim to have witnessed a variety of spirit entities.

While the case of Greg and the materialization of the entity Sofia directing him toward his true destined love, Gloria, is one of the most intriguing accounts in my files, the experience of Carol Larson Hickok is quite similar and equally eerie in its multilevel implications.

When Carol was a junior in high school, her parents moved out into the country, forcing her to leave her friends back in the city.

"In those days (the early 1950s), schoolbuses didn't travel far beyond the municipal limits of the medium-sized South Dakota city from which we had moved, and I found myself attending a much smaller township school. Every couple of weeks, my mother would take my sister Laura and me back to the city to borrow books from the library. I felt completely removed from my old school friends, except for an occasional chance meeting among the quiet library stacks. And because Mom would usually be back to pick us up after a hurried visit to the supermarket, there was never much time to maintain friendships."

One day at the library, about a year after her family had moved to the country, Carol quickly selected the books that she wished to check out, then sat on the library steps to await her mother's return.

"I had not sat there long," she recalled, "when I saw the familiar figure of Ronnie Broderson, a boy from my class in the city high school approaching. He was a handsome boy, a good athlete, and I remembered how all the girls always made a fuss over him. Just seeing him reminded me how miserable I was in that little township high school. There weren't any boys like Ronnie there."

Carol could hardly contain her excitement when she saw Ron really was walking in her direction.

"Hey, Carol," he called out, when he spotted her sitting on the library steps. "It is you, isn't it? Carol Larson? Boy, you've gotten even prettier since you moved. Must be that country living."

Carol remembered blushing and feeling embarrassed. "But I was putty in Ronnie's hands. I offered little resistance when he asked me to walk across the street to the park and sit on a bench with him. I had had a crush on Ronnie since fourth grade. We dated once when we were sophomores, just a plain, old unromantic movie date. I had always hoped for more, but I pretty much decided that Ronnie didn't really like me all that much.

"When we settled ourselves on the bench, Ronnie put his arm around my shoulders and my heart started thudding so hard it hurt. I thought I would faint when he bent down and kissed me on the cheek!"

Ronnie told her that he had always liked her. "I was sure sorry when you and your folks moved."

Carol said that she'd missed all the kids at first, but some of her new friends were nice, too. "I just wish there were some handsome boys like you out there. Boys I could care for the way I . . . I cared about you."

She felt instantly awkward and embarrassed once she had just come right out with her feelings about him.

"That's real nice of you to say that, Carol," Ron said. "As I said, I always liked you. But there's one boy out there in your school who I think is really neat. I know I like him, and I think you would, too."

"Who's that?" Carol asked, not really wanting to know. She had begun to create the most beautiful mental images of Ronnie and her writing love letters back and forth and meeting when she came into the city. She had even fashioned a perfectly marvelous picture of Ronnie driving down their lane in his old Ford.

"Bob Hickok," Ron answered her indifferent query.

Carol laughed. "Wild Bob?" She used the nickname the kids had taken from the Old West gunfighter, Wild Bill Hickok.

"Now, now," Ron scolded. "Bob gets teased enough about that. He's really a terrific guy."

Carol finally admitted that Bob was "kind of cute," but she kept wondering how she could maneuver the conversation back to *them* and getting Ronnie to come driving down their country lane.

"Are you going with anyone, Ronnie?" she asked, knowing that every minute counted, since her mother would soon be coming.

Ronnie surprised her by laughing heartily in response to her bold question. "Not any more. There's no need. You see, I'm going to go away from this town, too."

Carol's heart sank. "You . . . you're moving away?"

Ron sighed and tightened his one-armed embrace of her shoulders. "Far away, kid. Far, far away. You're never going to see this old boy ever again."

Carol remembered feeling terribly depressed, and she thought for certain that she would begin to cry. The image of Ronnie's Ford coming down their lane evaporated into a murky mist.

"How about a goodbye kiss?" Ron asked gently. "A farewell kiss for an old friend who's going to go far, far away."

This time, Ron kissed Carol on the lips. "He held the kiss for so long that I thought I really would faint this time."

When he finally released her, Carol looked up into the scowling features of her mother and the laughing face of Laura.

"Mama grabbed me by the hand, and I barely had time to wave goodbye to Ronnie before she dragged me off to the car," Carol said. "Ronnie was grinning from ear to ear. 'Don't forget to be nice to my friend Bob,' he yelled after us. 'Bob is a great guy. You two are made for each other!' "

Carol said she'd never forget the argument that she and her mother had all the way home that night.

"Finally, when I explained that Ronnie was going to be moving away and Laura supported my claims that he was a great guy, Mama became somewhat more understanding and sympathetic. She made it very clear, however, that she did not approve of any daughter of hers smooching on a bench in a public park."

It was nearly three weeks before Carol got back to the city and the library. Illness and farmwork had prevented her mother from taking them to town any sooner. Carol had begun looking at Bob Hickok with totally different eyes. He was a tall, ruggedly handsome boy, and since they were both juniors, they were together in most of their classes. It was becoming obvious that Bob was taking quite an interest in her as well.

By the time they got back to the library, they knew the books would have overdue fines. Celeste Motters, one of Carol's former classmates, was working at the library desk, and as Carol was paying the late charges, she could not resist boasting to Celeste about her rendezvous with Ronnie Broderson in the park.

"That's in really bad taste, kid," Celeste said. "Did you lose all your class, moving out with the chickens and the pigs?"

Carol's temper flared. "Just a bit jealous, are we, Celeste? Then you'll just be delighted to know that Ronnie kissed me while we sat on a park bench."

"Wow!" Celeste exclaimed, momentarily forgetting all about the QUIET sign over her head. "Either you're getting goofy out on that farm—or you are just getting plain crude!"

The head librarian came to shush the girls, and Carol's former classmate turned to walk away from her.

"Don't go, Celeste!" Carol whispered sharply, catching her friend's arm. "We always got along so well! Why do you accuse me of bad taste and call me goofy or crude because I let Ronnie kiss me? Is it just jealousy, or what?"

Celeste fixed her with a cold stare; then something within Carol's eyes caused her to thaw just a bit. "Look, Carol, we all tell fibs now and then. No big deal. But it was in bad taste to talk about Ronnie Broderson kissing you a couple of weeks ago. Maybe you didn't know because you live out in the country now, but Ronnie was killed in an automobile accident almost five months ago."

Carol could find no words to utter as she watched the back of her friend moving away from her. *Ronnie, dead?* It simply could not be.

She recognized another former classmate across the library reading room and nearly ran to the table where the girl sat flipping through a magazine. She sadly confirmed the news of Ron's death.

"I can provide no logical, rational explanation of my experience that will please everyone," Carol said, concluding her report. "I only know that forty years ago, I had an encounter with an affectionate ghost. I know that I sat on that park bench and received a warm kiss from a boy who had been dead for nearly five months—and I can offer the additional testimony of my mother and my sister, who saw Ron Broderson as clearly as I felt him.

"We could never really understand why Ronnie's ghost played Cupid for me and Bob Hickok. He and Bob weren't related, and Bob said he couldn't remember ever meeting Ron.

"Bob and I went together through our junior and senior years in high school, and we got married three years after graduation. We have two wonderful kids.

"Maybe it wasn't really Ronnie's ghost, but an angel that came to me disguised as the handsome boy I'd had a crush on. Maybe the angels decided it was our destiny to be together, and they used Ronnie to work it all out."

Twenty-nine

Fated to Be His True Love's Guardian Angel

One of my favorite stories from my files of those destined to love one another is about a man who became his lover's guardian spirit when an untimely fatal accident separated them.

Doreen Raney told me that she and Kevin Lawsky had known each other for many years and had become good friends long before they had begun to think romantically about each other.

"We had worked together in the same insurance company for nearly three years before we had a sudden awareness of each other as sweethearts," Doreen said. "There had been many times in the past when I had even taken my love-life problems to trusty and dependable Kevin, who at that time had seemed like a brother, someone in whom I could confide. Suddenly one evening after work, when we were sitting in his car just talking, he leaned over and kissed me—and that was that!"

Once they'd begun dating, Doreen soon learned that Kevin had a mystical side to his nature. "He would philosophize about why some Force-Greater-than-We had for some reason chosen to keep us apart, yet together, for so long. He wondered why, though we were attracted to one another as close friends, we had seemed more like brother and sister than lovers."

One night as they relaxed with wine and cheese in front of the fireplace in his apartment, Kevin theorized that maybe he had been Doreen's brother in another lifetime. Doreen had laughed, not completely certain if Kevin was serious. "You mean, like in reincarnation? Other lifetimes? That sort of thing?"

"Sure." Kevin grinned, refilling her glass. "Why not? All things are possible."

"All things are possible," she agreed.

Kevin suggested that they close their eyes, relax, and allow their minds to drift. "Maybe we can pick up on a time when we really *were* brother and sister."

Doreen took another sip of her wine and lay her head back on Kevin's chest. She felt as if she were a kid playing "let's pretend."

"I'm kind of picking up a really romantic period," Kevin said, "like Renaissance Italy. I think I was a painter, and I created a portrait of you in an elegant, flowing gown. It caused a sensation because you were so beautiful and I was so talented. Your portrait made me famous overnight."

Doreen laughed at the dual conceit of her beauty and his talent. "And I was your *sister?*"

Kevin squeezed his eyelids tighter together. "Wait. It's coming clearer. Aha! Got it! You were my best friend's sister. At first, I felt very protective toward you, like a brother. Then, later, as I became increasingly rich and famous, we fell deeply in love."

Doreen sat up, laughed at him over the rim of her wineglass. "You're a little strange, you know that, don't you?"

Kevin shrugged. "The really weird part is that we had thirteen children. Six boys and seven girls."

Doreen picked up a sofa pillow to pummel him. "You should have kept your brotherly feelings toward me. Thirteen kids! You satyr!"

Kevin sighed. "Well, it could have been. Who can say?"

Becoming serious, he said, "I only know that in this lifetime, the moment I first saw you, I felt very protective toward you. It was as if I wanted immediately to appoint myself your bodyguard."

Doreen snuggled up next to him. "Well, mister, you can guard my body forever."

"I will," he assured her, murmuring into her ear. "I will always protect you and look after you."

"When Kevin proposed to me, I did not hesitate to say yes," Doreen said. "He was twenty-eight; I was twenty-five. We were both old enough to know what we were doing—and young enough to enjoy doing it. We had not *fallen* in love; we had *grown* in love. Ours was the kind of ideal relationship that I had always read about in the women's magazines. Kevin and I had been friends before we'd become lovers."

Two months before their wedding date, Kevin was killed instantly in an automobile accident.

Doreen said that she had little memory of the first few weeks after Kevin's death.

"I was left to try to put back together the pieces of what seemed to be an irrevocably shattered life.

"It was well over a year before I began dating again, and I know that I was really hard on the men who asked me out. In my mind, no one could ever begin to compare to Kevin. No one could ever satisfy me on as many levels as Kevin had. There were a few men with whom I didn't mind being friends, but I was not ready to consider any of them as potential lovers."

Two years after Kevin's fatal accident, Doreen began to date Charles Mybeck.

"After three months, he asked me to marry him. I was unable to give him an answer, and asked for a few days to consider his proposal. I had tender feelings for Charlie, but I still felt I was not yet ready to marry." Doreen explained her feelings to him, but he continued to court her.

"Finally, after we'd been going together for nearly a year, I agreed to marry Charlie. He was a good-looking guy, probably better looking than Kevin had been. But in spite of his impeccable manners, Charlie did not have the depth of feeling that Kevin had shown me."

One night, less than a week before the wedding, Doreen lay tossing and turning in bed, unable to sleep.

"My mind was full of thoughts of Kevin. I figured it was kind of strange for a bride-to-be to be thinking about her dead fiancé, rather than her living husband-to-be; but I just lay there thinking about what might have been.

"I started wishing that Kevin was right there with me to talk the whole business over. Should I marry Charlie, or shouldn't I? I knew he'd be able to give me good advice, just as he had so many times in the past."

She began to cry, and in between her sobbings, she gradually became aware of Kevin's voice calling her name.

"I sat bolt upright in bed, struck with the sudden realization that I was not just imagining the sound of Kevin's voice, I was really hearing him calling to me! I looked in the direction from which his voice seemed to be coming, and I was startled to see him standing just as solid as life next to the dresser."

So many images began to flood Doreen's brain that she feared she might succumb to the shock of seeing Kevin standing there and faint dead away.

"I became strangely calm at the sound of his voice. He told me my marriage to Charlie Mybeck would be a serious mistake, that I must not marry the man. 'He's not the man for you,' Kevin said. 'He's not what he appears to be.' "

Doreen said that she was so moved, so impressed by the apparition of her dead fiancé, that she feigned illness and told Charles that they must postpone their marriage until she had recuperated.

"Two weeks to the day that Kevin had appeared to warn me

that Charles Mybeck was not who he pretended to be, he was arrested." Doreen and many others who had only seen one side of Mybeck were shocked by the charges of unsavory activities and his disturbing marital history.

"Two years later, just a few days before I turned thirty, Joel Raney asked me to marry him," Doreen said. "Joel was a kind, thoughtful man who from the very first had reminded me of Kevin. I felt almost certain that an apparition of my dear friend and lover would once again appear to let me know if my choice in men was a wise one.

"Three nights before my August wedding to Joel, Kevin appeared in my room. Once again, he looked just as solid as he had in life and as he had when he'd materialized to warn me about Charlie.

"I was not shocked this time, and I waited eagerly for some sign, some signal from him. This time, he only smiled at me, waved a hand, and disappeared.

"I knew," Doreen said, concluding her story of a love that had survived the grave, "that my dear Kevin had given my marriage to Joel his blessing and that he had waved his hand in a final farewell."

Thirty

The Spirit Gives Permission

Just before Jennifer Jonsson moved in with Marshall Satern, she was warned by some of his friends that she should never bother to have marriage plans in her future. At least, not to Marshall.

"That's fine if you want to move in together," Karyn Petrovsky told her one day over lunch. "Just don't have your heart set on marrying the guy."

Jennifer nibbled on some celery and cream cheese. "Why? You know he's the marrying kind. He was married before."

Karyn nodded. "That's just it. He was devoted to Susan during her long illness, and especially after she suffered the stroke."

"She was so young." Jennifer frowned. "Thirty-three, thirty-four, something like that."

"Only thirty-two. Susan had always been jealous of Marshall. After her stroke, when she lost the ability to speak, she got worse, and very possessive," Karyn said.

Karyn probed her salad with her fork. Jennifer could sense that she was trying to decide whether or not she should share something. After a few moments of silence, Karyn sighed and revealed some information that probably should have remained un-known to Jennifer.

"Once when Ken and I were visiting Marshall and Susan just a few days before she had the stroke, she started talking about life after death. Everyone knew she had been ill for some time and that her doctors had not been optimistic in their prognosis. We had heard that she'd developed complications and had only a few months to live. We tried to change the subject. It was morbid for someone so ill to be discussing funerals and such, but she continued talking on and on about what the afterlife must be like.

"Then she turned to Marshall and told him that she would come back to haunt him if he should ever remarry."

Jennifer felt a chill run through her. "Oh, I'm certain she must have been making some sort of joke."

"A joke in very bad taste," Karyn said somberly. "We tried to laugh it off at the time. But if you had seen the look in her eyes . . ."

Karyn could not suppress an involuntary shudder. She reached for her wineglass, and Jennifer saw that her hand was trembling.

"But surely Marshall would not take such a threat seriously," Jennifer protested.

Karyn had drained her glass and reached for the carafe to pour herself a refill. "After Susan's stroke . . . and her subsequent death, I think he learned to take it seriously. There are . . . things that go on in that house. I've heard them myself."

Jennifer felt a slight flush of anger. "Now you're trying to scare me. You're beginning to sound like a Gothic romance. You know, the scene where the new mistress of the mansion is warned about the master's terrible secret."

Karyn picked up the check and began to rise. Before she left the table, however, she took Jennifer's hand. "I'm sorry, dear. Truly I am. I've talked on and said far too much. The wine, I sup-pose. You know that Susan and I were dear friends. I sincerely wish you well, Jennifer. I like you. And Marshall certainly deserves some happiness in his life."

"I thought Karyn Petrovsky's comments to be in bad taste, and I hoped it was not her intention to undermine my relationship with Marshall," Jennifer said. "At first I didn't take her warning about Susan's malediction seriously, but during my first night in Marshall's home, I began to reconsider her words."

Jennifer and Marshall were preparing for bed one night when they heard a loud thumping sound from the room that Susan had occupied during the last months of her illness. Because of her stroke and her inability to speak, she had been forced to knock on the wall whenever she needed something.

"Marshall muttered something about a loose shutter," Jennifer said, "but I could see that he was very pale and shaken."

He breathed a deep sigh, as if he regretted the tradition that required the menfolk to investigate all strange night noises. He fastened the belt of his bathrobe securely about his waist, then stepped out into the hall.

"I sat nervously on the edge of the bed," Jennifer recalled. "I had resolved to give up smoking, but I snagged a butt from Marshall's pack on the nightstand. After a few minutes, the terrible pounding sound stopped.

"I turned to glance at the door and was startled to see a colorless, bony hand reach around the door and shut out the lights.

"I lost it," Jennifer admitted. "I sat there screaming until Marshall came back into the bedroom and snapped on the lights."

There were no further manifestations that night, but Jennifer told Marshall the next morning at breakfast that she did not want to sleep another night in that bedroom.

"Marshall agreed without a word of argument," she said. "He told me that as soon as he returned from work the next evening he would help me move the furniture to a back bedroom."

A freelance artist, Jennifer had set up her easel and sketch board in the front room, where there was a lot of natural light.

Now, she was beginning to regret that she would not be leaving the house to go to work.

Marshall had only been gone a few minutes, when a flurry of knockings and thumpings sounded throughout the house.

"The venetian blinds actually shook as if they were caught in a heavy breeze," Jennifer reported. "I was certain I could hear the sounds of things being moved around in the attic.

"I didn't think I'd be able to go on living in that house. It seemed obvious to me there was something living in the shadows that did not want me there.

"Karyn had not just been making silly girltalk about Susan promising to come back to haunt Marshall. Somehow, Susan's spirit was still in the house, and it was apparent that she didn't mind haunting me as well."

Jennifer decided to stick it out.

"For several days the pattern of the haunting didn't vary," she said. "There would be thumpings at bedtime, and knockings and scrapings during the day.

"On a number of occasions, as I worked in the kitchen, I heard what sounded like a sick person dragging her feet up the stairs. Whenever I pushed open the kitchen door and looked up the stairs, however, there was never anyone there."

Jennifer had tolerated the eerie manifestations for more than a week when she heard a loud pounding emanating from Susan's bedroom.

"I got up from my sketch board and glanced up the stairway. I saw nothing, but there had been a rather dramatic departure from what I had come to accept as part of the haunting's regular schedule. Up until that afternoon, the pounding from Susan's bedroom had sounded only at bedtime."

Jennifer continued to watch the top of the stairs. If she had not known for certain that she was alone in the house, she'd have sworn that there truly was an invalid in that bedroom who was trying desperately to signal her.

"The longer I concentrated on the sounds coming from Susan's bedroom, the more I became convinced that her spirit was actually attempting to communicate with me."

Although she has since stated that she will never know how she managed to summon the courage, Jennifer walked up the stairs and entered the bedroom where Susan had lived her last days.

"I don't know what I expected to see. I guess I feared I'd be confronted with the ghostly image of the poor, sick woman whose place and home I had taken."

Jennifer remembered that the room still had an antiseptic smell to it.

"It was apparent that the room had received only a superficial cleaning after Susan's death. I stood there in the middle of it, not really having the faintest idea what my next move should be."

A loud thump sounded next to the bed.

"Startled, I turned quickly, nearly losing my balance. Another thud sounded from the wall next to the bed where the poor dying woman must have lain and rapped out her pitiful signals to her part-time nurses."

To her complete astonishment, an envelope appeared to flutter down from somewhere. "It looked like an autumn leaf dropping from a tree. It simply fluttered down from some invisible hiding place."

Jennifer picked it up and saw that it was a letter Susan had written to Marshall. "It was sealed and had never been read by Marshall."

That night she gave the letter to him. Hesitantly, he took the envelope from her hands. "Tears streamed unashamedly down his cheeks as he read the letter," Jennifer said.

"When he had regained his composure, he told me that Susan must have written the letter just hours before her death. She told him how much she loved him and she prayed that he would forgive her for some of the selfish and thoughtless things she had written in bitterness during the course of her illness.

"When she had been deprived of her voice after the stroke, she had been forced to do more listening and more thinking. Contrary to what Marshall had feared and Karyn had supposed, Susan wrote that she hoped that he *would* remarry. But she begged him always to remember her with kindness and to think only of the good days they had shared."

According to Jennifer Jonsson Satern, she and Marshall still live in the same house, but they never again heard the eerie knockings and thumpings from Susan's room. They have been married for seven years.

"I don't really think that the surviving personality of my husband's first wife was ever trying to drive me away," Jennifer concluded, "but I do think that she wanted to make her position clear to me and to Marshall. It was as though she would not permit, or sanction, Marshall's remarrying until he had read her last letter to him."

Thirty-one

❖

Earthbound Spirit Releases Him to New Love

One of the most dramatic stories I have ever heard regarding two destined lovers and their encounter with the spirit world was told to me many years ago by an elderly spirit medium whom I have agreed to call "Sarah Woodward" to protect her privacy.

In 1921, Sarah married a rancher who lived in the Southwest. Chad Woodward had been a widower for nearly five years. He was a tall, ruggedly handsome man who owned a comfortable spread of grazing land and several hundred head of cattle. Matronly cupids in the county had been trying to play match-maker for Chad for so long that they had almost given up on him and stamped "not interested" across his forehead.

However, when he returned from a trip to Saint Louis with Sarah, his lovely new bride, his friends' wives once again felt that all was right with the world and held a happy chivaree for the newlyweds.

"After the chivaree, all the neighbors gave us their blessing and left us alone to enjoy our first night together in Chad's large ranch house." Sarah smiled at the memory. "I could not help overhearing the women clucking over what a quiet, soft-spoken, sensible lady I appeared to be. Well, I like to think that I was all those things, but I didn't feel that I could tell Chad or any of those nice ladies and courtly gentlemen that I was also something a good deal more than what I seemed."

Sarah possessed a secret she had not even shared with her husband. For several years before her marriage, she had been a well-known spirit medium in Cincinnati. Just a few months before she had met Chad, she had decided to disavow her mediumship and move to Saint Louis to begin a new life.

"I had found the physical and mental drain of mediumship to be too great for my rather frail constitution, and I had grown sad and weary of watching the eligible men pass me by in favor of more orthodox wife material. I was working as a very conventional shopgirl in a clothing store when Chad met me."

That night, more than ever, as her husband took her in his arms, Sarah was glad she had decided to keep her mediumship a secret. Even though Chad's rugged features made him appear that he would not be frightened by any earthly man or beast, she would not have wanted to do anything unearthly to scare him away.

"I was soon to learn, however, that my husband also harbored a secret he had kept from everyone," Sarah said. "We were preparing for bed when I was startled to see a woman walk unannounced into our master bedroom."

As Sarah watched in astonishment, the woman strode to the middle of the room, narrowed her eyes, and glared at her, obviously seething with rage.

Sarah looked at her husband, expecting him to speak to the woman, whoever she was—neighbor, relative, friend, or jilted sweetheart.

"But Chad seemed to be unaware of her presence," Sarah recalled. "Admittedly, I was unfamiliar with the local customs, but it seemed to me that invasion of privacy was rude no matter where one lived."

It was clear to Sarah that the woman had no business storming into their bedroom, so she decided to tell her so. "What do you want in this room?" she demanded. "All the guests have gone home."

Chad chuckled and turned to her somewhat awkwardly. "They sure have, sweetheart. I guess they figure that we're still kind of on our honeymoon. It was thoughtful of everyone to leave so early and leave us all alone."

He seemed oblivious to the intruder's presence.

"Dear." Sarah frowned her impatience. "We are not alone."

The woman had put her hands on her hips and had begun to tap an angry foot on the hardwood floors.

Chad turned in surprise from the clothes closet, where he had been hanging up his suit. "What are you talking about, hon? There's no one here but us. Everyone has left."

Sarah realized her husband could not see the woman. *She was in spirit.* Sarah had time only to shout a warning before the angry uninvited visitor from the spirit plane hurled a vase at Chad's head. He fielded the heavy glass vase on his left shoulder and it crashed to the floor, shattering into a dozen pieces.

"Louise! Louise!" Chad shouted in the direction from which the vase had been thrown. "Please stop!"

Sarah sensed that the violent psychic storm had abated, and as "Louise" left the bedroom, she passed a cold chill over Chad that made him shiver. The rancher sat on the edge of the bed and began to weep.

"She has a nasty temper, doesn't she?" Sarah said, after several moments of silence.

Chad's eyes pleaded for Sarah's understanding. "She . . . warned me that something like this would happen if . . . if I ever remarried. I've known she was still in the house . . . I've felt her presence on and off these five years since she died."

Sarah nodded. Chad didn't really need to tell her these things. She had already received strong psychic impressions that told her much of what he was saying. But she knew it would do him good to talk about it.

"Well," she said with a sigh, "Louise is certainly one redhead who really lives up to the reputation for having a quick temper." As soon as she had spoken the words, Sarah regretted having opened her mouth.

"How did you know Louise had red hair?" Chad was looking at her quizzically. "Surely none of the women here tonight would have been so rude as to tell you about Louise. Or did they?"

"No," Sarah assured him. "All of your friends were on their best behavior. No one said a word about your late wife."

Chad reached in his back pocket for a handkerchief. "You acted from the very first as if you could see her. You were talking to someone in the room before the disturbance began. Sarah," he demanded, "could you see her?"

Sarah admitted that she had seen Louise in spirit form.

Chad wiped away his tears with the white handkerchief, then blew his nose. "But how? How could you *see* her?"

Sarah chose to ignore the question. She knelt and began to pick splinters of glass from the floor. "Darling," she began in a soft voice. "I've always been able to see men and women like Louise. Ever since I was a little girl."

"You can see *ghosts?*" Her husband's voice sounded as if it had come from within a deep cavern.

"Sometimes I can see men and women who are in spirit. A spirit such as Louise has remained earthbound . . . probably because she felt possessive toward you while she was in the physical body. She was strong and proud, and she was taken away from you and from her life when she was young."

Chad nodded, silently agreeing.

"What people call 'ghosts,' are usually the restless spirits of those who died violent deaths and who cannot adjust to their sudden change of condition. In other cases, they are the spirits of men and women who are tied to the earth plane because of deeds left undone, lessons left unlearned—or because of earthly attractions that remain too strong."

Her husband leaned forward, cradled his head in trembling hands. She had not intended to say so much.

"Sarah," Chad spoke at last. "Can . . . can you also *talk* to ghosts?"

She considered her answer very carefully before she answered his question. "I am . . . I used to be . . . I used to be a spirit medium."

Chad could not suppress a sudden scowl. "You mean, you had a tent at carnivals and fairs and such, and told fortunes for people?"

"Of course not! I gave readings for a select clientele in my home or gave spirit messages in spiritualist churches in Ohio. Anyway, I gave all that up before I moved to Saint Louis."

"But you could *see* Louise," he reminded her.

Sarah had already considered this. Somehow, she had known that the gift of mediumship could not be surrendered so easily. Somehow she had known that her renunciation of a talent nurtured within her psyche by spiritual forces could not be accomplished as simply as resigning from a regular job. She knew now that she would remain a spirit medium until whoever had bequeathed her with such gifts decided to withdraw them.

Chad took her hands in his own and clasped them with his strong fingers. She knew what he was going to ask before he had found the courage to voice the words.

"Sarah, dear, could you . . . talk to Louise and ask her to please leave us alone? I mean, I did love her once, but now . . ."

He could no longer speak, but Sarah understood. He was a lonely man who sought to make a new life for himself with a new bride.

"I walked the hallways of the ranchhouse that night," Sarah said. "But I could neither see nor sense any sign of Louise. I searched every room and closet in the sprawling house, but it soon became apparent that the angry spirit of Louise had spent its wrath for that night.

"I told Chad I was quite certain Louise would return the next night when we prepared to go to bed. As an earthbound spirit, Louise would feel most jealous about her husband's intimate relationships, the ones she would least wish him to share with another woman."

Neither Sarah nor Chad felt like attempting to make love that night. Louise had won the first round.

Sarah's prediction proved true. The next night, as she and Chad were undressing for bed, she caught sight of Louise's spirit manifesting in the bedroom.

"Louise was shaking an angry finger at Chad, and I knew that the psychic fireworks were about to begin," Sarah said. "I shouted at the spirit being to listen to me."

The spirit turned to her with a look of shocked surprise. "You shameless hussy!" Louise shrieked at her. "How dare you shout at me? You come into my home like some common slut and try to take away my husband. And right in front of my eyes you try to carry on with him."

Sarah had already decided to confront the spirit head on. "Chad is *my* husband now."

"What in tarnation do you mean, *your* husband?"

The spirit crossed the room and stood eye to eye with her. Sarah could see the terrible hurt and the anger churning within the spirit's aura.

Chad had been sitting on the edge of the bed and was pulling off a boot when Sarah began speaking to the invisible Louise. He sat there with one hand on a boot heel—frozen, immobile, fearful lest some movement, some small sound, might break the connection Sarah had established with the other side.

In a firm, steady voice, Sarah told Louise she was now in the spirit world. "You are no longer a soul inhabiting a physical body.

You are no longer of the flesh. Remember the day you died. Remember the day they buried you."

The tormented spirit put its hands to its ears. "Stop it! Stop it! Or I'll scratch your eyes out!"

"You cannot harm me, Louise," Sarah told her. "This house is no longer your home. The earth plane is no longer your home. It is time for you to pass on."

Louise's features became a mask of anguish. "I cannot leave Chad. He still needs me."

"You need not worry about Chad," Sarah said in a soft, soothing voice. "He's with me now. It is time for you to pass on. You should have moved on five years ago. You came together to complete some karmic tie. You fulfilled your destiny together, and now it's time for Chad and me to work out our Karma."

Louise considered Sarah's counsel. "I know that Chad and I were meant to be together. I know that we had some lessons to learn together."

Sarah agreed. "And now Chad and I must walk together on the earth plane before we, too, pass to spirit. We, too, are meant to be together."

"But I will still worry so about him," the spirit protested.

"You need not worry about him," Sarah assured the spirit being. "The concerns of the earth plane should now mean nothing to you. Remember your loved ones with affection, but don't try to hang on to them. You must now be concerned only with things of the spirit."

Louise turned to look sadly at the confused rancher who sat on the edge of the bed. She began to weep. "I remember now. The minister standing over me. 'Ashes to ashes,' he said. All my relatives and friends were standing alongside him to agree.

"But I wasn't ready to leave. There was my husband to look after . . . and the ranch . . . and the hard times I knew were coming. I had to stick by Chad and help him. Two men came in white, shining suits and said that they would guide me, but I told them to go to blazes."

"Those men were your spirit helpers, your guardians," Sarah explained. "You should really have gone on with them. You should have realized that it was time for you to pass on."

"But I had to stay with my husband, don't you understand?" Louise shouted, the anger within her flaring again. "And he rewards my fidelity by bringing you home with him from Saint Louis!"

Sarah did not flinch in the face of the spirit's rage. "He is my husband now, Louise. You have been in spirit for five years. It is not good that man should live alone."

"Alone?" Louise scowled. "He had me!"

"He had you while you were in your material body," Sarah said. "But you have been in spirit for five years."

"In spirit . . . five years?" Louise's spirit form began to vibrate in a peculiar manner.

Sensing that she had at last managed to help Louise to achieve some degree of comprehension of her true status in the greater reality, Sarah once again told the entity that she had been in spirit for five years.

Louise sighed and approached Chad. "That's why he has not touched me for these five long years. It was so unlike him to be so distant. He was always so affectionate. Then he just stopped touching me."

"Because," Sarah reminded her, "now you are in spirit."

"Now I am in spirit," Louise echoed.

Her image was beginning to waver. Realization of her actual state of existence was beginning to pervade her total energy pattern.

A brilliant, glowing orb formed behind Louise, and Sarah could perceive the forms of two angelic beings standing within the golden light.

"They're here again," Louise said. "Those same two fellows are back again. The ones I told to go to blazes."

"Are you ready to go with them this time?" Sarah asked her.

Louise nodded. "Guess so. I have a greater understanding now. It's your turn to work out your own problems together. Just promise me that you'll be a good wife to him."

Before Sarah could reply, Louise stepped into the brilliant orb of golden, glowing light.

"I caught just a glimpse of two majestic figures in white," Sarah told me. "Behind them I saw a landscape of rich green grasses and multicolored flowers. Then there was nothing before me but my poor husband, still sitting on the edge of the bed, still holding on to his boot heel with one hand."

The spirit medium I have called Sarah Woodward eventually reentered the spiritualist ministry with the blessing of her husband. When she told me her story in 1973, she was nearly eighty years old and living in a nursing home in California—still alert, still studying, and writing down experiences taken from a lifetime spent fulfilling her destiny between two worlds.

Thirty-two

He Married His Personal Prophet

The night was made for love. The snows had retreated from the Michigan countryside before the advance of spring; during the day, the sun placed a warm, friendly hand upon the backs of the winter-weary and drew them outside to fill their lungs with sweet country air. For a week or more the warm evening breezes had tossed the stars around, and the moon had glowed with a special magic that awakened the promise of renewal in the minds of all and had intensified the deepest longings in the hearts of young lovers.

James Galper, in the full flush of his twenty years, was excited beyond mortal words as, with the appreciation of a seasoned taster of fine wines, he let his eyes sip slowly at the face of the beauty next to him on the front seat of his car.

She wore her black hair long and straight, and her eyes were softly sad, reflecting depths of warmth and emotion. Her slender figure and long legs could have inspired the designer of the miniskirt that she wore that night.

At last, James rediscovered his ability to form coherent thoughts and to speak.

"Bridget, I. . . ."

"Oh, thank you. I'm so glad that you think my hair looks lovely tonight, Jimmy. I washed it this afternoon, and I didn't really know if it would look good in time for the dance."

"Yeah, well, it looks fine. I was wondering. . . ."

"Why, Jimmy, you silly! Of course I had a wonderful time. I always have a good time with you."

James loosened his necktie. "Bridget is at it again," he thought. "I wonder if . . ."

"No way, Jimmy! I told you last time, none of that!"

James let out a deep sigh of resignation, then switched on the ignition. Carefully he guided his hardtop convertible out of the parking place by the river and back onto the main road.

"I'm glad," he dared to think, "that all the girls in Michigan aren't mind-readers!"

Today, nearly twenty years later, James Galper never tires of recounting anecdotes of those strangely romantic days when he was courting Bridget Muro, his "mindreader in a miniskirt."

"She always knew what I was thinking." He laughed. "How does a guy ever get ahead of a gal like that?"

"He never does, Jimmy," Bridget said with a winsome smile. "He never does. But I warned you that you were my destiny the first time we met at the municipal swimming pool."

James laughed even harder at that particular memory. "I was nearly eighteen, going into my senior year in high school, and I was lifeguarding that summer at the pool. I really felt that I was Mr. Cool, getting paid for working on my tan and for eyeballing the knockout chicks in their scanty swimsuits. Then up walks this pretty little jailbait fifteen-year-old in a teeny-weeny red bikini and tells me that I am destined to marry her."

"And after he recovered from that shock, he found out more about me and really had his mind blown," Bridget said.

"Yeah, I found out that she was a sexy little witch who had even been written up in the local newspapers for her psychic powers."

"I prefer 'psychic abilities,'" Bridget said. Then she explained: "I've always been psychic. When I was thirteen, I found a lost three-year-old boy who had been missing in the woods for a couple of days. I wanted to remain anonymous—you know, just a psychic Good Samaritan—but the local papers got wind of it, the wire services and the tabloids picked up on it, and all of a sudden I was being confronted by total strangers who were begging me to heal them or make them rich."

"She became quite a local celebrity," James said, "but I had been too busy with football practice and my car and stuff, so I had missed her early notoriety."

I asked Bridget how, as a teenager, she had handled her abilities and her celebrity.

"There were times when I really enjoyed having these gifts from God, the Holy Spirit, the angels—wherever they came from," she said. "For example, I could read the boys like they were open books. Or I should say, open *Playboy* magazines. They would always get so flustered when I told them exactly what they were thinking. Then it got so none of the boys would date me, and hardly any of the girls wanted to be my friend. Those were the times I wished that some Higher Power would take my psychic abilities away from me."

How did her parents and other members of the family respond to her extrasensory talents?

"Mom liked it because I always knew what she was going to ask me beforehand, and I usually had the chore done even before she thought of it."

"Her dad and her brother Marty liked her abilities because they made a lot of money off her betting on sports events!"

Bridget seemed embarrassed by her husband's charge, but she

didn't deny it. "I stopped giving them predictions, though. I'd always felt that there was something improper about using ESP to make money."

Intrigued by the lovely young psychic in the red bikini, James had begun dating Bridget. Although he sometimes became very frustrated and flustered by her extraordinary abilities, he learned to adjust to them and even to appreciate them.

"But then came the day when he didn't appreciate my abilities *enough*," Bridget recalled. "And it almost cost us our lives."

Somewhat sheepishly, James agreed. They had dated through his senior year in high school, and they continued their relationship when he went off to college.

"I was home for the summer, working at my dad's supermarket," he said. "I was twenty going on twenty-one. Bridget was eighteen. It was a beautiful Sunday, and I said we should go on a real excursion and drive to Chicago, about five hours away. But Bridget had had this dream . . ."

"I could remember the dream in very sharp detail," Bridget emphasized. "In my dream, Jimmy asked me to go riding with him into Illinois and on to Chicago. As we drove along the highway, we collided with another car, and both vehicles were badly damaged. Through drops of blood blurring my vision, I watched a woman with her arm bandaged and in a sling crawl out of the other car. I told Jimmy the dream and said we should definitely not drive out of town and out on the highway on that particular Sunday."

I asked James how he could have disobeyed Bridget's prophetic warning at this stage of their relationship. Surely the accuracy of her predictions had been proved time and time again.

He shook his head in wonder. "I don't believe it myself now, twenty years later," he admitted. "But you know, man, I kept saying to myself that it was just a *dream*. It wasn't like her usual predictions or her mind-reading. I mean, nearly every night you can see a lot of really nutty stuff in your dreams—thank the Lord they don't all come true!"

Bridget laughed. "He should have known that after all those years of having all these weird things happen to me, I *knew* the difference between a nutty dream and a prophetic one—but he just wouldn't listen."

"I wanted to see Chicago," was all James could offer in his defense.

"He coaxed and he begged and he pleaded with me to ride with him to Chicago," Bridget recalled with an exaggerated rolling of her eyes. "He kept asking me if I was going to let a silly dream interfere with an outing on such a gorgeous day. 'There won't be any wreck with old Steady Hand at the wheel,' he bragged."

Bridget's mother had been sitting on the front porch swing, reading the Sunday paper. "I think an automobile ride would be pleasant on such a fine day," she offered her opinion.

"Right on, Mrs. Muro," James had grinned, pleased to have her on his side. "And if we get started now, we can be back by just a little after midnight."

Against her better judgment and her psychic warning, Bridget finally yielded and followed the grinning James to his car.

"You drive carefully, Jimmy Galper," she admonished him, as she slid into the front seat.

And James did drive carefully—a point he has emphasized repeatedly—until they were halfway to Chicago. That was when they crashed into another car.

Bridget's head went through the windshield, and she staggered from James's automobile, wiping the blood out of her eyes.

"Dimly I saw the driver of the other car removing himself from behind the wheel with great effort," Bridget recalled. "The driver's wife was tugging at him with one good arm. Her other arm was bandaged and in a sling."

"While we sat in the emergency room, waiting to get Bridget's scalp stitched closed and my forehead bandaged, I kept begging her to forgive me for not listening to her dream warning," James said. "I said that I would never again doubt her predictions—especially when they concerned our welfare."

"And he never has," Bridget testified. "And Jimmy never again doubted that we were destined to be together."

James agreed. "And neither did I doubt her prediction that we would have three girls. I just started saving for their college fund."

Thirty-three

❖

Broadcasting on Destiny's Frequency

During a break between sessions when I was conducting an ESP seminar near Chicago in 1976, we began informally speaking about unusual things that various couples had done to spice up their relationships.

We had heard ideas such as feeding one another a meal using only fingers instead of utensils, leaving juicy love notes around the house in unexpected places, and wearing sexy lounging clothes to watch television.

Edgar, an attractive man in his early thirties, raised his hand and told of the time that he had rung their doorbell on Halloween. "And all I was wearing was a monster mask and a red jockstrap." He laughed at the memory. "And when Alice answered the doorbell, I yelled, 'Trick or treat, Baby!' She got so flustered, all she could say was, 'Where's your bag for the candy?'"

When the laughter from the seminar participants had died down, his wife added, "I think the neighbors were the ones who got the trick, looking at your bare bottom. I got the treat!"

Another time, according to Alice, Edgar had a grass skirt delivered to her office with a note telling her that he was preparing an exotic Hawaiian dinner at home and the only way she'd be admitted was if she was wearing the skirt and danced the hula.

"Edgar," I shook my head in mock wonder, "you have to be the Wizard of Wackiness and Marital Miracles to come up with these stunts to keep the sizzle in your marriage."

Alice, a full-figured redhead of seemingly perpetual cheerfulness, agreed. "He surely knows how to keep my fire glowing.

"One of my favorites was when he gave me a list before I left for work and asked me to pick up all the items he had written down before I came home. Well, it turned out to be a list for a sexy scavenger hunt. First, I went to a lingerie shop to pick up the nightie he'd bought for me. Then I went to the perfume section of a department store and got the bottles of perfume he'd reserved. And on and on, until I ended up at the liquor store to pick up the bottle of champagne that he had chilling.

"I arrived home to candlelight, soft music, a marvelous dinner, and the kids already at my mother's."

When everyone began to credit Edgar as the master of creating wild things to do to keep the spice in a marriage, he confessed that he had not always been Mr. Romantic, attuned to his lady love's needs and desires. He had, in fact, been a very self-centered and shallow young man—cold, emotionless, and intensely intellectual.

"I had to undergo a tough lesson about how we are all interconnected and how even our thoughts can affect the ones we love," Edgar said. "I had to find out for myself how it is possible to hurt the ones we love telepathically as well as emotionally."

Edgar Morris had always been a high academic achiever, and by the time he was a sophomore at a prestigious New England university, his classmates knew he raised the grading curve on any exam he took. For the academically oriented, Edgar Morris became *the* man to beat.

Near the end of his junior year, Edgar met Alice, and Cupid's deadly darts began to take a toll on his study time.

"The climax came after a big physics test," Edgar said. "When the grades were posted, I was mortified to see that I had received only an average mark. Some class members actually cheered, and nearly everyone was laughing at my humiliation. Later, one of my academic archrivals passed me in the corridor and whispered: 'Every Samson has his Delilah! I guess Alice is yours.' "

Edgar discovered to his embarrassment that he was not so academically aloof that he was immune to feeling the pinch of terrible pride.

"I went to a campus coffeehouse with Hank, my closest friend, and told him that I intended to break off with Alice," he recalled.

Hank was shocked. "Hey, c'mon, man. You can't dump a great chick like Alice because of a little nick in the old grade points. You've got to be kidding."

Edgar said that he was deadly serious. "I can't jeopardize my academic standing. I really don't know what got into me, wasting all those hours spending time with that girl."

"You're unreal," Hank protested, shaking his head. "Alice is one foxy lady. You'd be nuts to drop her. Just study harder, man."

Edgar said that he most certainly intended to study harder, immediately, to make up his low mark in physics class.

"Perhaps one day I might take up with Alice again when things are back on an even keel," Edgar said firmly. "But as of this afternoon, at 3:55 P.M., Alice and I are no longer a 'thing.' "

"When are you going to tell her?" Hank asked. "Are you going to take her to dinner and announce your breakup for dessert? Send her a note by Express Mail? Or maybe make a curt telephone call? Maybe you just won't call her at all but instead will let her suffer, not knowing what goes on in that cold, sadistic, intellectual brain of yours."

"Thanks Hank, old friend," Edgar glowered. "You make me sound like a complete jerk."

"Anyone who'd dump a terrific girl like Alice because he didn't get his usual highest mark on a test is a complete, total, quintessential jerk!"

Edgar bade his friend farewell and went back to his room to attack the books with vigor. He would notify Alice of the change in their relationship in his own good time.

"After two or three days had passed," he said, "I began to notice that I had not seen Alice in the coffeehouse or in the one class we shared. When I inquired about her, I learned from one of her friends that Alice lay in a near-coma at the campus health service.

"According to her friend, Alice had been perfectly well and her usual exuberant self until about four o'clock three days before. She had suddenly heaved a deep sigh and fainted. Neither the girls nor the campus doctor had been able to revive Alice to full consciousness for more than short periods at a time."

Edgar went directly to the health service and asked to see her.

"I really felt awful that she was ill—and so mysteriously so," he said. "Although I had made a vow to break off with her, I had not yet seen her to tell her of my intentions. But then, neither had I called her for several days."

When he entered her room, Edgar saw that she was lying on the bed in what appeared to be a light state of trance sleep. She became immediately animated the moment he stepped into the room.

"You deceitful creep!" she screamed at him. "So I no longer mean anything to you! So you're going to break off with me! You cruel . . . cruel . . ."

Edgar was struck dumb with astonishment. How had she known of his intentions? Surely Hank would not have informed her.

"I heard your voice inside my head," Alice said, weeping her humiliation and sorrow. "I heard your voice saying that you wanted to dump me. And all because you got a lower-than-usual grade on a test! I can't believe you're so shallow. I can't believe you'd blame your errors on me. After all we've meant to each other. . . ."

"For a moment, Alice couldn't think of anything more to say, so I awkwardly, stupidly, childishly asked her what on earth she was talking about," Edgar said. "How could she have gotten such notions?"

Alice blew her nose, then sat up in bed and looked me straight in the eye. "I don't know how I heard you, but I heard your voice saying you intended to break up with me."

Edgar wanted to know when she had supposedly heard his voice uttering such a statement.

"It was around four o'clock, three days ago," she answered. "I had just gotten back from my class in child psychology."

"Somehow," Edgar said, "Alice had picked up my thoughts and words telepathically. I was immediately touched by the fact that our psyches had so merged that we had become as one mind. The universe suddenly became a very different place to me, and I realized that we truly must be responsible for every thought we think and every word we utter. I also realized how very much Alice meant to me and how callous I had been toward her.

"I really didn't know what to say or think, so I walked over to her bed and kissed her and told her that there was nothing to worry about. I loved her and I would spend the rest of my life showing her, rather than telling her, how much I cherished her presence in my life.

"Alice was out of the infirmary that next morning," Edgar said by way of conclusion, "and for fifteen years now I have honored my vow. I always find the necessary hours to spend with Alice, and neither my work nor the love of my life is ever neglected."

Telepathy often delivers cries for help between people who deeply love each other, as the following two stories show.

When Evelyn Romano experienced extreme feelings of uneasiness and nausea, she somehow knew that the uncomfortable sensations were related to her absent husband.

"Tony was at work," she said. "Although he had looked well when he had left for his job, I *knew* he was ill. It was as if I could actually hear him saying, 'Evelyn, please come and get me. I'm terribly sick.' And then awful waves of nausea would hit me."

Evelyn reached the point where she could no longer bear her uneasiness, and she changed her clothes and drove to the factory where her husband worked. Asking at the desk, she was told Tony was not at his job, but was in the dispensary.

When she walked into the dispensary, she found her husband sitting down, extremely pale and in great pain. The nurse on duty said she'd been trying to call Evelyn at home.

Two of Tony's co-workers stood on either side of him, ready to assist, if need be. Evelyn accepted their offer to help her husband into their car.

"Honey, what made you come after me?" Tony asked, once she had him home and in bed.

"I really don't know," she admitted. "I felt I was just being silly at first . . . or coming down with some bug myself. But it became increasingly clear to me that the terrible feeling of uneasiness was related to you and that you were sick and in pain."

"Well, sweetheart, you were certainly right," Tony sighed. "You came just when I needed you. You amazed everyone when you came walking into the dispensary while the nurse was trying to call you at home."

In the case of Shirley Nakashima, a telepathic call from her husband's hospital bed prompted her to take the action necessary to save his life.

"Nick had come down with a bad case of flu," she said. "I was staying at home with our children while he received medical attention in the hospital. I had just started to drift off to sleep that night when I clearly heard Nick's voice calling to me, 'Honey, I'm dying! Help me, help me! I'm dying but no one knows it!'"

Shirley didn't hesitate. She saw no need to attempt to rationalize the source of the voice. She knew that she had not been dreaming, and she knew that she had heard the voice of her husband.

It was after midnight when she arrived at the hospital.

"I was coldly informed that visiting hours were over. Just as coldly, I insisted that they examine Nick," she said.

"Again, in a crisp, antiseptic manner, I was told that a night nurse had just looked in on my husband and that he was sleeping restfully. I was told that I should go home and leave the medical care of Nick to professionals."

Shirley would not be put off.

"I insisted that they call a doctor to examine Nick, or I would run into his room and look at him myself."

Shirley concedes that she is a rather small woman, but the nurses saw the determination in her eyes and could see that she meant exactly what she said. "My fierce look made me seven feet tall!"

The nurses summoned a doctor, who listened impatiently to Shirley's pleas.

"I know that it was just to humor me and to shut me up that he finally agreed to look in on Nick," Shirley said. "I waited at the desk for a few minutes, then I felt very strongly that my husband needed help immediately."

She brushed aside a nurse as she ran up the stairs toward Nick's room. "I heard the doctor say in a harsh whisper, 'Good Lord! This man is dying!'"

Quick work on the part of the doctor and the attending nurses saved Nick Nakashima's life.

Later, when he had regained consciousness, he told Shirley how he had lain there, knowing in the central core of his being that he was dying.

"I desperately sent a cry for help to you at home," Nick said. "We have always been so close, always knowing what the other would say before the words were spoken. I *knew* you would hear my thoughts and come to save me."

I am certain that many of us have known couples who have grown so close over the years that it is difficult to visualize one of them without the other. It may well be that such couples form an enormously powerful telepathic bond that becomes an integral element in their personal testament that they were destined to be together.

Highly respected experimental psychologist Dr. Stanley Krippner has expressed his opinion that the scientific establishment will soon have to revise its image of what it is to be human on the basis of telepathic evidence. At present, Dr. Krippner observes, psychology and psychiatry view each person as an entity separated from everyone else, as an alienated being.

"Telepathy," Dr. Krippner said, "may teach us that in the basic fabric of life, everything and everyone is linked, that man is continuously enmeshed, that he is always an integral part of all life on the face of the earth. So far, the scientific establishment has ignored this possibility; it will, for one thing, refute many of their basic concepts."

As the more than 20,000 respondents to our "Steiger Questionnaire of Mystical, Paranormal, and UFO Experiences" have testified, they are not at all respectful of the opposing dicta of scientific orthodoxy that decree that mental transmissions and receptions between humans are "impossible." In fact, 90 percent of our respondents said that they had experienced at least one dramatic episode of telepathic communication. We are certain there are hundreds of thousands—if not millions—of men and women who have discovered through some profound telepathic link-up in their own lives that they are, indeed, "continuously enmeshed."

* * *

Thousands of laboratory tests have indicated a number of interesting facts concerning the conditions under which telepathy—and, in general, all testable psychic phenomena—work.

Distance appears to have no effect on telepathy or clairvoyance. Equally remarkable results have been achieved when the receiver was a yard away from the agent or when the experimenters were separated by many hundreds of miles. As Dr. S. G. Soal, a British researcher, has observed, "In telepathic communication, it is personality, or the linkage of personalities, that counts, not the spatial separation of bodies."

Attitude is of great importance in achieving successful telepathic communication. Cheerful, friendly folks almost always achieve better results in laboratory ESP tests.

It has also been demonstrated many times that those men and women who "believe" in their psychic abilities score consistently higher than skeptics and doubters.

Spontaneous psychic communication seems to work best under conditions that Dr. Jan Ehrenwald termed a "state of psychological inadequacy." Naming this state of psychic readiness the "minus function," Dr. Ehrenwald believes that very often "... a necessary condition for telepathic functioning is a state of inadequacy or deficiency, such as loss or clouding of the consciousness," *i.e.,* sleep, hypnosis, trance, and so forth.

It is also fascinating to note that on the average, a man is more effective as the agent (the sender) and a woman is more effective as the receiver. This observation seems to apply to spontaneous instances of telepathy as well as to roles assumed under laboratory conditions. Other controlled experiments demonstrate that receivers often achieve better results if the agent is of the opposite sex.

All of which may be additional indications that such psychic abilities as telepathy are aspects of a fundamental and natural force that must be included in any total concept of humanhood and our world.

Thirty-four

❖

A Karmic Love Bond

"Seriously, Brad," Diana Coronado told me, "it really is possible to die of a broken heart."

I nodded my agreement. "Yes, I am familiar with serious scientific research into so-called 'voodoo' deaths, or 'broken hearts.'"

Diana had entered my office in Scottsdale, Arizona, with her handkerchief already dabbing at her tear-rimmed brown eyes. She was weeping quite openly when she sat down. She had made an appointment to explore the possibility of a past life that might be impinging on her present life experience, but it appeared that she had another agenda she first needed to satisfy.

"There's a doctor who's done experiments with both humans and rats, and he's found an area in the brain that controls the heart," Diana informed me, after she had regained her composure.

"I believe it's called the 'insular cortex,'" I said.

Diana paid little attention to my interruption. "Well, this part of the brain is very sensitive to stress, and when it is stressed, it accelerates the beating of the heart. If this area, this insular cortex, should suffer extreme emotional stress, it can cause sudden death."

"So I've heard."

"So that's very likely what happens when someone dies for no apparent reason after they've lost a lover or a spouse through death or the sudden termination of a love affair," she said. "They've literally died of a broken heart."

"All right, Diana." I leaned back in my chair. "I appreciate your flying in all the way from Houston and paying my fee just to keep my files up to date on medical research."

She blinked in astonishment, completely missing the teasing nature of my remark. "I've come here to get your help so my heart doesn't break. I know that William and I must have some terrible karma to work out."

I knew Diana was no past-life groupie flying from one researcher to another. She was stylishly dressed, about thirty-five, and a businesswoman.

"I'll do my very best to see that you won't die of a broken heart, Diana," I promised.

Diana told me she'd been haunted by a recurring dream since early adolescence. In it, she saw herself dying of a fever in a crudely built cabin.

"I sense other people in the room, but my attention is riveted by a man who stands at the foot of my bed, looking down on me with extreme distaste. He seems somehow afraid of me, as though I have some dread disease he doesn't want to be exposed to. He turns his back to me and the others and walks out the door. Then I see flames crackling up around my bed.

"That's when I wake, screaming my terror and my sorrow," Diana said. "I feel the man was my husband. I know we lived in a crude cabin; before he deserted me, he set fire to the cabin to destroy both me and my disease."

Although she'd first had the disturbing dream when she was

around eleven or twelve, Diana told me that she'd had an active adolescence and was not affected negatively by the vision.

"I firmly believed it to be a memory of a past life," she said. "I suppose I developed a healthy respect for fire and I was perhaps overly concerned about communicable diseases. I remember that I would go to great lengths to avoid contact with anyone who suffered a cold, but such an idiosyncrasy didn't cripple my social development."

Diana had married soon after graduation from college, and her union with Joseph Coronado produced two daughters, Beth and Lynn. Diana and Joe had legally separated nearly two years before. Numerous attempts at reconciliation had failed.

"I know our split was caused by my work," she said. "Joe wanted to marry Betty Homemaker. He didn't really believe I'd go back to work after Lynn was born. I know that he never believed I'd ever make more money than he did."

Seven months ago, Diana met William.

"He was getting off an elevator when I first saw him," she said. "His eyes seemed to pierce my very essence. I know that may sound like a purple passage from a romance novel, but I don't really care. I stood there as if I'd been turned to stone. Those were the eyes I had seen so often in my recurring dream. Those were the eyes of the husband who looked on me with revulsion and left me to die in a burning cabin."

Diana admitted that a strange rush of both love and hatred filled her trembling body. "I wanted to kiss him and strike him down at the same time. Somehow, I managed to push past him and get into the elevator."

When she returned to her office, she was shocked to find him waiting for her. "I know that I must have paled. I couldn't even manage to ask him his business. On the other hand, he seemed oblivious to my discomfort. He stood, flashed me a professional smile, and introduced himself as the new sales representative for one of our largest suppliers."

Diana remembered that she mumbled something that she hoped was reasonably appropriate, then sat down weakly behind her desk.

"When I began to calm down and gather some self-control, I wanted to laugh at the way Fate had reversed our positions," Diana said. "If I chose, I could cancel our order with that company and virtually destroy the man's career as a sales rep."

As they talked, she noticed William studying her. "I know this'll probably sound like a classic traveling salesman's line." He had grinned self-consciously. "But don't I know you from somewhere?"

"I think you probably do," Diana said frankly. For a moment, she thought she might blurt out the whole incredible story, but discretion prevailed.

"Are you originally from Houston?" he asked, seeking an answer. "We didn't go to college together, did we? I usually have such a good memory."

That might have been true, Diana mused, but did he have a memory that could stretch back a hundred years or more?

She accepted his invitation to dinner, and later, after several glasses of wine, she confronted him with her memory of his desertion and terrible deed in another lifetime.

William didn't run from the restaurant, shaking his head over his bizarre dinner with a lovely lunatic.

"He actually seemed contrite," Diana told me. "He listened to the account very attentively, and when I had concluded, he expressed his sorrow for having committed such a barbaric act."

I was skeptical. "Are you certain he hadn't had too much wine?"

Diana admitted freely that they had drunk a lot, but she denied that William could have been too drunk to follow the finer— and more startling—points of their conversation.

"Then you're telling me William believes in reincarnation?" I asked.

"He said he was open to the subject."

"So open that he didn't mind being called a vicious murdering swine over dinner? So open that he sat calmly through your accusations of betrayal and murder?"

"He said that while he couldn't imagine doing such a vile thing, he wanted to make reparation in this life," Diana said.

I could see that, in her mind, Diana was convinced she'd been reunited with William so he might work out his Karma and pay his debt to the Universe for his having deserted her in a prior life experience. She'd had the recurring dream to fortify her conviction.

I told Diana I was sorry, but I couldn't be certain William actually remembered a past life shared with her. He could be only a clever opportunist who sought to make his present life a bit more interesting.

"Not only does he have what to him may be nothing more than a flaky New Age excuse to have an affair with you," I pointed out quite bluntly, "it might cause you, as the buyer for the department store, to order larger shipments."

Diana's eyes misted over, and she reached once again for her handkerchief. "That's why I came to you, Brad. I wanted to be sure."

I was relieved to see that she was not that gullible. I reminded her that I was not a therapist.

"I know that." She nodded. "But I've read a number of your books, and I know that you do research with regressions into past lives. Besides, Joe has reentered the scene, and it seems as though a reconciliation might be possible. I want you to regress me so that I might determine which man is truly my destiny—William or Joseph."

I was willing to attempt a past-life exploration with her, but I stressed that any life-altering decision derived from the experience would be totally of her own volition.

* * *

While there are few tales more romantic than those of reincarnated lovers who have once again managed to find each other over the span of centuries, caution must be exercised so we don't fall into the trap of believing that every person who projects physical attractiveness or sex appeal to us indicates a past-life relationship between us.

I have conducted many regressions for people with marital maladjustment, emotional entanglements, and sexual traumas. Many obtained a release of present life phobias by reliving the origin of their trauma in some alleged former existence. I found it extremely effective to focus on the particular past life that I call the Karmic Counterpart, that former existence that appears to be directly responsible for the troublesome imbalance and/or confusion in the subject's present life experience. In many cases, we needed only one session to enable the person to see that he or she had been unknowingly allowing unconscious memories of a prior existence to threaten or to ruin a fruitful relationship or a productive existence in the present life experience. I decided I would use the Karmic Counterpart technique with Diana.

I used a relaxation technique to place Diana in a deeply altered state of consciousness.

Once she was as relaxed as possible, I called upon the real Diana within to become aware of a beautiful figure robed in violet standing near her tranquil, resting physical body. This beautiful figure, I told Diana, was her spiritual guide, her guardian angel, who would take the *Real Diana* out of her physical shell and travel with her to a higher dimension where she would be able to receive knowledge of a past life that she needed to know about—a past life that had greatly influenced her present life experience.

This particular past life, I told the entranced Diana, would be one in which she would see a good many individuals who had come with her to her present life experience to complete a task left unfinished, to learn a lesson left unaccomplished. *Whatever* she saw, I stressed, would be for her good and for her gaining. She had nothing to fear, I reassured her, for her guardian angel would be ever near, allowing nothing to harm her.

I moved Diana back in time and space to the past life that was primarily responsible for her present life experience. I instructed her to see the reasons why her soul chose the parents, the brothers or sisters, the friends, the lovers, the nationality, the race, the sex, the talents, the occupation that she had, and to see the soul-chosen purpose for the agonies, troubles, pains, and griefs that had entered her life.

When I asked her to speak and to identify where she was in terms of country and year, Diana said that she *felt* she was in Georgia, in about the year 1850.

Brad: What sex are you?

Diana: Female.

Brad: As you view yourself now, how old are you? And please describe yourself.

Diana: I'm in my late thirties, maybe forty. I am not too tall, and I have dark brown hair streaked with gray. I have blue eyes.

Brad: What is your name in that lifetime?

Diana: Magdalena . . . Magdalena Esta . . . Maybe Estabrook . . . Esterbrook. My back hurts.

Brad: Why does your back hurt? Go deep into the memory. *Be* Magdalena once again. Feel what she felt; know what she knew.

Diana: I've been carrying heavy pails of water in the slave quarters and lifting the coloreds who are too weak and helping them to get into their beds.

Brad: Why are you doing this?

Diana: There's some kind of terrible plague that is sweeping over the plantations here in Georgia. It's been striking down both fieldhands and house slaves. I'm doing my best to care for them . . . to help them get well. A lot of them are dying. A lot of white folks are dying, too. I'm doing my best to nurse them.

Brad: That must be a big job. No wonder your back hurts. Isn't there anyone to help you? What about your husband?

Diana: Arthur was working alongside me until he took sick. Most of our neighbors say that they're just slaves. They say we're damn fools to take any chance of catching the plague. Just let 'em die and burn the bodies. But me and Arthur believe that they're people, too. And we believe it's our Christian duty and our responsibility to look after them and care for them. Naomi, one of the house slaves, and Benjamin, her husband, been working right beside me day and night ever since Arthur collapsed.

I asked Diana to go even deeper into her past-life memory and to see if any one of those people—her husband, Naomi, or Benjamin—had come with her to her present life experience. Her features assumed an expression of shock and surprise.

"Arthur . . . he's my husband Joseph!" she gasped. "I can't believe it. And . . . and Naomi . . . she's Beth. And Lynn, my goodness to glory, she was Benjamin."

Tears were running unchecked over Diana's cheeks. Once a subject has been placed in an altered state of consciousness and regressed to a prior life experience, things don't always turn out the way the subject expected. I knew that prior to my placing her in a hypnotic state, Diana had believed William had been her past-life husband.

I told Diana to move ahead in that time one week.

Diana: I'm sick! Oh, Lordy, I am sick!

Brad: Did you catch the plague?

Diana: Dear God, I must have. I am really sick . . . I . . . can't talk . . .

I instructed her that all pain, distress, and agony would be taken from her and she would be able to speak freely.

Diana: Arthur . . . I think Arthur is dead. We're in one of the slave cabins. I was nursing Hannibal and his wife and child when I just keeled over. Hannibal, bless his heart, let me lie down in his bed. I . . . I'm too weak to move.

I inquired about Naomi and Benjamin.

Diana: Benjamin is either dead or dying; I don't know which. Naomi is here with me. She's still strong. No plague gonna be able to get her. Hey, there's someone coming!

Brad: Someone coming to help you?

Diana: I should say not. It's our overseer, Mr. Napier, he's got a torch in his hand. He's cursing Arthur and me for being such fools. He says we gave our lives for nothing . . . for trying to help a bunch of slaves.

Brad: What's he doing with the torch?

Diana: He's says he's going to burn down the slave quarters. That's the only way to get rid of the plague on the plantation. He says he's gonna burn us along with it. He's looking at me with such contempt and disgust. Then he sets fire to the cabin! He's going to burn me alive! Naomi tries to beat out the fire with her feet and hands and a blanket. Mr. Napier clubs her down with the butt of his shotgun. He hits her until she lies still. Flames are all around me now . . ."

I moved Diana ahead until she was past her death agony. When she said that her spirit was floating above the scene of fiery destruction and she felt unemotional and detached from the terrible events below, I told her she'd be able to see clearly Mr. Napier had come with her to her present life experience.

Diana: It's William. I knew him by the eyes. It's been those cruel eyes looking at me with distaste and disgust that have haunted me all my life.

Before I brought Diana back to the present, I told her that her angel guide would allow her to receive any lesson or teaching that she should know for her good.

"My spiritual guide showed me that Joseph had felt insecure when I'd received a promotion," she said. "This triggered his past-life memory of the life in which I took it upon myself to attempt to care for the victims of the plague. I had asserted myself more than the average woman of that time period, and I had paid for my independent action with my life. Somehow, he had become insecure and frightened that my rising above the crowd, so to speak, would once again cause my destruction. These fears led to the senseless arguments that brought about our separation."

How did she feel now about her unresolved karma with William?

"I'm going to keep him at arm's length and maintain our relationship at a professional level," she answered without hesitation. "He has yet to receive any kind of noticeable level of higher awareness. Perhaps, slowly, I can help him raise his consciousness.

"I can see clearly now that Joe really is my destiny. I know now that we were brought together in our present lives to continue our love bond. Thank you, Brad, for not allowing me to die of a broken heart!"

Thirty-five

❖

The Romantic Mystery of Soul Mates

When I met Bix Carter in 1977, he was in his early sixties and internationally recognized for his ability to blend aspects of traditional African art with contemporary surrealistic expression. We had become friends, and whenever I was in San Francisco, I tried to make time to visit the combination studio and apartment he shared with his third wife, Lois, an author of children's books. One night after I had lectured at a metaphysical conference, a group of us followed Bix and Lois back to their place.

"Brad, you were so correct during the question-and-answer period when you cautioned that young woman about pursuing the man she believed to be her soul mate," Alisha, an astrologer, said to me, as we talked over wine and sliced apples and cheese. "Unless they were fated to be together again in this life, she could truly be opening herself up to a lot of heartache."

I was pleased with her agreement. "I always caution people about the soul mate concept. So many unscrupulous Don Juan types use the old 'You are my soul mate' or 'We must have been lovers in a past life' lines just to chalk up another sexual conquest."

Sandy, a past-life reader from the Bay area, asked, "But you *do* believe in soul mates, don't you, Brad?"

"Yes, I believe we may come together with our 'other half,' in many lifetimes, for the growth of our souls. I just think we should be more judicious in awarding the title. I know some metaphysicians who seem to have a 'soul mate of the month.' "

Alisha laughed at my observation along with the others, then shook her head in sad reflection. "You're right. Too many guys and gals in the New Age field use the old soul mate line as a justification for their current love affair."

Bix Carter laughed. "That is so disgustingly true," he said. "Yet no tale is quite so romantic as that of two lovers who have found each other again after a past lifetime of love."

He reached inside his coat pocket and withdrew his wallet. "I recognized Lois as my soul mate the moment I saw her," he said, handing me a photograph.

The photograph was of a very young girl standing at a ship's railing. Just to her side was an older woman. The picture was very wrinkled and had been pressed between adhesive plastic sheets to preserve it. At first I thought that it might be a snapshot of one of their daughters, but the picture was too old, older than either of their teenaged girls. Judging from the older woman's dress, I guessed the picture had been taken sometime in the forties.

"That's a picture of Lois when she was nine," Bix said, after we had studied the photograph. "I took that picture the first time I set eyes on her because I recognized her immediately as my soul mate."

Everyone knew Bix was a couple of decades older than his wife, so a lot of silent arithmetic was going on inside a lot of heads.

"I really was nine years old in that photograph," Lois smiled affirmation. "Bix took that picture in 1940, when my family traveled by boat to Hawaii."

"I was going on twenty-seven," Bix said. "I had already knocked around the country for quite a few years when I got a job as a merchant seaman sailing out of San Francisco."

Alisha's eyes were wide with amazement. "And you, as a grown man of twenty-seven, took one look at this nine-year-old girl—and *knew* she was your soul mate?"

Bix nodded. "I was getting ready to load some cargo into the hold when I happened to glance toward the gangplank and see a family of five coming on board—husband, wife, two young boys, one little girl. When I saw that little girl, it was as if she was suddenly bathed in a bright, golden light—and I knew that I had rediscovered my soul mate."

Sandy could not suppress a giggle. "That's all well and good, Bix, but what did you do with such knowledge? You surely didn't run up and try to hit on a nine-year-old! There are laws against such things."

The man who had accompanied Sandy agreed. "She was even younger than Lolita," he scolded Bix in mock seriousness. "Bad form."

Bix shrugged his broad shoulders. "Obviously, I didn't want to be thrown overboard and fed to the sharks as a pervert. So I did nothing. Nothing, that is, except take this picture one sunny afternoon."

Bix is a natural storyteller who loves to play to an audience. It didn't take any coaxing to get him to tell us the story of their second meeting.

Two weeks after the United States entered the war in December 1941, Bix enlisted in the army. He was wounded in 1944 during heavy fighting in Italy and sent back to the States.

"After my discharge in '45, I started painting. I had experienced a series of visions while I was in the hospital that showed me how I could use my African roots in new and exciting ways. I had my first one-man show in New York in 1950, then moved back to San Francisco."

Lois was the daughter of teachers who had accepted positions in the Honolulu school system. Although her parents looked upon the job in Oahu as a temporary change of scene before a return to the mainland, the attack on Pearl Harbor altered their plans significantly.

"We became permanent residents," she said. "My parents and one of my brothers still live on the big island of Hawaii. I returned to the mainland to attend Berkeley in 1950. I wanted to be a professional painter, but I knew I wasn't good enough to be more than a weekend dabbler. I decided to write about the arts and contemporary culture instead."

In 1963, Lois was given an assignment by a national magazine to interview Bix Carter.

"By that time," Bix chuckled, "I had gone through two wives who seemed dedicated to the proposition that my life should be a living hell on earth. I was not looking for romance, believe me. I had decided to devote all my energies to my painting. But when Lois walked into my studio, I swear to God that I recognized her at once. I was fifty-two . . . she was thirty-four . . . but I knew exactly who she was. She was my soul mate. And that same bright golden glow was all around her!"

Lois had arrived at his studio and nervously approached the celebrated painter with the tentative preamble: "I hear you're easy to talk with."

Bix laughed at the memory and gave his wife an affectionate squeeze. "I said, 'Sister, I've got a whole lot of talking to do with you. I've been waiting for you to walk through my door for twenty-five years!'"

Lois reached up and kissed her husband's cheek. "I thought it was some corny line until he reached in his pocket and dug out that picture."

Sandy wanted to know if Lois had recognized herself in the old photo.

"Of course I did," Lois said. "But I wanted to know how the hell he had been able to get into our family scrapbooks."

When Bix had explained and told her the entire story of his twenty-five years of waiting for her to reappear in his life, she was so stunned she postponed the interview for a couple of days.

"That night, I experienced a powerful past-life dream that identified Bix as my husband in ancient Greece. It was an idyllic life experience, filled with love and intimacy. I woke up crying, and I could hardly wait to return to Bix's studio. Later, during a regression, we both recalled other past lives in Egypt and Peru. We really were born again to be together!"

Someone asked why there had been such a disparity in their ages in their present life experience and why it had taken them so long to be reunited.

"I don't think anyone has the answers to those kinds of questions," Bix said. "The important thing is that we did find each other somewhere along the way and that we are privileged to journey on our earthwalk together just as long as we can."

There can be no question in anyone's mind that Bix and Lois Carter are destined lovers and that they truly are soul mates. But not all soul mate reunions are as smoothly accomplished. Witness the following account from a well-known professional educator:

I met my twin spirit in 1959. I knew in an instant that I had known him for 10,000 years. At that time I had no knowledge whatsoever of psychic matters—nor did I know anything of twin spirits. I simply felt a pull so strong that I was overwhelmed. He was a teacher and I was his student.

After the initial meeting, we did not see each other for several years. But he was brought back into my life at least two dozen times for extended periods of time. We have worked together, have traveled the world together, and are aware of our twin spirit relationship. However, even though there are pleasant memories, the relationship has been a tortured one as well.

My soul mate, a brilliant academic, does not have a high enough level of awareness to pursue our twin spirit relationship to its zenith. Our energy together is so strong that it frightens him—and he must back away from it whenever he can to recover. I have tried through the years to raise his level of awareness—and have succeeded to a great degree.

About four years ago, I decided never to see him again. It was just too painful for me. But we are working together again in very close proximity on a number of important projects. My family and friends are afraid because along with his support through thirty-three years, there has also been betrayal.

We are completely telepathic. I can "pick him up" regardless of where in the world he is. This telepathy has caused us problems because I think he has said something aloud when he has only thought it.

Our relationship has torn me up, but I finally learned to live with it—by continuing to love him, but breaking the attachment to his karmic destiny. By doing that, I no longer anguish when we are not together—nor do I have dreams of what could be or what might have been.

I have no idea what the future holds for us. Perhaps we'll only remain friends in this lifetime. The universe works in strange ways, and I can't predict what might happen.

I'm really happy that I met my twin spirit, because I know what it feels like to be truly happy with the opposite sex. I also know what it's like to have my soul energy multiplied by ten so that I feel like I'm soaring when we are together. My life has changed enormously since I met my soul mate three decades ago—and over all, it has been a fortuitous encounter.

My friend Benjamin Smith is also one who knows that he met and married his soul mate—but it was not ordained that they should stay together in this lifetime. Ben told me their story:

I first met Nancy when I was president of a service club and was interviewed by her on a local television station in Eugene, Oregon. I fell in love with her on that day, but I didn't follow up on my feelings because she was wearing a wedding ring (even though I found out later that she wasn't married at the time). I admired her from afar, and I went through another marriage before I asked her out.

On our first date, we had an almost instant bonding, and we stayed up until 5 A.M. just talking . . . within four months we were living together, and we were married the following March. It had been ten years from the first time I'd met and fallen in love with her until I married my soul mate.

I believe a soul mate is someone with whom you have built up a karmic bond over several lifetimes. Upon investigation, Nancy and I discovered that we had spent at least seven lifetimes together.

We were able to communicate without speaking. Once we went on a two-hour drive and spoke perhaps a dozen words out loud—but we held an intensely deep conversation for the entire drive. Many times I would know what she wanted or what she was going to say before she uttered a word.

Ours wasn't necessarily the happiest of relationships, but it was the deepest love I have ever felt—and the most complete psychic connection I have experienced. I learned a great deal in the relationship, and I'm certain she did as well.

We explored metaphysics together, and we joined a group of fellow explorers who met weekly for several years.

I knew a year before she did that we had to go our separate ways. We had completed what we had come together to do. But I also knew that she was the one who had to make the split. I had left her in previous lifetimes and I couldn't do it this time around.

Our marriage lasted ten years—and our friendship still endures. She has remarried and lives in the Southeast, but we still correspond; and I know that if I really needed her, she would be there for me—and I for her. We became close enough that we lived together in the same house for about a year after the divorce became final.

I still love Nancy a great deal, even though I know that we've completed what we needed to do in this lifetime and that we had to go different directions. Someday I know that we will be together again, but not in this lifetime—and perhaps not even on this level of knowing.

Thirty-six

❖

The Universe Brought Him to Her

Clarisa Bernhardt is the only psychic-sensitive in modern times to predict an earthquake to the day, the location, the magnitude—and even the minute. The astonishing documented prediction was made on her radio show *Exploration* and referred exactly to the 1974 Thanksgiving Day quake in San Jose, California.

Although the attractive blonde bears the oft-bestowed title of "Earthquake Lady" with a tolerant smile, her paranormal talents are not limited to quake predictions. She has demonstrated an additional use of ESP by locating lost people and by cooperating with law enforcement agencies as a psychic sleuth. She is regularly consulted by business executives who seek her assistance in making top-level decisions, and she is an extremely gifted medium.

I first became acquainted with Clarisa in 1973, when I was researching my book *Medicine Power: The American Indian's Revival of His Spiritual Heritage and Its Relevance for Modern Man* (Doubleday, 1974). Clarisa, who is half Cherokee, the granddaughter of Chief John Muskrat of Tahlequah, Oklahoma, told me of her experience in a haunted California ranchhouse with the ghost of a Shumash chief who liked to greet guests with a hotfoot.

As one of the spirit's victims put it, "You'll believe it for your-self after he comes into the room while you're in bed and burns your foot. Then nobody will believe *you!*"

Clarisa's friend Flo owned the house but had not experienced any unusual spirit phenomena until after she'd remodeled the place—then no one could spend the night there without waking up with red marks on fingers or toes and without experiencing burning sensations.

"The house had been built over a Shumash graveyard," Clarisa recalled. "You could feel a presence in that house as soon as you entered. Since I have the spiritual privilege of seeing people on the other plane, I met the chief in the hallway, where there was a very high vibration. The Shumash were apparently a very evolved people. At first the spirit was hostile to me, but after a couple of visits, he was all right."

I had grieved with Clarisa when she'd lost her husband, Russ; and I had commiserated with her when she'd later found herself in an unproductive and negative relationship. I could not have been happier when she met and married Norman, her present husband.

"He's a wonderful human being and a very spiritual man," she said. "It's been a great blessing in my life that the universe brought me Norman, and I'm thankful for the events that occurred at just the right time in my life to allow me to make the right decisions. You and Sherry know that it's important to be with a person who's spiritual, as well as interested in worldly things, who treats you well, and who professes to be in love with you."

Clarisa said that the manner in which she first met Norman and the strange way they got together was like something right out of a novel.

In the summer of 1984, Clarisa's good friends, the scientists Patrick and Gael Crystal Flanagan invited her to present a lecture on "Earthquake Predictions and Visions" at a one-day seminar they were hosting in Scottsdale, Arizona.

After she'd completed her presentation and had instructed audience members on how they might apply the sixth sense in a practical way in everyday life, Clarisa noticed one man standing back from the others crowding around her for the opportunity to speak with her personally. She could not help noticing him, for he had an extremely brilliant auric field surrounding him. Since childhood, Clarisa has had the ability to perceive the human aura, the magnetic field every individual possesses.

"As he walked toward me," she recalled, "I thought he had the most engaging smile, and he looked as though he'd just stepped out of a men's fashion magazine. He was very handsome and very magnetic."

He introduced himself as Norman, a Canadian from Winnipeg, and he requested a psychic reading. He explained that he was short on time, as he had to catch a plane to Mexico early the next morning.

Later that afternoon, they met outside the conference room, and Clarisa attuned herself to receive the answers to his many questions.

As he rose to leave, he looked at her very intently and asked a final question: "Do you feel I'll ever meet someone very special in my life?"

Clarisa took a deep breath and gazed steadily into Norman's aura. "As I continued to gaze, a figure began to become visible. The features became very clear. In fact, it was like looking into a mirror!"

She could not suppress a sudden gasp of surprise. It couldn't be! But the image in her vision was . . . *her own!*

"Is something wrong?" Norman wanted to know.

"Oh, no, nothing at all," Clarisa said, trying desperately to regain her composure. "I . . . I see that . . . in the next twelve months, approximately, you will definitely meet this person."

"But how will I know her?" Norman asked, wanting to be certain he didn't miss his golden opportunity.

Clarisa was in a quandary. She certainly was not going to give Norman a description of herself.

"Oh, you'll know her," Clarisa finally answered, hoping a general reply would suffice. "Just follow your heart."

"But what does she look like?" Norman persisted.

Clarisa hesitated, praying for the right words to come out of her mouth. "Well, she's sort of blondish."

Clarisa is very blond and she didn't want to push her own image on Norman. "But . . . maybe more of a sandy blonde . . . a sandy blonde leaning to a darker blonde . . . sometimes bordering on a light brown. Yes, that's it . . . light brown."

Norman smiled. "Sounds good," he said, as he walked away.

All that day Clarisa remained baffled by the unusual experience. Why had she seen herself in this stranger's aura? Certainly he had an extraordinarily positive vibration around him, but he had struck a most peculiar chord in her heart, as if he were someone very special to her.

She had always believed in maintaining a professional and impersonal attitude toward her clients. She had been nothing but professional with Norman, but she had never felt like this before. She had made it a point never to allow her personal feelings to cause any distraction from her work.

Perhaps she needed to take a vacation. She had to admit that she had been under stress because of an unhappy personal relationship. She had been too vulnerable during a period when she was recovering from the loss of her late husband.

"I became aware that it was a beautiful day in Scottsdale. As I rose from the area where I had given Norman his reading and placed various papers in my briefcase, I decided it had been very nice to meet him, and I hoped all good things happened for him. We were worlds apart. There was no advantage to be wasting time with 'what ifs,' so I flew back to California."

In the months to follow, Clarisa was surprised to receive a couple of telephone calls from Norman. She was delighted to hear that he was pleased with the information and guidance she'd given him on several of his projects. He also arranged a telephone consultation with her for additional psychic guidance. Before he ended the call, he told her he'd missed seeing her at another conference in Scottsdale.

In August 1985, she experienced a vivid dream of being in an elegant airplane. She was seated on the aisle, and when a voice announced, "You are to change now," she immediately got up and was ushered into an extravagantly decorated section of the craft. Just as she was settling into the harmony and comfort of the plush environment, the plane suddenly encountered turbulence—and she awakened.

She knew the dream had to be symbolic, and she was certainly going through a period of turbulance in her personal life. Feeling too off balance to be objective enough to use her own psychic talents, she called her friend Gael Crystal Flanagan.

"Gael, who has her own special brand of spiritual magic, said I should come to visit them in Arizona. Then she asked if I remembered Norman."

Gael told Clarisa that Norman had asked about her when he'd attended the Flanagans' conference that summer.

"He said he found you fascinating," Gael continued, "and if you hadn't been involved in a relationship, he'd have liked to have had the opportunity to get to know you better. He even went so far as to say that under the right circumstances, he felt he could easily fall in love with you."

Clarisa listened to Gael without saying a word. She remembered how nice Norman had seemed.

She was startled to hear Gael telling her to stay by the phone. "I'm making a call, and I'll get back to you."

"Gael," she protested, "you're not calling Norman?"

The telephone line only buzzed at her. Gael had hung up.

Twenty minutes later, Clarisa answered the phone to hear Norman's voice.

"Although I was a bit embarrassed," Clarisa admitted, "his openness and his charm quickly put me at ease. Norman said I should come to Canada to visit him for a few days—no strings attached. The vibrations felt very good again. I accepted Norman's invitation; in less than forty-eight hours, I was on the plane flying to Canada—and into the most wonderful and romantic adventure of my life. And it continues to this day, ten years later!"

Before Clarisa's visit ended, she and Norman decided they wanted to be together to see how things would work out.

"We traveled to Arizona for the winter, first visiting the area in Scottsdale where we'd first met, then spending five marvelous months in Sedona.

"When we arrived in Sedona, we stayed for a few days at the lovely Phantom Ranch, atop the mesa near the airport. We were so pleased when Gael and Patrick arranged to meet us for an afternoon. Gael brought us a gift of some crystals she had taken with them on their wedding night in the great Pyramid at Giza.

"That night, in meditation, I received a beautiful vision of having known and loved Norman in many lifetimes, including one in Egypt and another when we were students in an ancient Aztec pyramid.

"I am so thankful that Norman and I were able to meet in this lifetime and to be together," Clarisa said. "He has been a great inspiration to me. There has been an incredible magic between us . . . and it continues!"

Thirty-seven

Two Souls Reconnect

Readers will recall that I said in chapter one it was at an event sponsored by my friend Stan Kalson that I encountered the lovely blonde, Mary-Caroline Meadows, whose physical body was temporarily usurped by an angelic being to see that I got together with Sherry Hansen. When Stan and I later discussed this miracle of love, I asked if he'd consider sharing his own story of how he reconnected with his past-life love, Lee Lagé.

When Stan and I first met in 1977, he was already recognized as an authority in the field of holistic health, and soon after our meeting he traveled worldwide, teaching concepts of nutrition and energy healing.

After a few years of using Phoenix, Arizona, as a base, Stan became undecided as to whether he should stay in Phoenix to continue his networking activities or return to Honolulu. He remembered the decision as a truly tough one.

"I attended the Human Unity Conference in Vancouver, British Columbia, and received the inspiration to start a holistic resource, the *Arizona Networking News,*" he said. "When I returned to Phoenix, I needed a place to live, an automobile, and individuals to support my new brainchild. I boldly stated that if all these things did not manifest quickly, I would gladly return to Honolulu."

Finding an automobile was easy, and new living quarters were found through an ad in the newspaper. When John Cheney, the owner of the house for rent, opened his door, he took one look at Stan and asked, "Have we met each other before?"

"Later, as we visited at greater length, we both realized we'd never met before that evening. I inquired about John's occupation. He was a graphic artist. The Angels of Love were working quickly to keep me in Phoenix to meet my past-life love."

She, however, did not arrive immediately.

"I obviously had more lessons to learn as I sought to develop the *Arizona Networking News.* For the first three issues, I did most of the work, struggling to the point of exhaustion. I was feeling largely unsupported by most of the others involved in the project."

At this time, Stan received a letter from Vince Halpin, whom he'd met briefly while on tour in Australia. Vince wrote that he'd be in Phoenix and would like to spend some time with Stan.

"Upon Vince's arrival, I discovered that he was a devotee of Paramahansa Yogananda. The Self Realization Fellowship had been my spiritual refuge. Although I had never formally studied their teachings, I had always felt spiritually connected to Yogananda."

When they visited the temple of the Self Realization Fellowship in Phoenix, Stan opened his eyes during a meditation and noticed that a particular photograph of Yogananda seemed alive.

"Especially his eyes," Stan recalled. "I kept opening and closing my eyes to see if my observation would change, but it stayed the same."

After an hour of meditation, Stan nudged Vince to indicate that he was ready to go.

As they were leaving the temple, Vince said that Yogananda had spoken and given him a message for Stan.

"For me?" Stan asked, quite surprised.

"Yes," Vince replied. "He is sending a special woman to you who will join you in your work and life."

Stan smiled, thanked him for the message—and quickly dismissed it.

"Shortly after Vince had left Phoenix to return home, I was invited to discuss holistic health concepts on the radio," Stan said. "The interviewer was unprepared, and we did not have a good rapport. Once before, he had scheduled an interview with me— and he had not even shown up at the studio to conduct it. He had never offered a word of explanation or apology. Patiently, I sought to create a positive situation out of a negative one, and I guided the interviewer through one very *long* hour. Later, I wondered why I'd ever agreed to do the interview."

Two weeks after the awkward radio interview, the announcer left the radio station to work at a public relations firm for which Lee Lagé produced health-oriented radio programs. One day she announced out loud that she needed a guest who was well-informed about holistic concepts for one of her health shows.

The former radio host said that he knew someone. "But look out," he warned. "This Kalson guy will try to take charge of the interview."

Somewhat reluctantly, Lee called Stan and arranged a time for him to be interviewed. Stan liked her pleasant voice and agreed to do the radio program.

"The day of the scheduled interview had been a terribly busy and hectic one for me," Stan remembered. "In order to help reduce stress, I was hanging upside down on a gravity inversion machine when I realized the live radio show on which I'd agreed to appear would begin in twenty minutes!"

Stan dashed out the door unshaven and dressed only in T-shirt, shorts, and sandals, and he arrived at the studio with only seconds to spare.

Nervous and stressed because she feared her guest was about

to become a no-show, a relieved but disoriented Lee Lagé introduced their guest authority as Stan *Kalston* and the interview
began.

"The interview proceeded without my being in my body!" Stan
emphasized. "To this day I do not know what I said. However, the
host loved the interview—and Lee followed me to my car."

Both Stan and Lee felt a wonderful rapport and a strong attraction to each other, as if they had known one another for a long
time.

After they had talked for a time, Lee told Stan she was a member of Self Realization Fellowship and that his image had once appeared in her meditation so strongly that she had waited for him
at the door.

While Stan had not appeared physically at the temple for Lee
on that occasion, he had manifested for her that afternoon at the
radio studio.

"Lee's confession definitely excited me," Stan admitted, "and
I began to think that she must be the special woman Paramahansa
Yogananda was sending me."

The two parted that day, not yet comprehending the bigger
plan for their spiritual love connection. Lee recalled that she returned to her office and told all the secretaries that she and Stan
Kalson would soon be living and working together.

"You just met him!" they all screamed at her.

"Never mind that!" she told them. "It *will* happen."

That evening she told her best friend, Georgia Ross, all the details of her meeting Stan Kalson.

Georgia screamed out, "That's who I've been telling you
about! How many times have I told you the two of you should
meet? I just knew the two of you would like each other."

It all came back to Lee. "I put that name completely out of
mind," she laughed. "I remember now your mentioning your
meeting Stan, but I thought you said he was married, so I just
mentally erased his name."

Not long after their initial meeting, Stan and Lee began to date and to develop deep feelings for one another. Stan wanted her to work with him on the newspaper and to become a part of the International Holistic Center. Lee did not want to leave the security of her public relations job.

One night Georgia, Lee, and a few other friends went to a nightclub that featured Richard Ireland, a most remarkable psychic of wide reputation.

Blindfolded, Ireland placed slips of paper with questions from the audience up to his forehead. "Is there a Lee Lagé present here tonight?" he asked.

Startled, Lee managed to answer, "Here I am!"

As he held her folded paper to his forehead, he said aloud: "The question is, 'Where will I be working?' "

Lee could hardly contain her amazement. "That's right. That's my question."

"Yes, I see that you will change jobs. I see that you will be working with Stan Kalson of the International Holistic Center!"

Lee screamed her wonderment—and so did the rest of her friends.

Lee did work with Stan, and for many years they coproduced the *Arizona Networking News,* as well as organizing successful events in Phoenix.

"Often when we are alone together," Stan said, "I will speak Lee's thoughts as she thinks them."

A psychic acquaintance once told them that they had experienced many lifetimes together in very powerful positions.

"In this present life experience," Stan explains, "we would be of service to the many people who were our loyal followers in many previous lifetimes."

To this day, Stan Kalson and Lee Lagé continue to give each other personal love and support—and this translates into positive energy for spreading the concepts of holistic health to the widest possible audience.

Thirty-eight

✦

Two Opposites Together

To the best of my recollection, I first met Lawrence Kennedy, Ph.D., in 1978. As a teacher of parapsychology who had undergone a number of dramatic metaphysical and E.T. (extraterrestrial) experiences, he had responded with great enthusiasm to my book *The Gods of Aquarius: UFOs and the Transformation of Man*. He arranged to meet me and we became friends and colleagues.

As Sherry has often remarked, one cannot help liking Lawrence, a robust, smiling, rugged man with contagious enthusiasm. He always has at least a dozen ideas scrambling around in his brain for immediate attention, and he tries to give as many of them equal time as he possibly can in any given hour of conversation.

Late in 1982, he came to my office with an attractive, well-spoken, well-educated young woman he introduced as his partner and business associate. I suspected the beginnings of a romantic involvement, despite the two seeming in nearly all ways to be complete opposites.

I liked Sandra Sitzmann immediately, but my inner voice kept whispering that their relationship would never last. But it is four-teen years later, and Lawrence and Sandra have truly found their destiny together.

"Our story is not one of love at first sight," Sandra admits. "It is, however, a tale of the 'gods at play,' and we often laugh about our love story being a grand cosmic joke."

I asked Sandra if she would help me tell their story of their destined love.

In the summer of 1981 in Omaha, Nebraska, Sandra Sitz-mann, M.S., L.M.T., was busily packing and preparing for new and unknown adventures.

"I had just retired from the school system with fourteen years' experience as a professional teacher and guidance counselor. For the past seven years I had been feeling a growing restlessness to do something else with my life and my career."

But what? That was the nagging question. Why was she feeling this urgency to be somewhere else, doing something different?

She had no reason to be dissatisfied with her teaching career. She was well educated, proudly earning her master's degree by age twenty-seven. She had many good friends and a secure job guaranteeing a strong, steady income.

What else did she need?

Despite being well-read and well traveled, Sandra had discov-ered she craved a deeper spiritual sense of herself and the uni-verse. Humanistic, psychological, herbal, and health studies, extensive reading, and a well-developed social consciousness were not enough to quench the thirst of a searching soul that wanted to explore and experience life without conventional re-strictions.

"With supportive input from some friends and the assistance of my astrologer friend Bob Mulligan, I began to break down the walls of fear I had tenaciously clung to during my 'seven-year itch.' I knew there was more to life than Nebraska's Big Red football team, apple pie, and the American dream."

Mulligan encouraged her to eliminate her worldly possessions—even to the extent of selling her house. Sandra was proud of having bought a house by herself at twenty-nine. When Bob told her the house would sell by August 25, she began packing, cleaning, and preparing to relocate and adjust to a new life.

Mulligan had introduced her to the massage technique called foot reflexology, and Sandra had realized the deep, profound benefits of bodywork combined with mental, emotional, and intuitive levels of healing. Sandra applied and was accepted as a student at the Boulder School of Massage Therapy (also known as the Rocky Mountain Healing Arts Institute). She had decided a career in massage therapy would enable her to work more effectively with the whole person.

Training started the first week in September, and Sandra began to get a little nervous from the time pressure. Was her house really going to sell by August 25 and provide her with the money she needed to move to Colorado and enroll in classes?

"Angels must have worked overtime to relieve me of my worries," Sandra said, "because my house sold on the exact day Bob Mulligan said it would. As destiny would have it, a couple soon purchased my house so I could traipse off to Colorado. I made it to Boulder safe and sound for my first day of classes after driving all night. More angelic assistance!"

Simultaneous with the stresses, fears, and doubts of preparing for a major change in her life, Sandra underwent several unusual experiences that were synchronisitic to the story of how she met her destined love.

"I now have a better understanding as to the meaning and significance of these events. I remember participating in a heavenly initiation that was held specifically in my honor celebrating my rebirth and my decision to begin a new cycle in my life. It was so real—and I felt ecstatic and joyous! Evidently I passed my test of initiation and it was time to acknowledge that."

In August, Sandra's mother came to help her pack. Even with the assistance, Sandra felt overtired. She was emotionally sensitive to the fact that she was about to leave her home and friends.

"When I finally went to bed in the wee hours of the morning," Sandra said, "I heard computer-like sounds and saw multiple blinking lights—with my eyes open or closed! It all seemed so real in the physical sense, and it appeared to be occurring simultaneously inside my head and in another dimension, at another level of reality. I pinched my eyes tightly shut—and then played an 'open-and-closed game' for a while with the impressions persisting. After a while, the phantom images disappeared.

"Years later, after becoming involved with the E.T. phenomenon and hearing how contact often happens during emotionally trying times, I realized that this experience was preparing me for yet another scenario in the next phase of my life."

During the late 1970s and early 1980s, Dr. Lawrence Kennedy taught a series of classes entitled "I Can" in Lake Tahoe, California. The theme was mind over matter, also known as psychokinesis. Lawrence says his life underwent a 360-degree turn after undergoing a near-death experience in 1971.

"Previously, I had undergone two near-death experiences, but this time I was clinically dead for thirty minutes after two bleeding ulcers ruptured simultaneously. Drastic changes occurred in my life. My personality, beliefs, and values completely reversed, and I left a lucrative job with a high-paying salary as an advertising executive. I willingly eliminated my material possessions and terminated my marriage. The 'new' me returned to postgraduate study, and after receiving a doctoral degree in parapsychology in 1973 and completing a course in mind control, I began to research and teach about paranormal events, including spiritual psychic healing. I applied what I had learned in the I Can classes."

Explaining his near-death experience, Lawrence said:

> I recall leaving my body and peering down at it from the upper corner of the condo ceiling. The physical me was doubled up into a fetal position, hoping to alleviate the excruciating pain. As I began to move through a tunnel toward a bright light, I no longer felt pain—nor did I have any feelings of concern for my physical form—as images of my life and emotions passed before my eyes. I continued to move toward the light and was absorbed in it. I was overwhelmed with feelings of love and ecstasy. It was no longer important that my physical body was nonfunctioning as it lay on a blood-drenched carpet. I basked in the brilliant light and felt unattached to everything—except a nagging, tugging force that seemed to be pulling me back to the room where my body lay.

Lawrence said two radiant beings who called themselves "Counselors" appeared to him in two swirling cylinders of living light.

> The frequency was almost more than I could handle. Even though the two beings looked like creatures from out of this world, the first was so dazzlingly beautiful and radiated so much love energy that I could barely stand to look at her.
> The female entity had white hair with almost violet highlights, lavender eyes, and appeared to be youthful, perhaps twenty-seven years of age. She spoke telepathically in a high girlish, sing-song voice and told me that her name was Flameen, that she was from a place called Venusia, and that we had known each other in a past lifetime. I understood

that *Venusia* had nothing to do with the planet Venus, but existed on another level of reality. Her voice and words soothed me and sounded like music in my head.

The other Counselor was male. At first his appearance frightened me. He resembled a kind of fish-man, and though he was decidedly 'different' looking, he was strangely handsome. He wore a form-fitting silver lamé suit that covered his muscular form. He had large reptilian eyes and a slightly pointed rise to his hairless forehead and scalp. I saw scaley webbed hands, and he wore boots on his feet.

In my head, I heard him say, 'If you cannot handle this appearance, I will change to a form you can accept.' In a flash, he became another swirling cylinder of light. He put me further at ease by changing his form to one portraying the image of a handsome Greek god, with a blond pageboy-style hairdo and a short white tunic, trimmed in electric blue.

The words that the two entities spoke to Lawrence in unison astonished him. They said Lawrence was about to lose his physical form because he had not completed what he had come to Earth to do in his present life experience.

"I was shocked," Lawrence recalled. "I had been programmed to believe I was a portrait of success. After all, I had a great portfolio by the age of thirty-three—comfort, recognition, female companionship, an exciting nightlife, and all the 'toys' that money could buy."

The Counselors shocked him even further by pressing him to make a choice between staying and completing what he came to do—or leaving.

As a single father, Lawrence was concerned about leaving his young son. Who would take care of him? Was he ready to leave his family and friends to face the unknown?

"And then," Lawrence said, "the universe silently spoke to

me, enlightening me with profound truths, instilling within me an incredible knowledge and an awesome sense of the God-force."

Lawrence remembered how at the age of seven, he had boldly proclaimed himself never to be spiritually controlled by the dogmatic rules of the church which had denied his mother communion after she had become a divorcee. He had argued that no loving God would allow such an injustice, questioned the authority of the church, and vowed never again to return to that particular church's rigid beliefs and regulations.

But now he was embracing and comprehending God beyond what mere words could ever describe.

"I made my decision," Lawrence said. "I knew that I must return and begin the real work of my life. I could not precisely define it, but I knew it was to deliver truth and love to others.

"The Counselors knew my every thought and telepathically responded: 'We are here to assist you on your return to the body. After a while, others will follow us to continue helping you progress into your new states of consciousness.' "

Lawrence quickly and repeatedly received the assistance that the other-worldly entities had promised.

"My medical doctor examined my 'after-death' x-rays and was amazed to find my bleeding ulcers completely gone, with no scars remaining! After this experience, I became a believer. Of *what,* I did not yet fully comprehend!"

Inspired by Spirit, Lawrence became driven to speak on free will and choice, teaching about the existence of life at other levels and universes. He taught the I Can classes, graduating nine hundred eager participants over a seven-year period. In 1980, he was mysteriously funded to participate in an expedition to Egypt to research the ancient Egyptian-Pleiadian connection, to prove their existence, and review their history.

After meeting with retired colonel Wendelle Stevens, a UFO investigator, and becoming involved in the Billy Meiers-Pleiadian connection, he moved to Sedona, Arizona. The Meiers case had left an indelible imprint on Lawrence, and he began to work on the *Pleiadian Connection* film series that later became a part of the *Cosmic Connection* video.

In 1982, Lawrence Kennedy was in Colorado, making a guest appearance at Dael Walker's crystallography class. Walker had invited Lawrence to take some Kirlian aura photos of participating members to show how the crystal healing work affected their bioelectric energy. Sandra Sitzmann was a member of the class, but neither took much notice of the other.

"Later, at a party, I was demonstrating spoon bending through PK (psychokinesis) to an interested audience that had crowded into a small room," Lawrence recalled. "Sandra entered the room and sat next to me on the couch. I do not recall accidentally sloshing wine on her, but she insists that this was her second brief introduction to me—and she was not too impressed with it. However, Spirit continued to play cupid."

Sandra remembered that Lawrence's assistant, Lenore Cullin, kept encouraging her to try Dr. Kennedy's special eye treatment program because he had been achieving some remarkable results.

"I was involved in another holistic eye program with a local doctor, and I was excited to find someone who might be able to assist me with new methods," Sandra said. "It was an extraordinary experience, and my eyes showed signs of improvement after only one session."

She was so impressed that she arranged for Dr. Kennedy to take Kirlian photographs at a group meeting of Reiki healers that she had organized in Boulder.

"He very effectively demonstrated the affects before and after a healing session," Sandra said. "But afterward, he began to converse about extraterrestrial intelligence. I was now sure this man was far out, and I had no intention of getting mixed up with a space cadet!"

At the same time, Sandra couldn't deny she was intrigued by Dr. Kennedy's knowledge and understanding of things she had never heard about before. Seemingly out of nowhere, he asked her to assist him in putting together an E.T. ball in Boulder on Halloween eve of 1982.

"Why me?" Sandra exclaimed. Her reluctance turned to enthusiasm and the E.T. Ball was an event to remember.

They managed to pull it off with two bands playing and a radio disc jockey announcing and awarding prizes to the best-costumed "extraterrestrials" at the "Come as You Were" Ball. They still talk about this fun-filled event as a significant catalyst to the beginning of their relationship.

After successfully accomplishing the showy event, Lawrence suggested that they travel to Arizona and meet with me, retired Colonel Wendelle Stevens and Jim Diletoso, a computer analyst who was expert at detecting the authenticity of UFO evidence.

"Why not?" Sandra thought. "I had just graduated from massage school. I could work in Phoenix as well as anywhere else. It was as good a time as any to pursue the dream. Lawrence and I were then more involved as partners in business than in a romantic relationship."

Many seasons have come and gone as Sandra and Lawrence have traveled throughout the Southwest and Northwest. The threads of their encounters primarily weave together the Pleiadian-cosmic-universal theme and the interrelated themes of health, electrophotography, earth changes, and the environment.

The two have bonded on many multidimensional levels and have created Starline Unlimited, a service-product-oriented company; High Quest, a community-focused project; Link-Up/Up-Link, a networking vehicle; the *Cosmic Connection,* a videotape with a right-brain approach to the E.T.-Star People connection; and the Hiva, a sustainable prefab structure using natural, recycled materials for shelters, greenhouses, and therapeutic centers.

* * *

How do apparently extreme opposites such as Lawrence Kennedy and Sandra Sitzmann manage to stay together and accomplish so many high-energy projects?

Sandra suggests that a partial answer may be that wholeness can be achieved when opposite qualities exist in harmony and balance through nonjudgment, acceptance, and lack of fear.

"He speaks and I write. He is objective and I am subjective. He dreams about the architectural drawings, and I attend to the details as we build foundations together. It takes two sides of a coin to create the whole, the balance, the unity.

"We continue to transmute addictions, ego issues, and power struggles within a relationship between two strong-willed and independent individuals. Transmuting the dross of the base metal (ego) by fire through endurance, patience, courage, and commitment to a greater universal cause has polished our stars to a brighter sheen of gold. When our halos get tarnished, more polishing with tolerance and more buffing with tender loving care is required. Just as fine, minute particles of sand constantly irritate the shell of the oyster to produce a beautiful pearl, so, too, are our annoying, repetitive, and addictive habits eventually transmuted to the wonderful gifts of acceptance, unconditional love, joy, and consciousness.

"We do not pretend that our relationship is easy or even perfected yet. Life continues in a never-ending and ever-expanding circle and spiral on the humanistic and dualistic merry-go-round.

"Our ties to each other have universal origins, and the assistance and support of a greater energy force from beyond the stars is recognized.

"Our journey continues with a spiritual commitment to a Higher Power and each other, knowing that we are evolving as greater galactic beings in the sea of energy for our own benefit and for the good of all."

Thirty-nine

✦

Destiny Reunites Twin Flames

Patrick Flanagan and Gael Crystal Flanagan regard the story of how they got together as a modern-day fairy tale. In their opinion, there is no question that destiny played an important role in re-uniting "twin flames."

I first met Patrick in Honolulu in February of 1972. At that time, he encouraged me to join him inside a large plastic pyramid he had built as a portable meditation device.

Since that time, he has greatly enlarged his research program on pyramidal energies, written numerous books on the subject, marketed a wide variety of items, and established workshops on the transformation of various body energy fields into higher consciousness. As one of the "fathers" of longevity research, Patrick believes that we can eliminate practically all disease, purify our polluted air and water, and prolong human life for decades by applications of various scientific health modalities he has developed over many years.

People are more inclined to believe Patrick Flanagan when he makes extraordinary claims because he has been harvesting the groves of science since he was eleven years old. When he was seventeen, he gained international recognition for his invention of the Neurophone, an electronic hearing aid that allows deaf people to hear by bypassing the ears and transmitting sounds directly to the brain. Before he was out of his teens, *Life* magazine had listed Patrick as one of the top scientists in the nation.

In July 1982, ten years after I had met Patrick, I met his destined love, Gael Crystal, a nationally known writer and health and longevity researcher, when I was filming a seminar at the Camelback Inn in Scottsdale, Arizona, for inclusion in a video on past life research that I was producing.

"I had been living on the island of Eleuthera in the Bahamas," Gael said. "One night I had a very vivid dream in which I saw myself in a beautiful room full of many bright and unusual objects that looked like crystals of all shapes and sizes. I was sitting across from a little brown-haired man with a beard who seemed to be predicting my future. Just before the dream ended, he levitated the table between us. When I woke up, I tried to remember what was being said, but all I could recall was that he was predicting some important event in my future."

About two years later, after she'd packed for a trip to Australia and the Orient, Gael received a brochure advertising a seminar in Scottsdale. Among the featured key speakers would be scientist Patrick Flanagan, inventor and "Father of Pyramid Power."

Although she rarely attended seminars, Gael said that she was drawn to this particular gathering by an inner prompting from Spirit that was quite strong. Without further deliberation, she decided to postpone her world travel plans and head for Scottsdale.

The first time she and Patrick came into physical contact in their present life experience was on stage in front of hundreds of people as he selected her from the audience to demonstrate the secret Hopi handshake.

Later Patrick told her, "I thought you were a most beautiful soul, and I felt that somehow I had always known you. I knew that we would meet again."

Both knew that they had felt a special connection on a Higher-Self plane, and the resonance of their initial meeting continued even after they had returned to their homes. Patrick was living in Brentwood, on the western edge of Los Angeles, and Gael had decided to move to the middle of the Angeles National Forest to live in a house full of quartz crystals and semiprecious stones.

"The forest offered me a quiet environment of tall pine trees and a creek that ran through the property a few feet from my door," Gael said. "I spent my days in meditation, writing, and research."

On a day that Gael comfortably terms "fateful," she received a telephone call from a friend who wanted to tell her of an amazingly accurate reading that she had just received from a very special psychic-sensitive.

As they spoke, Gael felt a tremendous sensation of *déjà vu,* and she vividly recalled the dream she'd had two years before, in the Bahamas, about the brown-haired, bearded man who levitated a table and made a prediction.

"I realized that something important was about to happen in my life," she said. "Tell me," she asked her friend, "Does this amazing psychic of yours have brown hair and a beard?"

"Why, yes, he does."

"And does he also levitate tables?"

Once again, she received an affirmative answer.

"But how do you know . . . ?" the woman asked.

Gael told her friend about her dream, and she asked her to bring the psychic-sensitive to her house as soon as it could be arranged.

"When the psychic arrived, I immediately recognized him from my dream," Gael said. "He responded to the energy of my house full of crystals, and he remarked, 'I don't know if it is you or all these crystals, but I've never experienced so much energy in my life!' "

During the course of the reading he did for Gael, he asked her, "Who is Pat?"

Gael paused, then remembered her meeting with Patrick Flanagan a few months earlier.

"Yes, that's him," the psychic affirmed. "You will meet again soon, and you will cross the ocean together. You will help him to discover something that will greatly benefit humankind. It has something to do with water and rejuvenation. You will do great things together as you have done in past lifetimes, and you will be together for the rest of your lives."

Gael's head was spinning as the psychic spoke on, making seemingly outrageous predictions.

"I am getting strong impressions of the importance of the discoveries you'll both make together," the psychic continued. "They'll help a great many people all over the world."

Gael asked when these things would occur.

"Soon. Very soon," he said.

Before he left, Gael told him about the dream in which she had watched him levitating a table.

"From time to time, if the energy is right, I can use combined energies to lift a table an inch or two off the floor," he said, then demonstrated his remarkable ability.

Less than three months later, Gael was invited to be a keynote speaker at a seminar in Scottsdale. Patrick Flanagan was invited to speak at the same seminar.

Earlier that year, Patrick had been contacted by a well-known psychic-astrologer who told him that he would meet his lifemate at a seminar where he would be speaking. His destined mate would have long, dark hair with reddish highlights. She would be a Taurus and would have come originally from northeastern United States.

At the time, Patrick was conducting seminars all over the country on a variety of subjects, so he knew that it was not out of the question for him to connect with his preordained mate at such a gathering.

In July 1983, Patrick entered a large room at the seminar in Scottsdale where hundreds of people were milling around between lectures. The moment he spotted Gael standing near the seminar registration desk, he walked straight up to her.

"Are you a Taurus by any chance?" he asked.

Gael smiled at the direct question. "Yes."

"Are you originally from the Northeast?" Patrick pushed onward with his spontaneous interrogation.

"Yes," she said. "Do I win some kind of prize for answering both questions correctly?"

Patrick laughed and took her hand. "Yes, you win me!"

While Gael studied him for some clue, he quickly explained: "It sounds incredible, but a psychic-astrologer told me that I would meet my lifemate at a seminar and that she would be a Taurus from the Northeast who had long, dark hair with reddish highlights. You match the description perfectly! I just knew it was you the moment I saw you."

Patrick's facial expressions seemed to be begging her to understand that he was not some raving lunatic, and Gael felt an instant connection. She was already beginning the process of recognition that Patrick Flanagan truly was her twin flame.

"What else did this astrologer tell you?" Gael asked.

Encouraged by her willingness to hear him out, Patrick continued, "She said that you would give me the love, support, and commitment that no one else could provide."

"Really?" Gael said, feeling a surge of love toward him.

"She also said we'd marry, move to the mountains, and be happy for the rest of our lives."

Soon after the seminar was over, Patrick invited Gael to join him for a weekend. "It was a weekend from which neither of us returned to our former life," Gael commented.

Once, while meditating together, they experienced a simultaneously received past-life memory. In a prior life experience, they were Alessandro and Seraphina Cagliostro, eighteenth-century metaphysicians, healers, and alchemists. The Cagliostros were very close to the Count St. Germain, and they were initiated by him into the order of the Knights Templar. Seraphina enjoyed the honor of being the first woman initiated into the order.

"Like the Cagliostros, we also work together formulating rejuvenating elixirs and sharing teachings on the development of the higher spiritual self," Gael said.

The Flanagans have had their previous lifetime together as Alessandro and Seraphina confirmed by several well-known psychic-sensitives, including Lazaris.

When Patrick and Gael decided to get married, they travelled to Egypt to be joined as one in the Great Pyramid of Giza during the Pleiadian alignment of 1983.

"This auspicious astrological alignment happens only once every 4,800 years," Gael said. "It occurs when the full moon is directly over the top of the pyramid, in direct alignment with the Pleiades."

In Egypt, destiny once more played its part in their lives. There was no precedent for the Egyptian officials to grant permission for them to get married in the Great Pyramid, as it had never been done before.

"Permission was granted," Gael said, "and we spent three intense days and nights meditating and celebrating in the king's and queen's chambers with a small circle of friends. On the third night of the Pleiadian alignment, with the full moon shining directly over the top of the Great Pyramid, we climbed to the top and spent the entire night in meditation."

After visiting the sacred temples of Egypt and Greece, the Flanagans returned to their secluded home near Sedona, Arizona, and began a fast.

On the twenty-second day of their fast, Patrick and Gael

began speaking about the spiritual, as well as the physiological, importance of water. They discussed how, throughout history, sacred temples and sites had usually been built on special energy locations where water played a significant role in the generation of certain specific and powerful energies.

Patrick told Gael about his lifelong quest to duplicate the special energy properties of Hunza water. (Hunza is a remote valley in Pakistan enclosed by Himalayan mountain peaks. The residents there are said to possess certain health secrets which enable some of them to live in excess of 150 years.) He told her how his friend and mentor, Dr. Henri Coanda, had started him on the quest over twenty years before.

"That night," Gael said, "we went into our laboratory and created our Crystal Energy™ concentrate. Through a special thirty-three-step process, we created a laboratory analog of the water that is found in the Hunza Valley.

"We went six months living on juices and smoothies, putting our Crystal Energy™ into all our beverages. During this period we were exercising, writing, creating, and feeling better than ever."

Impressed by the Flanagans' bright eyes and robust health, their friends began to request the "elixir," and soon Patrick and Gael began producing it in ever increasing quantities. It is now used by tens of thousands of people all over the world. They have even written a book on the concentrate entitled *Elixir of the Ageless*.

Like the alchemists of old, Patrick and Gael spend almost all their time creating life-enhancing and health-giving formulations in their laboratory-home, venturing out into the world on rare occasions. They work with the latest high-tech equipment—some of which they have specially designed for their pioneering research into longevity and bioenergy systems.

The Flanagans live a quietly active lifestyle on a remote, twenty-odd acre "hermitage," surrounded by wildlife. Although my wife, Sherry, and I have known them for decades, we have not seen them for many years, keeping in touch mainly by telephone and fax. We respect their need for seclusion, and we know their pets keep them from being lonely.

As a mutual friend and reincarnationist has commented, "Patrick and Gael Flanagan are a perfect example of soul mates with shared dharma in the areas of science and service."

Dharma is defined as your duty to yourself and to society. Some see it as their true purpose in life.

As longtime spiritual beings, the twin-flames of Patrick and Gael Flanagan have embarked once again on a journey of discovery on all levels. They have now been married for over twelve years, and their love and their life together continue to flourish.

Forty

***

She Found Her Knight

One of the marvelous benefits of being an author is the opportunity to meet many colorful people. In some instances, such a meeting develops into a friendship spanning many years. In 1983, I was introduced to John Hobson by a mutual friend and we have remained constant allies and confidants ever since.

Although the public may know John as the tough, two-fisted former cop who headed his own "A-Team," a select handful of men who flew to foreign countries to rescue U.S. citizens held captive by terrorists, I know him as an excellent artist and wood-carver.

While government officials recognize him as the specialist responsible for having established the security systems of many nuclear plants, I recognize him as a sensitive man who unashamedly allows his tears to flow.

While dozens of Hollywood celebrities regard him as their highly capable personal bodyguard, I regard him as a friend who blushes if I compliment him and gets goosebumps if I share a spooky story.

In addition to all of the above, I know John as an individual

296 / *She Found Her Knight*

who came to rely on all six of his senses and his guardian angel to get him out of tight spots. Not long ago, John and I met with representatives of a major Hollywood studio who have expressed interest in dramatizing some of our adventures in a television series.

Although John was on the periphery of the movieland scene for years, working sometimes as a technical adviser, other times as a bodyguard, and on occasion, as an actor, about thirteen years ago, the cinema bug bit him hard.

"I've lived the kinds of roles Sly Stallone and Chuck Norris play," John would grouse. "My true-life adventures beat anything that I see in the movies or on television. I feel I've got to go to Hollywood to give it a try."

"Go for it," I encouraged him. "You're no kid anymore, but you've still got a good physique and more ambition than any ten thirty-year-olds. Besides, you're a damn good storyteller. You can write your own scripts and act in them."

In 1992, when I was in Los Angeles to give a speech, I got a call from John.

"I'm coming to your lecture," he said.

I told him I would leave a pass for him at the registration desk.

"I'm bringing my attorney with me," he added.

No problem, I assured him. I would leave two passes.

When I met the lovely young woman John introduced as his attorney, my inner guidance tickled my solar plexus, and I picked up that Lisa the lawyer was most definitely a "keeper." As someone who wished only the very best for John, I prayed that he knew it.

Thanks to the angels of love, on August 18, 1995, John and Lisa were married, and they left on a European honeymoon.

But before they went, I got their separate stories on how they felt the sure hand of destiny brought them together.

"I guess I was always too busy getting my life together to allow time for a serious relationship," Lisa said. "My mother, Loretta, was always trying to get me interested in the guys who visited our home. Although they were usually friends of mine, I would always end up finding fault with them.

"My friends and family would comment that I was too picky. I usually did not go out with a fellow for more than one or two dates, because I knew I just wasn't interested. In my opinion, I was just being a smart girl. I was determined to do something with my life before I settled down and had a family."

During law school, Lisa began to feel an overwhelming loneliness, as if a void in her life needed to be filled. "After I broke up with a young man who had chased me from high school to college to law school, I felt I was never going to find someone just right for me. On the other hand, I was glad I hadn't gotten married earlier, because I'd changed my expectations of what a relationship should be. I'm certain an earlier marriage would only have ended in divorce or an outside affair."

Lisa decided to develop her spiritual side. "I began to meditate. I attended New Age courses, began to interpret signs, and kept a journal of my dreams. I prayed to God that I would find a husband with whom I could spend the rest of my life. I even bought a stone in the shape of a frog and stroked it while meditating to attract true love."

Sensing Lisa's frustrations, her mother asked her if she wanted to meet an actor friend who hung out with her crowd.

"Oh, great," Lisa sighed, unfairly equating "actor" with "flake."

Loretta tried to tell her that this man was far more than just an actor.

Lisa was beginning to become a bit more interested, but when her mother indicated that he was an older man, Lisa nixed the meeting.

But Loretta was persistent, and eventually, Lisa met John Hobson.

"Although John is an attractive man with a strong physique," Lisa acknowledged, "there were no sparks flying."

Then, through one of those little twists of fate, John came to live temporarily at Loretta's place.

"I would have long talks with him when I came to visit," Lisa said. "Soon we would just hang out together, and we became good friends. We went to museums, movies, and lunch. I began to notice that it was nice to be close to him."

One evening her mother asked John to tell Lisa some stories about his "other life."

"That night, I heard about so many courageous adventures that he had undergone that my head was spinning," Lisa recalled. "I couldn't put John in any mold. It seemed he'd always pursued truth and justice from many different careers.

"That same evening he gave me a collection of the articles written about him. I was impressed. When I read the article by Brad Steiger that referred to John as a modern Knight Errant, tears welled up in my eyes, and I asked myself if he could be the knight for whom I had searched all my life."

It was soon after that fateful evening that John asked her to represent him in his career as actor and screenwriter.

"I took this as an invitation to get more involved with him. We met for lunch to discuss our plans. Soon after, we began dating— nine months after we had met."

Their first trip together was a ski weekend in Arizona. "We talked all the way on the drive," Lisa said. "It was then that John confided in me that he had learned through a past-life regression that he had a spirit guide in the form of a wolf that had followed him through time from a life where he and the woman he loved had been killed by angry villagers. The wolf had promised always to be his protector.

"When he told me this, John had goosebumps. There were tears in his eyes. Because he had confided in me, I was deeply touched, and I felt very close to him—which was a good thing, because when we got to the hotel, there was only one bed in the room!

"The first time I told John I loved him, he was dumbfounded. I said it a number of times that evening. Later, he told me that each time he had mentally asked his spirit guide what I was thinking, I had told him that I loved him.

"Soon after this trip, we moved in together. One day I hugged John and blurted, 'Would you marry me?' It kind of fell off my tongue before I even thought about it. He said yes."

John Hobson had always been a responsible father to his two sons. Although he had traveled the globe rescuing U.S. citizens kidnapped in foreign countries, he was always home on the holidays and special days.

"But I had been divorced for many years," he recalled, "and there was always something missing. I don't believe man was made to live alone. I wanted so much to have that certain woman in my life—but she just wasn't there. Don't get me wrong—I had plenty of opportunities—but nobody had come into my life that I wanted to spend forever with."

John painfully remembers many a Christmas Eve wrapping gifts for his children and his parents with tearing eyes, feeling empty in his heart, "Not for lack of love from my family, but for someone other than family to love."

Superficially, John tried to project the macho image others held of him, but he admitted that he steadily prayed for that special woman to come into his lonely life.

Nor could he ever talk to his fellow operatives about something so heavenly as his guardian angel. "She had the brightest blond hair. I was never able to see her features. In time of danger, she would often appear as one of God's creatures. I knew that she was real, and she proved her powers to me many times."

About the same time that John got the movie bug and Hollywood began expressing interest in his unique talents and the incredible stories that he had to tell, his boys were reaching their "own life" age, somewhere, he joked, between "knowing wrong and doing wrong."

"My oldest son was getting married, and my youngest was in his second year of college," he said, "so I left a million-dollar home, a new Porsche, my family, and, it seemed, everything I had worked for, and moved to Tinseltown to become a movie star."

John's new home in California was a storage room above his cousin's roller-skating rink.

"No windows, no toilet, and the pigeons flew in and out of the broken-down building," John recalled with a grimace. "Every weekend, the various teen gangs would patronize the rink, and there was always the threat of a shootout. I would sit alone in my storage-room home and wonder if I was an idiot for trying to become a movie star at my age—an idol for the aged."

During the first six months of his new life, John tried to go back to Phoenix and his old life as often as possible. Sometimes on those long drives, he would think about predictions that psychic Jan Ross had made in 1985.

"She told me I was going to become involved in the movie business and write about my exploits. I would move to California, meet a blonde-blonde woman, get married, and have two children. I would not stay in California because of the negative atmosphere, and I would probably move to the East Coast to live out my life. But now, here I was, six years later, living in a skid row apartment and broke, even though Orion had optioned a screenplay and I had costarred in a movie."

John had just decided to desert Tinseltown and head back for Phoenix for good when his friend Loretta invited him to move into her guestroom. He wouldn't have to pay rent; he could get out of his pigeon-infested dump; and he could still pursue his movie career.

It was on an outing with Loretta, her daughter, Gina, and her boyfriend, Rick, that John met Loretta's older daughter, an attorney named Lisa.

"Lisa sat next me," John remembered, "but I felt that neither of us had any interest in the other. The music was loud. At one point I forgot myself and made a comment about attorneys being like sharks. That didn't help to cement our relationship."

The night ended so uneventfully that a few weeks later, John talked a recently divorced friend of his into asking Lisa out. No sparks there, either. Both later reported to John that the other had a "nice personality."

John still travelled to Phoenix every other weekend. "It was during these long hours on the empty road that I would speak to God and my guardian angel. Though I'm Irish Catholic, religion was never a part of my upbringing.

"But through my own pain and turmoil, I had developed my own relationship with the Supreme Power. On more than one occasion, my guardian angel came to me, dodging bullets and kept me alive. I had spent many hours speaking to this angel, asking her for help. I truly wanted a love relationship in my life. It wasn't happening, but I didn't give up."

During the next several months, Lisa would visit her mother's house regularly. As a group, they would go to the beach or to dinner.

"It felt so relaxed to be with Lisa," John said. "She was so genuine in her heart. I had never met anyone who could laugh at herself like Lisa could. She didn't get angry. She enjoyed herself. I was learning something of life."

John can't quite put his finger on the point when Lisa changed. Or maybe he changed. Or maybe there was no change at all.

"But we were spending more and more time together. And it was all very different for me. Lisa was becoming my best friend. I was feeling something for my friend Lisa that I had never felt before.

"Then I'd become frightened, fearing that I was reading something into our relationship that wasn't mutual. Did she really care for me the way I cared for her? Oh, dear guardian angel, please help me!"

John recalled very clearly the Tuesday night when Lisa was

leaving on an overnight in Riverside for a trial. He was heading again for Phoenix. They had agreed to meet for dinner before she left that night.

While they were saying goodbye, John asked himself if he was prepared to be humiliated. "I leaned into Lisa's car and kissed her. Rain made the parking lot very wet, and while I was making myself vulnerable, my feet were sliding on the pavement and I was shrinking, getting shorter and shorter. Lisa didn't notice. But more important, she kissed me back."

From that point on, John said, they became even closer friends, and he began to share things with Lisa that he had never before shared with anyone—powerful, spiritual events that had taken place in his life. He was experiencing something that he had never before felt in a relationship—absolute trust.

Lisa said that on Thanksgiving Day 1994, she and John were in Wilmington, North Carolina. "For some reason I had worn a ring made of crystal baguettes to dinner. While we waited in the bar for our table, I joked with John about marrying me. Didn't he remember giving me this crystal engagement ring?

"After we moved to our table, I asked him again if he was going to marry me, and he said, 'Well, where's *my* ring?' I gave him the crystal ring I was wearing. He then asked me if I would marry him and said, 'Here's *your* ring.' Out came a case with my engagement ring! He had switched the rings like a magician!

"Thank you, Mom! Thank you, Wolf! Thank you, Angel!"

Forty-one

Angelic Beings Saved Him for His Soul Mate

David Jungclaus told me that he and his wife, Barbara, are firm believers that the Mother-Father God's love blesses us mortals with angelic beings, soul mates, spiritual guides, teachers, and spirit helpers.

David, author of *The City Beneath the Bermuda Triangle,* says he and Barbara freely acknowledge that Divine Guidance from the Cosmos has played an instrumental part in their lives—on both aware and subconscious levels.

"Angelic Beings not only brought us together as man and wife, but we have both been guided by such entities throughout our lives.

"The most interesting part of such spiritual guidance, is that you don't have to be a religious person or have any real understanding of the spiritual process involved. Such guidance is part of the Divine Plan to help all souls. Once you *do* become aware of the work of angelic entities, you realize that it is one of the greatest gifts you can receive."

David admitted that although Barbara and he are acutely aware of the guidance of angelic beings today, it was not always so.

"Neither of us knew until much later in our lives that angelic entities were helping to chart our spiritual destiny—both apart and together."

David believes we choose our parents and our birth environments for many different reasons—from wishing to return to be with those who form our spiritual family, to working out painful karmic lessons.

He knows very little about his parents because they were killed in a car accident when he was only a year old.

"I had the misfortune of being placed in a San Francisco orphanage at the time of the 1929 Depression, and such institutions were filled to overflowing and very underfinanced.

"But angelic guidance was already at work to compensate. Two wealthy volunteers at the orphanage told a couple they knew about the new baby."

The Jungclauses were warned of the baby's ill health. "Thankfully, it posed no problems to my new parents, for they were Christian Scientists and my mother was a healer. An act of true angelic guidance manifested at a time of financial crises. My father became a first reader at the First Christian Science Church in San Francisco and received a large salary."

David remembers that at the age of five he had a regular nocturnal visitor.

"I had my own bedroom, which faced the backyard, the fence, and the forest behind it. In the evenings, I would often see a dwarf sitting on the fence. In recent years, I have spoken to many UFO contactees who have shared similar experiences with dwarfs, fairies, and other magical beings. I believe that they are the guardians that monitor, communicate, guide, and protect us."

When David was nine, the invisible force of angelic protection saved him from being murdered by a man who preyed upon children.

"Even today, when I remember the incident, I can feel the chill wind of death's wings.

"Parents can only warn their children and establish rules to help them and protect them. Sooner or later, however, the child is probably going to break some of those rules. One rule that I broke often was to thumb a ride home from school."

David recalls that it was late one afternoon when he thumbed a ride home from downtown San Francisco.

"An inner alarm of fear sounded as I got into the paneled meat delivery truck and discovered that there were no door handles. A cold chill made me shudder. The truck was not air conditioned, and it had a foul smell to it. The driver was behaving in a weird manner. His clothes were dirty, just like the inside of the truck."

David was frightened by the man's eyes, which leered at him through thick lenses. The man began talking dirty, and he was nearly paralyzed with fear when he noticed for the first time a coil of rope and a roll of tape at his feet.

But a soft angelic voice told David to remain calm. "Try to act natural," the voice said. "If you make him uneasy, he will hurt you. Stay very calm."

David said it was as if the angelic being was sitting directly behind him.

"Face the man and talk to him. Don't let him know that you're afraid of him. Take your hand and slowly move it behind you—and roll down the window."

Somehow, David managed to get the window rolled down without the driver noticing.

"He was starting to get very excited as we neared an uninhabited mountain area. The angelic being said, 'Be alert and don't show fear.' The soothing voice calmed me as I fought the panic inside me. My heart was beating so loud I was certain the driver could hear it."

David did his best to fight fear as the driver started rubbing his crotch and slowed the truck to a near stop. A sick smile stretched the man's lips, and sweat moistened the grime on his face.

"Be ready!" the angelic being warned.

The driver slowly unzipped his fly. "He started laughing, then asked, 'Do you want to see my forty-five?'

"My angel guide told me to make my move. I don't know how I jumped out the window, but I did. The last glance I had of the driver was of his pulling a .45 automatic out of his pants.

"I ran and ran until I reached people. I didn't tell anyone what had happened—especially my parents, as I knew I'd be in big trouble for having thumbed a ride. The angelic voice had saved me from a killer!"

At a Halloween party in college, David met the girl of his dreams.

"She was just gorgeous. Her blue eyes drew me like a moth to a flame. It was instant love. It was as if two magnets had been pulled together. From that moment on, I couldn't eat, dream, or sleep without longing for her."

Barbara was a senior in high school, and the two of them soon began dating and spending all their free time together. Weekdays they would do their homework at her house.

"We were soon going steady, but neither of us was seriously thinking of marriage. We both said we weren't ready to settle down. Barbara didn't want to get married until after she had done a lot of traveling.

"All the traveling she got, however, was a honeymoon trip to Palm Springs!"

David and Barbara let their love grow and soon were planning for parenthood.

"Angelic guidance found us a home out of the city, and our life was very happy. We have brought into the world five wonderful children—four girls and a boy."

David remembered one morning rather early in their marriage when Barbara lay in bed, looking out the window and watching a family of birds in a large oak tree.

"Suddenly, she exclaimed, 'There's a dwarf sitting in the tree looking at us!'

"I turned just in time to get a quick look," David said. "It was *him,* my dwarf friend from childhood. I had a total recall of my earlier experiences, and I told Barbara all about him."

Forty-two

✦

She Could Not Resist
Her Destined Love

In January 1987, thirty-six-year-old Laura Wesson found herself
dumped in Barbados without a clue as to what she would do next.

"I had been in show business since I was eleven," she said,
"and on my own since I was eighteen. I had been an entertainer
on cruise ships for ten years, and my goal was to become a cruise
director. I was literally the darling of this particular ship—until a
new assistant cruise director came on board. For some reason, he
didn't like me. I tried to rise above his negativity, but he kept at
management until he got me fired."

As a practicing Christian Scientist for over twenty years, Laura
had the spiritual stamina to resist falling apart emotionally over
such unfair treatment.

"I somehow felt that everything would be all right," she recalled. "I had an inner knowing that I was being directed else-
where. I just had no idea at the time where that would be."

From the age of eighteen until her late twenties, Laura had
been gifted with psychic ability.

"My angels were with me whenever I most needed them during those years," she said. "I often heard a male voice directing

me and providing me with accurate predictions. When I needed the most help, I would receive messages through jewelry pieces that I found in the streets.

"Perhaps the most outrageous example of this unusual angelic process is the time when I was in New York, sitting in a rented car, feeling very depressed. I was actually thinking of ending it all when my hand fell to the spot where the back seat meets the bottom cushion and my finger touched something metallic. When I grabbed the object and held it up in front of my face, I saw that it was a piece of jewelry that had four letters hanging horizontally, reading 'L . . . I . . . V . . . E.' The funny thing is, all those life-saving jewelry pieces that I had collected over the years have simply disappeared."

At the age of twenty-three, Laura planned to marry a man she believed to be her soul mate.

"Robert was also twenty-three, separated, with two small children. When I told the good news to an acquaintance of mine, an accomplished palmist, her response was, 'Oh, no, dear, I don't think so. You won't marry until you're thirty-six. And when you do, it will be to a man who'll change your life forever.'

"Sadly, Robert became deathly ill due to internal conflict from his love for me and his responsibility to his young family."

One evening, as he lay in his bed gasping for air and Laura sat prayerfully in the living room, she heard a male voice say loudly in her head, "Robert must go back to his wife, Holly!"

Robert stood in the doorway, perfectly healed and almost glowing, and said quietly, "I must tell you something. I heard a male voice . . . that . . . told me that I must return to Holly. And then I was instantly healed."

The moment she'd seen him in the doorway, Laura had known what he was going to say. She said she'd been told the same thing, then they both began to cry.

It took Laura two years to get over her loss. Her palmist friend had been correct. But she had also promised Laura a man that would change her life forever.

"I had to wait thirteen years!" Laura said. "But I used to 'talk' to him all the time. I would climb to the upper decks of the ships on which I entertained and yell at the stars, 'Where the hell are you? Why do I have to wait so long?'"

What Laura did not know during those lonely nights aboard ship is that sometime during those thirteen years a successful Houston businessman named Dan Clausing was standing at the bay window of his office penthouse, suddenly realizing that even with all his wealth, he was very unhappy. At that moment of awareness, he heard a male voice in the room say very clearly, *"Either get on with what you came here to do—or check out!"*

As a rational businessman, he had difficulty accepting an unsolicited ultimatum from an unseen source, but the voice came again: *"Either get on with what you came here to do—or leave the vehicle!"*

Dan sat down at his desk in bewilderment—and resolved to ignore this unknown, unseen intruder.

Three weeks later, when he came down with a life-threatening illness, he recalled the warning voice.

Three months later, he gave up everything that he thought he had held dear—his failed marriage, his estate, his wealth, his businesses—and set out to make an avocation in metaphysics his new vocation. He worked with Bob Monroe for three years, and took his program on the road.

In January 1987 Laura was left in Barbados by the cruise ship on which she had been so happily employed, with her luggage and little else. She remained calm and assured that wonderful new opportunities were waiting for her right around some marvelous cosmic corner.

Laura's mother had always been her number-one supporter, so she eventually went to her mother's home in Los Altos, California. Soon after her arrival, Laura decided to drive to Santa Cruz to attend a seminar at a Roman Catholic retreat sponsored by the Monroe Institute.

"Mother was intensely adamant that I *not* attend the Gateway Voyager seminar in Santa Cruz," Laura recalled. "She even threatened to disown me if I attended. She carried on about the event being occult, New Age, satanic, and everything else, and she was afraid that I would end up brainwashed and in a cult."

At last, with Laura's promise to leave immediately if there were any satanic shenanigans, her mother relented, and Laura made plans to drive the forty miles to Santa Cruz. The seminar brochure indicated that the facilitator of the event was Dan Clausing—a name that meant nothing to Laura.

Neither did the name mean anything to a talented psychic-sensitive named Mary, who kept hearing the name in meditation one evening. A male voice had intruded in her reverie and told her to "call Dan Clausing."

After the command had repeated itself, Mary decided to call her friend Vicki, another talented psychic, to see if she might have any insight into the matter.

"Yes," Vicki surprised her. "I know Dan Clausing. In fact, in a few days I will be cofacilitating with him in Santa Cruz."

Vicki suggested that Mary call Dan and see what connection they might have with one another that had prompted a summons from a cosmic source.

After a conversation that was pleasant, but didn't provide any meaningful clues, Dan mentioned that his airline tickets had been improperly dated and that he would be flying out three days earlier than was necessary.

"That must be the connection," the psychic told him. "Vicki and I are driving to Mount Shasta to attend a seminar by Mafu. Come with us. It would seem that you are supposed to be at this seminar."

Dan accompanied Vicki and Mary to Mount Shasta, but he became somewhat uneasy when the channeled entity repeated over and over to the audience that they must all open their heart chakras. Dan had survived a nasty divorce, so he was not entirely certain that he wished to open his heart chakra any wider than was absolutely necessary. Not long before, a channeled entity named Solano had told him that his twin flame was on the horizon. As pleasant as that seemed, memories of a shattered marriage had left him in no hurry to be bound to another.

But by the time he left the seminar with Mafu's nearly incessant urging to open the heart chakra, Dan was fired up to maximum heat—and his heart chakra was wide open.

Two days later, he saw *her*—the very same woman he'd seen in a precognitive dream. The one of whom Solano had spoken. She was getting out of a car in the convent parking lot, obviously intending to attend the seminar he was facilitating! *And his heart chakra was wide open.*

Dan felt his knees buckle. Was he having a heart attack? He fell to his knees and was only capable of crawling to the door of the convent.

Amazingly, once the door had closed, blocking his view of *her,* he was able to stand. His heart resumed a normal pace.

Laura's first meeting with Dan was hardly impressive.

"I thought the guy had to be a total jerk," she chuckled at the memory. "He just stood there, trying to shape a coherent sentence. 'H . . . h . . . how are . . . y . . . you?' I thought, *this* is the facilitator? And he can't even make a sentence? What a wonderful weekend this is going to be!"

Dan finally managed to complete the sentence. Laura said she was fine, thank you.

"Then he did it again! 'H . . . how . . . are . . . y . . . y . . . you?' I told him again that I was fine—and I got away as fast as I could to sit beside Vicki on the couch. According to the brochure, Dan Clausing was a hypnotherapist, a channel, a lecturer, a radio personality, and an entrepreneur with a degree in psychology. Terrific! And he couldn't even make small talk.

"Later, Vicki said that from her psychic perspective, what she saw was two enormous balls of energy collide. She said she knew she was watching the reunion of two intimate lovers, and it was so intense that she felt she just wanted to disappear and leave us alone."

That might have been the view from a talented psychic's perspective, but it was just the opposite of what was being enacted on the physical level.

"I had absolutely no attraction to this flustered, stammering, pathetic guy," Laura said.

Later that evening, she found herself alone with Dan, and somehow she could not stand up.

"I didn't want to be alone with him—but there we were."

Laura managed to salvage the awkward moment by giving expression to her talent as a numerologist.

"Pretty soon, I was outlining his life for him. I know I was making solid hits, because his face kept getting redder and redder."

When she discovered that their rooms were opposite one another, she slammed her door in anger, unable to explain her rage.

The next day, during an exercise in an altered state of consciousness, members of the group came back to full wakefulness with stories of having seen Laura together with Dan in past-life love relationships.

"Everyone kept seeing Dan and me in passionate circumstances," Laura said. "I kept wondering what on earth was going on!"

That evening, as she stood alone looking out to sea, Dan approached her and came right out with it. He said that he was having strong feelings toward her. He was falling madly in love with her.

"I thought, 'Spare me, dear Lord!' For ten years on cruise ships I had heard every line in the book. But then I thought, Don't crucify the guy. Be nice."

Laura put on her most professional smile. "Look, please try to understand. I'm not attracted to you. You're just not at all my type. I'm simply not interested in you."

Dan could not be put off. "Laura, I'm forty-five years old, and I've just realized that I have never been in love."

"Don't fall in love with me," she warned him. "Because I feel nothing toward you!"

Laura uttered a prayer that he not try to kiss her, and then she was completely astonished to hear a voice that she eventually recognized as her own saying, "But I could learn to love you."

Had she really said that? She wanted to stuff the words back into her mouth. Where had that come from?

She had to get away from him, and she left him standing there.

When she returned to her room, she saw that Dan had left his door open.

"I became so angry that he would leave his door open, as if inviting me in," Laura said. "And there he was, sitting on his bed, looking like a forlorn little boy. I walked into my room and slammed the door. I told myself that there was no way I was going to go over there!"

But she found herself of two minds: one that didn't want to be with Dan, and another that was beginning to remember, to achieve a deep level of knowing.

It was as if her feet carried her to Dan's room without the consent of her mind and body.

When he looked up, she told him that she would only stay a minute or two to talk. Three hours later, she was still there.

Somehow, although her conscious mind could not believe it, they went to bed together.

"I was not an easy lady," Laura said emphatically. "All those years on the cruise lines had made me immune to the concept of one-night stands. I had been celibate two years just to prove that I was in control.

"When we began to make love, Dan went into terrible convulsions. I had never seen such intense body shakes. He was like a human earthquake, that's the best description I can come up with. I was afraid he was dying. I thought, 'Oh, my God! I've slept with the facilitator and killed him in a nunnery!'"

Laura learned later that the instant their bodies had joined, Dan's physical cells and soul energy had experienced 100 percent remembrance of her and 100 percent knowing that she was his twin flame.

But that night, as soon as she had calmed Dan, she slunk off to her own room, resolved to put an end to things before they really got started.

"The next day, I tried to make it as plain as possible to Dan that he was just not my type," Laura said. "I don't know why I'm even talking to you now," I told him.

As if he had not heard a single one of her protests, Dan asked her to fly back east with him when he facilitated another seminar in New Jersey.

"My brain intended to scream, 'No!'" Laura said, "but the words that came out were, 'Yes, I'll be there.'"

What's happening to me? Laura demanded of the universe. Dan began to channel for her.

"He started out by calling me 'Beloved Entity' and telling me that I was right on schedule," Laura said. "He said that we had been together in three past lives and that we were twin flames. Coming together in our present lifetime was our reward, so to speak. We were to be teachers to the people and to each other we were to be helpmates and companions through the coming time of transition.

"I thought it was all some act that Dan had come up with to try to manipulate me. I had been in show business and I wasn't about to fall for this gimmick."

When Laura left the seminar, she visited her father in another part of California.

"An old back injury returned with such pain and violence that my father had to take me to the emergency room. As I recuperated in the hospital, I had lots of time to think, and I realized that symbolically, my back injury was my 'turning my back' on my old ways, my former life.

"Dan called me daily on the telephone, and even though I was brutal and abusive to him, he remained calm and loving."

A week later, Laura was taken to a California airport in a wheelchair to join Dan, who met her with a wheelchair at the New Jersey airport. It had been five weeks since their first meeting in this lifetime.

"I was exhausted from the ordeal, and I was still very confused," Laura said. "Yet I saw nothing but the purest love streaming from Dan's eyes. I made a vow to shut off my intellect, to allow love to enter, to be in my heart and my feelings."

When Laura's full realization came, it arrived with such force that she was temporarily rendered speechless. "I felt intense heat throughout my body as my two opposing selves merged. Immediately, I was madly in love with Dan. Since I had lost my voice, I stated in sign language, 'I love you.' "

Two weeks later, Dan and Laura hiked 14,000 feet up to the snow-line on Mount Shasta and spoke their marriage vows to each other.

"The birds were our witnesses," Laura remembered fondly. "Our wedding rings were fashioned from moss. Later, we had an 'official wedding' for members of our families."

Dan and Laura Clausing have now been as one for eight years and state firmly that they still honor their being together.

"Every day we express our gratitude for this creation. We view our relationship as the distinction for passing through the fires of past lives. We spend twenty-four hours a day together—and it still is not enough. We truly communicate moment to moment. We may have two sentences of frustration between us—and then the very next words between us have no carry-over from the previous emotion. We hold no ill-will. It would seem that our purpose in being together is to be a constant catalyst to the other's growth. We are continually employed through the light of one another."

Author's Note

❖

Many of the people who contributed their own experiences also happen to be men and women who offer their own research, counsel, artistic expression, or inspiration to those who seek more information about the subjects described in this book.

For further details, readers may contact these individuals directly at the addresses listed below:

Lori Jean and Charles Flory, Post Office Box 1328, Conifer, Colorado 80433.

Vera and Joshua Shapiro, V&J Enterprises (The Peruvian Connection) 9737 Fox Glen Dr. #1K, Niles, Illinois 60714.

Jon Marc and Anastasia Hammer, Heartlight, Post Office Box 22877, Santa Fe, New Mexico 87502-2877.

Lois and Clay East, Angelic Images, Post Office Box 280843, Lakewood, Colorado 80228.

David and Barbara Jungclaus, Lost World Publishing, 2899 Agoura Road, Suite 381, Westlake Village, California 91361.

Judith Richardson Haimes, Pentacle Publications, 10710 Seminole Blvd. Suite #3, Seminole, Florida 34648.

John Harricharan, 1401 Johnson Ferry Road, Suite 328-M7, Marrietta, Georgia 30062.

Moi-RA and RA-Ja Dove, Rose Petals Star Ranch Community of Light, 3357 Cerillos Road, Suite 232, Santa Fe, New Mexico 87505.

Laura and Dan Clausing, Evening Star Ranch, 2376 Egland Road, Addy, Washington 99101.

Tara and Raymond Buckland, P.O. Box 892, Wooster, Ohio 44691-0892.

Patrick and Gael Crystal Flanagan, Vortex Industries, 1109 S. Plaza Way, Suite 399, Flagstaff, Arizona 86001.

Ben Smith, 2929 S.E. Mile Hill Drive, #A-6, Port Orchard, Washington 98366.

Dr. Lawrence Kennedy and Sandra Sitzmann, P. O. Box 611, Kalispell, Montana 59903.

Clarisa Bernhardt, P.O. Box 669, Winnipeg, Manitoba, R3C 2K3, Canada.

Lee Lagé and Stan Kalson, International Holistic Center, 5515 North 7th, #5-129, Phoenix, Arizona, 85014.

Those readers who may wish to share their own stories of destined love or participate in the research of Brad Steiger and Sherry Hansen Steiger may obtain a copy of the **Steiger Questionnaire of Mystical, Paranormal, and UFO Experiences** by sending a stamped, self-addressed business envelope to Timewalker Productions, P.O. Box 434, Forest City, Iowa 50436, or check their web site at: www.bradandsherry.com